« BLUES VISION »

Blues Vision

AFRICAN AMERICAN WRITING FROM MINNESOTA

Alexs Pate, Editor

Pamela R. Fletcher and J. Otis Powell‽, Coeditors

MINNESOTA HISTORICAL SOCIETY PRESS

Minnesota Humanities Center

CLEAN
WATER
LAND &
LEGACY
AMENDMENT

Co-published by the Minnesota Historical Society Press and the Minnesota Humanities Center. © 2015 Minnesota Humanities Center and Alexs Pate. Copyright in individual pieces is retained by their authors. All rights reserved. No part of this book may be used or reproduced in any manner whatsoever without written permission except in the case of brief quotations embodied in critical articles and reviews. For information, write to the Minnesota Historical Society Press, 345 Kellogg Blvd. W., St. Paul, MN 55102-1906.

Credits for previously published works listed on pages 285–86.

www.mnhspress.org
The Minnesota Historical Society Press is a member of the Association of American University Presses.

Manufactured in the United States of America
10 9 8 7 6 5 4 3 2 1

∞ The paper used in this publication meets the minimum requirements of the American National Standard for Information Sciences—Permanence for Printed Library Materials, ANSI Z39.48-1984.

International Standard Book Number
ISBN: 978-0-87351-973-1 (paper)
ISBN: 978-0-87351-974-8 (e-book)

Library of Congress Cataloging-in-Publication Data

Blues Vision : African American writing from Minnesota / Alexs Pate, editor ; Pamela R. Fletcher and J. Otis Powell?, coeditors.
    pages   cm
Summary: "A rich Minnesota literary tradition is brought into the spotlight in this groundbreaking collection of incisive prose and powerful poetry by forty-three black writers who educate, inspire, and reveal the unabashed truth" — Provided by publisher.
"Co-published with the Minnesota Humanities Center"
    ISBN 978-0-87351-973-1 (paperback) — ISBN 978-0-87351-974-8 (ebook)
    1. African Americans—Minnesota—Literary collections. 2. American literature—African American authors. 3. American literature—Minnesota. 4. Minnesota—Literary collections. I. Pate, Alexs D., 1950– editor. II. Fletcher, Pamela R., editor. III. Powell?, J. Otis, editor.
    PS283.M6B57   2015
    810.8'08960730776—dc23

                                                                    2014046118

This and other Minnesota Historical Society Press books are available from popular e-book vendors.

Contents

SCENE 7 » SPOKEN

Introduction

Blues Vision: African American Writing from Minnesotan is the culmination of a dream I've had for many years. I've always wondered: what would a collection of works by African American writers who've lived in Minnesota for significant portions of their lives look like? What stories, what poems? Would a theme or thread emerge? How much would we talk about the weather? About isolation? How much would we display an embrace of midwestern values, and how would we talk about the nature and the geography of this great state? Indeed, this collection is predicated on the intersection of race and geography in creative literary expression.

When I arrived here in the early 1980s, I was routinely told by many of the white Minnesotans I encountered about the liberal, inclusive, and supportive environment where I was lucky enough to find myself. There was, most definitely, a profound difference from the place that I'd left, Philadelphia, Pennsylvania. Yes, it did feel more open. I could sometimes see to the edge of the sky here. It was momentarily kind of breathtaking. After all, I was an inner-city kid, and there was always a building somewhere ahead. But that sense of openness was *momentary*. The state was nearly 97 percent white, less than 1.5 percent Black, at the time. It didn't take long to realize that as beautiful (and brief) as spring and fall are here, I had chosen to live in a place where I felt hyper-visible and completely unknown— and, perhaps worst, unknowable. Of course, over time, as I changed and as the world I inhabited changed, I began to redefine what home could be. I suppose I became more knowable. Minnesota became the place where I surrendered to writing in earnest. I was a writer here. And I know that being a transplanted Minnesotan has affected my voice and my vision. I see differently because I moved here.

So I have wondered, over the years, about other Black writers who have grown up in Minnesota or relocated here. What are they writing about? How does *who you are* and *where you are* change *what you see* and *how you feel* about it? And how do you remember and write about it? And when you do write about it, what does it look like? Or sound like? And finally, what would it look like to bring as many of those voices together in one book? I admit those are more than a few questions. But that is what anthologies are for, it seems to me: to answer a lot questions in one text.

When I approached the Minnesota Humanities Center with this idea, there was an immediate response of support and desire to make it happen. Under the leadership of David O'Fallon, the Humanities Center made a commitment to find the necessary resources, which have come from Minnesota's Arts and Cultural Heritage Fund and from the National Endowment for the Humanities. It has taken some time, but through this long process, the Humanities Center never flagged in their effort to make this book a reality. Davu Seru, Phillips Graduate Fellow for the Givens Collection from the University of Minnesota, began research into the history of Black Minnesota writers, and we were off and running. I was very fortunate that coeditors Pamela R. Fletcher and J. Otis Powell‽, two important Minnesota writers, were generous enough to bring their hearts and eyes and join me in this effort.

And thus, finally we have *Blues Vision: Writing by Black Minnesotans*.

Of course, any project like this has its limitations. We wanted this book to be as inclusive as possible, to hold the voices of Black writers who have lived and passed on here as well as those who still walk with us. We wanted *Blues Vision* to be a usable, accessible book that would allow high school and college students and teachers to experience the literary history of Minnesota's Black community. And, of course, we wanted it to reach all who are curious about the flow of language and meaning that is represented here. But those limitations kept manifesting. The most significant of them was simply a matter of space. Size matters, and that, as much as anything else, prevented this book from being much bigger. So no matter how comprehensive we've tried to be, many fine writers are absent.

Still, the writers included here make great representations for those who aren't. Gordon Parks takes us back into the history of his formative years in St. Paul. Legendary Nellie Stone Johnson does the same for her early years in Minneapolis. Others, including Taylor Gordon and Lloyd Brown, provide excursions through the early years of the last century. Both Kofi Bobby Hickman and Kemet Imhotep provide a tribute to the late Kwame McDonald of St. Paul.

Many of the writers in this book lived in Minnesota through the Civil Rights Movement, the Black Power Movement, the advent of hip hop, and the election of America's first Black president. You will find their visions expressed as memoir, essay, fiction, nonfiction, plays, performance pieces, and poems. And they write about specific communities, like St. Paul's Rondo neighborhood and Minneapolis's Kenwood neighborhood, as well as places well outside of the larger metropolitan areas. These writers reflect the lives of Black folks who have lived or who continue to live in Minnesota.

But, to be clear, this anthology tilts toward the contemporary. We wanted to capture the power of the Black literary explosion that has taken place in Minnesota over the last twenty years. Poets and writers like Angela Shannon, Tish Jones, Philip Bryant, G. E. Patterson, Carolyn Holbrook, David Haynes, Mary Moore Easter, E. G. Bailey, Shannon Gibney, and Frank B. Wilderson III, just to mention some, take us into their present-day lives and struggles.

Blues Vision does something else as well. Here we make real the literary contributions of talented and creative minds that are often overlooked when people come together to talk about the literary tradition of Minnesota. Indeed, it is a wonderful and rich tradition. And many of the writers who are represented here must naturally be recognized as a part of that tradition.

There have always been Black folks writing in Minnesota. There have been Black newspapers and journals. Black poets and storytellers. There have even been other anthologies of Black writers (one of which, *The Butterfly Tree*, was edited by the late Conrad Balfour). We have always been here. And we have always seen the landscape and life in Minnesota the same and differently from our white counterparts.

With *Blues Vision*, we set out to claim a space, to mark a period of time and the voices of a community that has seemed, over the years, to grow exponentially more powerful, more skilled and clearer about the Minnesota they live(d) in.

If you consider the blues, as many critics do, to be more than a music—to be, rather, a way of being and a way of seeing—then you will enter the poems and stories presented here open to the beauty and power of their expression.

A lot of what this book is about has to do with sight and voice. It is a sample of the way Black writers in Minnesota have processed their lives as Minnesotans. How they see the world move around and through them. Black writers see the Minnesota landscape differently, and because they are of this region, they see their *world* differently as well. There is a flow, a rhythm, to the seeing. Sometimes we are told what it is we are looking at. Sometimes we define it. And what the writer's eye sees, especially in a world where the history of the writer is saturated in struggle, affects everything. The way our sight is connected to memory, to people, to places, and even to sound and touch, leads some of us to anger, redefinition, or simple befuddlement. As Etheridge Knight writes, "Soft songs, like birds, die in poison air/So my song cannot now be candy."

There is precious little candy (at least not in Knight's meaning) in this collection, but there is considerable sweetness. There are moments of tenderness and wonder. Memories and experiences that are revealed as only the poets and writers who wrote them could have. The poets and writers here speak through their hearts. They make us see what they remember, go where they've been, and feel what they've felt. These authors introduce us to the people they loved, the stories they've heard, and they've finally spoken to us in pictures made of words. All from the perspective of living and writing as African Americans in Minnesota. We benefit from their collective vision.

Acknowledgments

To be truthful, I'm not sure this book would have happened without the dedicated and passionate work of poet J. Otis Powell‽ and prose writer Pamela R. Fletcher. They both brought a degree of professional commitment to the process and to the final product that will forever put me in their debt. They both worked very hard. But I knew when I asked what I was getting. Their keen sense of aesthetics and understanding of how important this book might become was enough to make our collaboration successful. So to each of them, I simply want to say thanks and to express how much their friendship means to me.

I would also like to thank the folks at the Minnesota Humanities Center. David O'Fallon, from the beginning, has supported this project and cleared the way for it to happen. At the time, then–Vice President Matthew Brandt embraced the need and began marshalling the resources necessary to get us started. This project was launched with money from the Arts and Cultural Heritage Fund that was created with the vote of the people of Minnesota on November 4, 2008 and with support from the National Endowment for the Humanities. Throughout the long process, Eden Bart took on the responsibility of communicating with the writers and handling all of the considerable details to take us to completion. Finally, it was the Humanities Center's director of programs, Casey DeMarais, who brought everything together. I can't thank the Humanities Center and its staff enough.

But all of that administrative support would have meant nothing if the writers who are collected here, and even some who aren't, hadn't taken the time to respond to our call for submissions. Thanks to all of you for taking this effort seriously and giving us the best of your creative expressions, and for your strident voices that continue to contribute to and shape this cultural landscape.

The early research that Davu Seru performed also deserves mention. His work convinced me that there was clearly a wealth of material to try to track down. I also want to thank Jess Annabelle who promised to help me "do this" and did. And thanks to Joe Leadly for his assistance.

Thanks also to the Givens Foundation and its staff who support African

American writers and literature in this region. In the same way, I want to thank John Wright, scholar and critic at the University of Minnesota. His impact on the way I think about literature is indelible.

To our publisher, Minnesota Historical Society Press, much appreciation and thanks are also given. From the moment I met and talked with Ann Regan, I knew we were in good hands. Her sensitive yet intense engagement with the editors and authors of this book, from both a logistical and an editing standpoint, has been nothing short of astounding. It's kind of stunning, really, how many people contributed to this project, but without Ann, it might still be languishing.

And finally, thanks to my daughter, who I hope one day will read this work and understand better what world she was born into, and to SooJin, who will help make that real.

Heart

Birth of the Cool: Minnesota

I know, Miles,
you didn't have rural southern Minnesota
in mind when you
blew your classic mute
on your famous *Birth of the Cool*
sessions in New York, circa 1949.
But it's the way the paper-thin
ice forms on the edge of the lake
in late October:
meeting at the cold dark water's edge
—still open and free
though not for long—
with the ripples of these short choppy
muted notes of yours
blown just out of reach
this cool windy autumn morning.

from A Choice of Weapons

After his mother's death in 1928, sixteen-year-old Gordon Parks moved to St. Paul to live with a sister. Within just a few weeks, his brother-in-law threw him out of the house, forcing him to find his own way in the dead of a Minnesota winter.

March came and held at fifteen below for several days; then a warm front pushed in and brought relief. But a big snow followed. It started around eight one evening, and by the next morning the city was buried beneath its whiteness. Twenty-foot drifts blocked the highways. Stores and schools closed and nothing moved but snowplows and trolley cars. I borrowed a shovel from George and in two days I made over twenty-five dollars—enough to get a room for a month and a few meals. It was Friday when I moved into the rooming house, and I had bought a newspaper and gone to bed when I saw the ad. The Stumble Inn near Bemidji, Minnesota, wanted a piano player. The salary was eighteen dollars a week—and tips. The room and board were free and the hours from eight until two in the morning. I reasoned that I could stay in school with a job like that. I stood in the dimly lit room trying to decide. I had paid five dollars toward my rent, which I knew I couldn't get back. And it would mean leaving St. Paul. But the prospect of eating and sleeping regularly made it seem worthwhile. I got up, dressed, stuffed the paper in my pocket and hurried to the Western Union office.

My telegram naively advised that I would take the job and they could expect me within two days. And at six the next morning I was at the out-skirts of town trying to thumb a ride to Bemidji. Car after car passed; and I stamped about in the snow trying to kill the numbness in my feet. The cold wind rose and began to whip fright into me and I was ready to turn back when a big truck slid to a stop. I jumped up on the running board, but my hands were too cold to turn the handle. The driver leaned over and opened the door and I jumped up into the cab.

"Where you headin'?" His accent was Southern.

"Bemidji."

"You're lucky. Goin' within fifteen miles of it."

We rode the next few miles in silence. Now and then he would curse the drifts as we approached them, gun his motor and burst through, sending flurries in every direction. The silences were awkward and I finally told him I was glad that he had picked me up.

"It's okay," he drawled, "'cause I git sleepy on long hauls. A little comp'ny keeps me goin.'" Another drift was coming up. "Damn useless snow! I cain't see why people settle in ass-freezin' country like this anyhow. Cain't figger it out." We plowed through and snow shot high above the cab, blinding us for a moment or so—then the road was before us again.

I wanted to ask him where he came from, but he was a white Southerner and this might have led to some uncomfortable North-South talk. He had done me a big favor, and I was in no position to argue in case his views opposed mine—and I was sure they did. Then, as if he were clairvoyant, "I got a boy 'bout your size back in Florida, and bet you a hound's tooth to a dollar he's lazyin' 'neath a orange tree in the back yard."

"He's lucky," I said.

"Maybe yes. Maybe no." I didn't know how to take that, so I kept quiet, waiting, so that he might clarify himself. "He ain't exactly a good boy, and he ain't exactly a bad one. Main thing wrong is he's got a lot of screwed-up ideas."

"Like what?"

"Well, he got us into a peck of trouble 'bout a week ago. We ain't out of it yet. It's not that my wife and me is against you people, but there's a time and place for everything. Well, my boy he gives a birthday party last week, and right in the middle of it a nigra boy who he invited walks smack through the front door, and my boy starts feedin' him cake and ice cream. Well, you don't know the commotion it started."

"What happened?"

"One of my boy's pals called him a nigga, and my boy hit him for doin' it. His own friend, mind you. Now every white boy in town wants to beat up on him. He's got hisself in a peck of trouble. He should never done such a thing in the first place. You think so?"

"I don't know."

"Would your paw like it if you invited a white boy to your birthday party?"

"I never had a birthday party."

"But s'pose you did . . . you think he'd like it?"

"He wouldn't care one bit."

"How do you know if you never had a birthday party?"

"I just know my poppa, that's all."

"Well, what you are saying is my boy don't know me."

"I didn't say that."

We were silent for some time after that. His manner told me he was thinking deeply. "You ever sleep with a white girl, boy?"

"Did you ever sleep with a colored girl?"

"Yeh, I did. And it was good. Now how 'bout you?"

I stiffened and got ready to thumb the rest of the way to Bemidji. "Yessir, I have," I lied, "and it wasn't so good."

To my surprise he roared with laughter. "Just wait till my boy hears what you said. It'll kill him. By god, it'll kill him." He continued laughing for almost another mile. After that I went to sleep, deeply puzzled by his reaction.

Sometime later in the night he nudged me in the ribs. "I quit you here. Bemidji's about fifteen miles down the road. Market trucks'll be goin' in for the weekend. You oughta git a lift 'fore long."

I rubbed sleep from my eyes and peered out. The highway marker, caught in the glare of the headlights, fixed my destination as exactly fifteen and a half miles. I thanked him and jumped down to the snowbank. As the truck roared off, I watched the whiteness swirl upward and around it, obscuring the only thing moving through the blackness. The sound of the motor gradually faded, and I turned and started down the road. The wind had died, but the temperature this far north was still far below zero. Past Kansas winters had taught me in such instances to keep moving, not too fast, not too slow—just enough, as my dad used to warn, to keep the blood running hot. A few market trucks did come along, but they didn't stop, and I made the whole distance on foot, reaching the outskirts a little after one o'clock in the morning. I saw a garage and stopped there to get warm.

The white garage keeper was kind. He gave me a cheese sandwich and three cups of coffee and, as I sat in the heat of his pot-bellied stove, I remarked that it was the same type as we had back in Kansas. He asked me where I was going, and I proudly mentioned the job I had come to take at Stumble Inn.

"When you starting?"

"Soon as I can find the place."

"Why, didn't you come down the main road?"

"That's right."

"Good Lord, fellow, you passed it about three and a half miles back." My expression must have been most lamentable, for he immediately asked me if I would like to sleep there until morning. Wearily I accepted. There were two bales of hay in the corner, and I collapsed on them. The garage keeper threw me a horse blanket. I covered myself with it and slept as soundly as I had ever slept in my life.

As far as the owner of Stumble Inn was concerned, I could have remained in the garage forever. When I knocked at his place the next morning, he came to the door in his long underwear. I had awakened him and he regarded me impatiently as I explained who I was. "Hell," he said, "that job's already taken." Then he slammed the door in my face.

I went back to town and looked about for work all day, without success. By eleven o'clock that night a blizzard raged. The streets were deserted. I went back to the garage, but it was closed. Through the driving snow I saw a lighted sign that said EAT. Already weak, I felt faint as I was pushed along by the strong gusts. I reached the door and went inside.

"What do you want?" the waitress asked.

"A cup of coffee," I said, then I collapsed on a stool. Three white men and a woman sat at a table alongside the wall. They had been drinking. "Well, ah declare!" one of the men said in a heavy Southern drawl. "Ah seen eva'thing now. A nigga eatin' in the very same place as white folks. Ain't nothin' gonna happen like that down where ah come from."

I ignored him. He went on. "Black bastards'll be wantin' to git in our beds next!"

Suddenly my control was gone. I grabbed my cup and dashed the scalding coffee on him. He yelled. The woman next to him screamed. I began throwing sugar bowls, salt and pepper shakers, ketchup bottles, anything that I could get my hands on.

All at once the waitress shouted a warning, but it was too late. A chair knocked me unconscious. I came to while being hauled from the diner by two policemen. They took me to jail.

When they released me from jail the following morning, there was a soreness where the chair had struck my temple. The day was cold but clear, and I started walking toward the highway. As I passed the café, it appeared innocent of the violence that had erupted there only a few hours before. It was like passing a tombstone one had defaced, and I hurried on. Soon Bemidji and Stumble Inn were far behind me, and two hours later I was picked up by another trucker. Luck was with me. He was going all the way to St. Paul. It was easier to relax now, for I would be back in time for school on Monday morning, and I had a room—for at least the rest of the month.

As the truck bumped over the highway, I thought back over the fruitless journey. I couldn't understand that Southern truck driver. Had he picked me up out of kindness, or was he trying to expiate his feeling about Negroes? Why, after asking such a question, had he roared with laughter at my flippant answer? Was he trying to understand his own son through me, or maybe understand me through his son? I didn't know. It was impossible to judge him in terms of his actions. Then there were the garage man and the innkeeper, both white, but as different as summer and winter. Next, the other Southerner with whom I had fought in the café. He had obviously deserved his lumps. But had I handled that situation the way my mother would have wanted me to? No, she would have found some other way to defeat him and yet maintain her dignity and pride. But this man's tongue had hurt worse than a fist, and I had reacted out of an impulse fed by despair. My conscience told me that my actions were wrong, but my heart approved them. Momma used to say that strength came through prayer. I prayed these nights, but I was beginning to wonder about a God who would test me so severely.

I had come north to prove my worth, and I was discovering that there was a lot more to it than just the desire for recognition or success. The naiveté of youth, the frustrations of being black had me trapped, and achievement seemed almost impossible. It was becoming more and more difficult to live with the indifference, the hate, and at the same time endure the poverty. But even then I knew I couldn't go on feeling condemned because of my color. I made up my mind, there in the cab of that truck, that I wouldn't allow my life to be conditioned by what others thought or did, or give in to anyone who would have me be subservient. We rolled into St. Paul about three in the morning. The disappointing trip had left me tired and wounded; I was glad to be back.

Finally after a month, the snow was gone, and spring was over the land, but the memory of this first winter stayed with me. Yet, as I stood on a corner warming beneath the sun, I was glad I had stayed in school, and thankful that somewhere I had a family. My father, sisters and brothers were scattered, but at that moment they seemed as close to me as the poverty. I hadn't heard from any of them, but I felt that somewhere they were extending their hopes and love.

I could no longer consider myself just a boy. I knew that youth as it should be at seventeen was not for me, and that full manhood must come quickly if I was going to make it. There wasn't much good to extract from the memory of that never-to-be-forgotten winter. I had come out of it frightened and dispirited, stripped of nearly everything but hope.

Poetryapolis

I love poetry. Little old poems afraid to go out after dark. Teenage rowdy poems spilling energy on street corners and buses. Pompous middle-aged poems pausing to adjust their ties before entering another literary meeting. Big-bad mucho-macho sexist poems. Big-bad lesbian feminist separatist poems. Any poem that gets going and gets there. I love it.

> From the ancient ruins of Babylon,
> Athens and Rome—down Sonnet Av.
> to the McDonalds on Trope St. Hop
> on the Free Verse Bus. Get off at
> Prose Poem. Look for the Street Poets.
> Say hi!

Remember the first poetry reading I ever attended. At the Unitarian Society on Mt. Curve. Open reading. In the basement. Organized by Michael Kincaid. Robert Bly was there. He had just won the National Book Award. I had never heard of Robert Bly. I had never heard of the National Book Award! He read a wonderful poem about three presidents. He cracked the binding on his newly arrived soft-covered edition. Frank Brainerd read poems about his parents. He published a magazine called Plainsong. He was from New Brighton. I thought New Brighton was in the Boundary Waters. Poetry coming together in Mpls. in 1967. I wanted to come along. That night I wrote a poem about a duck in Loring Park.

Poet: worshipper of language transcending fear, loneliness, despair.

Etheridge hadn't shown up. They were going in alphabetical order and his name was coming up. Etheridge had called several people and asked them to come and give him moral support in his denunciation of the anthology that the reading was celebrating. It was time for Etheridge and the m.c. was just apologizing for his absence when the door swung open and Etheridge majestically lurched down the steep stairs of The Walker Art Center auditorium. He graciously apologized for his lateness and then recited two of his finest poems before launching into his attack on the racism of the anthology and the Minnesota Arts establishment. "You can start the poetry now!" a woman shouted from the audience. "You can start the poetry now!" She shouted again. Can this be real, I thought, is she a plant? Tom McGrath was next. He has this great poem, "YOU CAN START THE POETRY NOW" about a mad Indian taking over a poetry reading, etc . . . (read it.) McGrath was frantically rummaging through his bag looking for the poem as the m.c. tried to get Etheridge off the stage, and he couldn't find it. The woman shouted it a couple more times. Etheridge finished and marched out with a few supporters. Tom couldn't find the poem. He started to read another poem as Jenne looked frantically through her bag for a book with the poem in it. She found it and took it to him. It wasn't as effective as it could have/should have, would have been. Etheridge left town. Jenne left town. McGrath left town. You can start the poetry now.

> black poet. white poet. red poet. yellow poet. brown poet.
>   woman poet.
> black. white. red. yellow. brown. woman. poet.
> black. black. black. black. black. black. black.
> poet. poet. poet.
> white. white. white.
> poet. poet. poet.
> within the circles of Poetryapolis. root fruit. history. herstory.
>   ourstories.

ROY C. MCAPOLIS

Tracks

Before I was born
There was movement
Paddles pushing pent up people through oceans of pain
That explains my fear of water

When I was born
There was movement still

Lines
Paths
Roads
Circles
And tracks

Check it
I had my first perm in elementary school
Went from coarse
Curly black hair
To straight
Thin
Then what you gon' do with this 'do

After that I did braids
Weave
Ponytails
Extensions
This faux hawk Mohawk ducktail design on the side type thing
But before all of that
I also wore
Tracks

Then there was high school
Saint Paul Central

Big gray five floor and a basement building
Kinda looks like a prison kinda ran like one too

The fifth floor was for the academic acronyms like *AP* and *IB*
The fourth floor was for the *Quest* learners
Second to the best grade point average earners
The third
Well the third was whatever
The second was *pass*
And the first was primarily the theatre class
How we were placed in this system
Tracks

Pause

My name is Tish Jones and I have been called here to represent

Ancestors
Whose blood sift through the palms of my little brothers hands
As he plays in the sand and they bless him
Forefathers
Who existed before my four fathers
And raised men to raise men
Hence the sun and the raisin
Then
A generation of beautiful black women
Born and bred to believe that beauty belongs to everyone but them
So
They dye and they fry and they try to fit in
In many ways allowing trains to leave tracks on their thighs
Because the tracks attached to the root of her naps which hang to the mid
    of her back
Reduce self-respect and she is alright with that
They call her a runner
Making laps on laps
Known as a track star
The best at her craft and she
Is right on
Track

Then
There is the little boy whose father was sent away yesterday
He's having a bad day so he answered the test questions in the wrong way
Now he's in the hallway with extra help
Frustrated
Fighting to keep his tears to himself
And she
Well she's lived in the inner city since the beginning
Light skin
Long hair
And just a little bit skinny
Smart
She makes failing a test seem hard
Don't believe me peep her report card

Well
She and he were cool
Went to the same school
Hung in the same crew
Did things that two best friends would normally do
Until one day after taking that test
She got labeled advanced and he got labeled a fool
Dropped outta school and did what he felt he had to
Became a star mathematician
A genius in the kitchen
Studied how different greens and whites would help with his addition
Financial advisor for women
Pimpin' and flippin'
Now
He fights his tears inside of a prison

Pause

Forget it
Play track black boy
Or football or basketball
Or just ball black boy
Rob steal fail get money and go to jail
You do the same black girl

Read *Cosmo People VIBE* and *Vixen*
Try all your life to find the place that you fit into

You see I represent broken histories
Missing texts from textbooks
Kinesthetic learners that don't test good
Products of society
Twenty-four hours of good clean sobriety
A language that I play with because mine was taken
And a country that shuns me yet I have so much stake in it

A people
Who are a direct result of an action taken
And people who fear those people so they've created laws to evade and
    contain them
Inside of lines
Paths
Roads
Circles
And tracks

My name is Tish Jones
And I have been called to represent the missing piece

Ottawa, MN, Cemetery—1992

In memory of Otto Spavek

I

A million years ago
all these white people weren't even born
only this
layer of soft clay
like the clouds that now
quietly roll over the lush green hills of
the Ottawa, Minnesota, cemetery.

II

    Otto Spavek
    Born 1892 Prussia
    Died 1957 Ottawa, MN
Survived by his wife
Amelia and his daughters
Gretchen and Ruth, grandsons Otto II and Wilhelm—
And now Phil Bryant,
Who traveled this lonesome road to southern Minnesota
All the way from
The Southside of Chicago.

III

Otto Spavek, you probably knew nothing about slavery, Jim Crow,
the W. E. B. Dubois and Booker T. Washington debate, Fred Douglass,
Nat Turner, jazz, blues, or gospel, Civil Rights or Black Power. In
turn, I know nothing about howling blizzards and killer ice storms,
diphtheria, failed crops, farm foreclosure, loneliness and death on
the prairie.

IV

Otto Spavek, I'm thinking about you
exactly a hundred years after your birth.
I, a black man born in the City of Big Shoulders
a long way from here,
seven years before your death.
Standing here beside your grave,
in the grand scheme of the universe,
it's like we missed each other by just minutes
on the express train of American history.
The crows perched high atop the dead cottonwoods
unfurl their black wings like they have for a thousand years or so and
seem to squawk at the thought of it.

Coming to Minnesota

Emily, Population 348. That's what the sign read as we came into the little town. "Well, it's 352 now!" Our family was moving to Emily, Minnesota, from Chicago, Illinois. Despite very verbal protests from family and friends, my parents made the decision to transplant us from America's third largest city to a town that had about as many residents as there were students in my high school graduating class.

"They're going to eat you alive!"

"You'll starve up there!"

"Are there any colored folks up there?"

"You don't know anything about living in the country, you're city folk!"

"What will you do up there?"

The people who knew and loved us were concerned because we were an African American family moving to what we Chicagoans called "the northern woods of Minnesota." For us, going Up North meant a sixteen-hour car ride up through and across Wisconsin, into Minnesota, and then north and west to the north-central part of the state. To our family and friends, it meant going into the deep, dark wilderness where Black folks didn't exist.

We made the trek to Minnesota early in the summer of 1966. Interstate 94 had only two lanes, and we were often stuck behind the military convoys going to Wisconsin's Camp Douglas. Passing the jeeps and military trucks was one of the most frightening things for me, because it usually meant passing several vehicles at once. In fact, most of the roads were two lanes, except for certain sections near the larger cities, which were four. Roads in Minnesota had lots of bends and curves, and I hated it when we pulled out to pass a slow driver or a tractor pulling hay bales. But even with the fear factors of travel and being among the only Blacks for miles around, I, for one, was happy that we were moving. I loved the country. I loved the peace and quiet, and our new home was on one of the most beautiful lakes around.

Mom and Dad had decided that it was time to leave Chicago years before we actually left. Mom was a teacher and Dad had a dental practice, so in the summer we were free to take long vacations and travel around the country. The latter trips were explorations to places where we might possibly move. The choices had been narrowed to Minnesota or Colorado. I didn't know that as a kid, but both were wonderful to me. Providence chose Minnesota.

In 1965 my parents settled a lawsuit in which they won the right to move into a house they wanted to purchase in the Beverly Hills area of Chicago. The white neighbors were outraged that a "Negro" family would move into their area, so the owner had reneged on the sale. Even though we won the case, my father didn't want us to live in a neighborhood where we would most likely have a cross burned on the front lawn. We ended up moving to a nice ranch home on the other side of Chatham-Avalon Park area, the well-to-do African American community where we had been living.

Moving day was of course hectic, as moving days usually are. My father was a rather independent sort, so we hired a truck and did most of the moving ourselves. Because our street was posted as a dead end, there was little traffic, and that's what made meeting Mr. Hooks so odd.

It was night, we had gotten down to the last of our belongings to load up, and the piano had yet to be moved. My father and his cousin were struggling to get it down the porch steps when this odd little brown-skinned man drove up and jumped out of his car to help. "Don't you Negroes know you need help to move a piano? You can't do it by yourselves!" He wore kaki work pants and a thin, white half-buttoned cotton shirt. His words tumbled out with the speed of a New Yorker, but he was a local guy. Friendly, loud, opinionated, and very talkative. He moved like a mini-tornado. My independent dad, sure that he and his cousin could move the piano by themselves, graciously accepted the help.

The next day, the strange little man showed up on the doorstep of our new home. Daddy was at work and Mom was home alone with my two brothers and me. Mr. Hooks introduced himself and said he had left his briefcase and just stopped by to pick it up. Mom was obviously a little put off, but she engaged in polite conversation and in the course mentioned the fact that my dad was a dentist. Then, as most people would do once they found out Daddy's profession, he began to talk about all the dental work he needed done and asked for the office phone number. He retrieved his briefcase and left in a flurry.

Not long after that encounter, we found ourselves going on a road trip to Minnesota with this stranger from out of the blue. "Doc, I got a place you just gotta see!" was what Mr. Hooks told Daddy. Dad quoted Mr. Hooks when he told Mom we were going to take a road trip north for a few days.

"Daddy, do you know this guy?" I asked.

"Nope, just met him when he stopped to help with the piano."

"Do you know where we are going?"

"Nope, just going somewhere up north in Minnesota."

In *my* mind, my dad had lost *his!* I was only twelve at the time, but I knew that you don't go traveling across the country with a stranger that you just met and knew nothing about. But my dad was like that. He had a special way of relating to folks and always seemed to know who the good ones were and who was a little shady. It was not unusual for us to find some questionable character working on the yard or doing some handiwork around the house. "Oh, he's okay. He's just down on his luck, so we need to help him out," Dad would say.

That day we piled into the station wagon, all except Billy, my older brother who spent the weekend with a friend. Mr. Hooks climbed in with us, and we started on our way north. I found it curious that he didn't have a bag or suitcase, he just came as he was, wearing work pants and a half-buttoned-up cotton shirt. My mind went wild with imaginary news reports: "FAMILY OF FOUR FOUND MURDERED IN WISCONSIN." "DENTIST AND FAMILY LEFT FOR DEAD OFF INTERSTATE 94." I imagined poor Billy, left with no family. But actually, Mr. Hooks was pretty funny, very nice, and he talked a lot. He used the term "Negro" all the time and detested people calling themselves "Black." He had great appreciation for Negroes who spoke the King's English and didn't "mush mouth their words like idiots."

We drove all night and into the morning and stopped at a roadside restaurant in Mille Lacs for breakfast. We didn't know it at the time, but it was on an Ojibwe reservation. The place smelled old and rustic, but in a good way. It was made out of huge logs and decorated with a variety of Native American artifacts, including snowshoes, which I had heard about but had never seen. The menu had a wide selection of pancakes along with other tasty breakfast fare. There was something special about that particular breakfast in Minnesota; perhaps it was the beginning of my love affair with the state.

After breakfast, we drove on a little further and finally reached our destination. We pulled up to a small home located on what was then called "Squaw Lake" (since renamed "Little Emily," because the Anglo name was derogatory). To my surprise, this was the home of another African American family, the Thomases. They had moved to Emily Township from Harvey, Illinois, several years earlier. I was thrilled because they had a daughter, Sherry, who was my age. They also had two sons, one closer in age to my older brother and another a little older than my younger brother, Reggie, who was two at the time.

Their home was modest and sat atop a hill, peering over the lake. There was a steep path leading down to the water, and though the fishing was good, the swimming was not: there was a drop-off and the water was rather muddy.

Parents and kids got to know one another for a bit before it was time for us to get settled in. Off to the side of their home, the Thomases had a little cabin with a smaller yard, and since we had come prepared to camp, we set up the foldout camper in this little area. Sherry was curious about our setup, so I invited her in, but she didn't stay long. She said she didn't want to wear her welcome out. She was a very pretty girl with beautiful dark skin, and she had a strong Minnesota accent. Back then, we would say she "talked like she was white." She wasn't aware of her accent, however it was very noticeable to me because Black folks in Chicago just didn't sound like her.

Sherry and I became fast friends and spent hours together going for walks along the road searching for agates and comparing notes on life in Chicago and life in the country. She took me to meet one of her friends who lived across the highway, and the three of us hiked down a little dirt road to Lake Roosevelt, which was a very nice lake with a small, inviting beach area. The water was crystal clear. You could see the rippled sand at the bottom. We waded in the water for a bit, then the other girl went home and Sherry and I went back to her place.

We stayed with the Thomases for a few days. Each day Mom and Dad would go off for a while, taking my brother with them, and I would hang out with Sherry. The day before we were due to leave, Mom told me that they had found some property. I was curious to see what this new place looked like. We drove across the highway and down the little dirt road, and we stopped at a little beach, the same little beach Sherry and I enjoyed just a day earlier. "Well, this is it!" Dad said, getting out of the car. He lit his pipe and strolled around the grounds. There were cabins hidden in the wild brush that grew all around. Seven, to be exact. "What do you think?" he asked, surveying his new kingdom.

All I could think of is that we now owned a beach! We could go swimming all summer if we wanted. We could also go boating and fishing, and the really cool part was that it was just right across the road from Sherry's place, so I'd have a friend handy to share all this with.

At the time of the sale, the owners knew only that their property had gone to a very nice dentist and his wife the schoolteacher. Mom and Dad dealt directly with the Realtor and didn't meet the owners of the land until later. Then once again, the color issue reared its ugly head, but the deal had already been sealed, and there was nothing that could be done about it. The property was ours. We heard that "Negroes" were not welcome on Lake Roosevelt. There were other lakes for *those people* to have their summer homes and Lake Roosevelt was not one of them.

Mr. Hooks and his wife Anna had property on a lake in Little Pine Township, just east of Emily; a retired Chicago policeman, Mr. Flagg, and his wife owned a resort on Lake Mary outside of Emily; and of course there were the Thomases across the road. None of these families lived on the lakes apparently reserved for the "Negroes," and each seemed relatively happy, though each family had had to forge their way into the local community life. At that time, only the Thomases were full time, year-round residents and had kids who attended the local school.

Now that we owned property in Minnesota, we no longer took trips all over the country. Dad and Mom had plans for the resort. Their vision was to make it into a camp for inner-city youth so they could have a taste of the country. They believed that part of the solution to the gang issue and teenage violence was to let kids experience the beauty and healing aspects of nature along with a good dose of positive role modeling.

There was much to do to fix up the cabins and get the brush tamed so that we wouldn't have to camp every time we came up. Daddy and Billy did most of the work on the property, clearing the brush with sickles and scythes. Then one day my father found this motorized contraption on wheels called a weed eater that looked kind of like a mechanical dragonfly's head with shark teeth attached at the bottom and two large handles on top. It made life a lot easier, still, much had to be done by hand since the property included a steep hill.

One time Dad came up a few days before us to get a head start on the work. We arrived in the wee hours of the morning, and when Mom asked him how he was doing, he just looked at her and said, "I'm so tired and sore. Even my hair hurts!"

Mom and I worked on scraping the old paint off the cabins and Billy spent his time digging holes for septic tanks. None of the cabins had indoor bathrooms, though they all had running water—but no hot water. So that meant that business had to be taken care of in the outhouses, of which there were three on the property. Fortunately, the cabin we chose to make our home-away-from-home had one very near. Unfortunately, it was an old, smelly, dank, dark, creepy place with spider webs all over, and I had serious issues with it . . . even after it was cleaned out.

There was a much nicer one located up by the house where the former owners had lived. So Daddy, being the kind man that he was, managed to replace the creepy biffy with the nicer outhouse. It was clean and bright and

Mom even painted it yellow with pink trim to make it look special. Still, I really appreciated the work my brother was doing and couldn't wait (but had to) until the new bathrooms were installed.

The first year we owned the resort, family and friends came up from the Chicago area with us to help get the place up to snuff. We made curtains, installed plumbing, painted buildings, scraped old paint off wooden fishing boats, caulked them and repainted them, cut weeds, shopped for linens and blankets, bought pots and pans and dishes, scoured second-hand shops for tables and chairs, and on and on. Our rewards for our hard work were fresh fish from the lake, swimming every day, campfires, and just a great time.

Sometimes Mom and Dad went up north without us kids, and Mom came back with stories about the Northern Lights. She talked about how they shimmered and danced back and forth across the sky. Sometimes they were colored with red, yellow, green and purple. It seemed the most exciting things happened when she and Daddy went up there without us. Then came the day when I got to see the Northern Lights for myself.

My brother and I and the kids who came up with us sometimes went over to Flagg's resort and hung out with the teens over there, playing pool, listening to music, and dancing. This particular night, we went to one of the other towns to hang out. We happened to be out in the parking lot when someone noticed a light in the sky. We looked up and there they were, the shimmering, dancing lights of the Aurora Borealis. I had never seen anything so amazing in my life! Some of us watched the sky till our necks started aching; others got bored and went on to other things. Personally, I was having a spiritual moment.

Minnesota nights remain amazing to me. The first night I looked at the sky I remarked to my mom how it looked like someone had spilled grits all over a black floor. I'd never seen so many stars in my life. And now I was witnessing something happening in the sky that no one I knew besides my parents had ever seen. I felt humbled by the experience.

Each time we left Minnesota to go back to Chicago, I got depressed. Generally, we left Sunday afternoon and got home by nine or ten in the morning. For some reason, I always felt that Minnesota was more like home than Chicago. I seemed to *fit* up there on the lake in the country much better than I did in the hustle and bustle of the Windy City.

Each spring, before school was out, we began the trek to Emily, sixteen long hours of travel, a little rest, then work to get the cabins cleaned out and ready for summer. There was always so much to be done, but things were coming along. Mom took a hotel management course to learn how to handle the resort. Daddy looked into special equipment for the grounds and for handling the care and feeding of campers. They were both always looking out for good deals to procure something that was needed.

Army surplus provided bunk beds and mattresses for the cabins; the post office auctions provided fabric for making curtains and seat covers; second-hand stores provided furniture; and some fortuitous connections provided sheets for the beds. Slowly things began to take shape.

In 1968 the Boulder Lodge Resort and Camp Boulder Bay really looked like it was going to happen. The cabins were pretty decent, at least the livable ones were, and the old house, the residence of the former owners, had been turned into the commons area. There was a nice-sized kitchen with stainless steel sinks and work space, room for a large group to eat, a couple of smaller rooms for sleeping if necessary, and a large, walk-in closet that had been added to serve as storage and a place to keep the linens.

Cabin #1 at the top of the hill was turned into the recreation area. It was just a one-room cabin with no plumbing, so it became the hangout for the kids we brought up from Chicago. There was a piano, a stereo, a pool table, a couple of sofas, and a few chairs. We could relax here after working, or hang out if it was raining outside. We could dance or have talent shows, play charades, or just sit around and listen to music. Sometimes Mom played the piano and we all sang along. Though it never quite became the youth camp my parents envisioned, it did eventually become a working resort, and families from Chicago and the Twin Cities area, both Black and white, did come to enjoy the beauty of the area. We even had the occasional church youth group come to stay.

My parents decided to move permanently to Minnesota in the summer of 1972. Daddy had his practice to close out, so he wasn't able to move right away. Bill had been going to school at Carleton College, and he had already decided to make his home in Minneapolis. I was in college at Ripon, so Reggie was the only one of us kids to really be affected by the move. He was eight at the time.

We hadn't yet built a permanent home on the property, so when we moved, most of our things went into one of the cabins for storage. We were still staying in cabin #4, which was halfway up the hill and had a beautiful view of the lake, but it wasn't winterized. So we worked all summer to get the old house in shape for winter. The linen closet had to be insulated, and it became my room. There was an old barrel stove for heat, and though there was a bathroom, there was no tub or shower, so we bathed in an old washtub, just like the pioneers in movies.

None of us had it as hard as Mom and Reggie. They spent that first winter alone during the week. Bill was living in Minneapolis and I had the luxury of being on campus in Wisconsin. Daddy had to close out his practice in Chicago and find a buyer for his share of the medical building that housed his office. He drove up to Emily every weekend and sometimes picked me up at Ripon, so I could see Mom and my brother. Sometimes Mr. Hooks rode with him. The only thing that ever stopped Dad from coming up was the occasional snowstorm, and even then he tried but sometimes had to turn back.

In the old house, as we came to call it, Mom and Reggie had to literally keep the home fires burning by shoving logs into the old barrel stove. Daddy made sure there was plenty of wood for them, but during the week it was mainly Reggie's job to bring in more and see to it that Mom had a sufficient supply on hand.

The phone was a rotary dial contraption on a party line, which means several families shared the same line and each family had a particular ring pattern. If someone else was using the phone, you had to wait until they finished; if you were using the phone, you sometimes had to endure the quiet invasion of a nosy neighbor listening in on your conversation. Mom remembered party lines from her childhood. I remembered them from watching *Lassie* on television. It took a lot of getting used to after having had my own Princess touch-tone phone back in Chicago. The phone was now pretty much relegated to emergency use only. Conversations with friends were short.

In Chicago, we had all the local TV channels and we could pull in one or two extra by using UHF. Before cable TV, that was pretty good. In Emily, we could get Channel 12. Period. The local news was full of information about corn, soybeans, and pork bellies. There were very few if any stories about shootings, robberies, and other crimes. The news from the Twin Cities was a little less pristine. And always when a crime was committed by a Black person it always started, "Today a Black man . . ." During football, basketball, and baseball seasons, that was all there was on Channel 12. We did a lot of reading.

For the most part, things went decently for Mom and Reggie that winter. There was much to get used to, besides the washtub and only having one television channel. There were a couple of neighbors feuding with each other all the time. We had run-ins with one of them during the summers. He would complain about the music being too loud. Sometimes it was because teenagers like to play their music in the ear-splitting range, but most of the time, we just chalked it up to him being a crotchety old man.

One evening in the winter, this particular neighbor, who was known to shoot at his other neighbor from time to time, apparently got it into his mind that he needed to terrorize Mom and Reggie. He came over to the house with a tree and began yelling at them and beating the house with it. Mom called the police, who eventually came, calmed him down, and took him to the local hospital for evaluation. When Mom shared the story with us, I thought she must be exaggerating, because who is going to haul a tree around like a Neanderthal and attack someone's home? Yet he did indeed have a small tree, bigger than a sapling, and he used it to beat on the house. I used to think Mom was brave and a little nuts when she went out during bad thunderstorms to make sure all the cabins were closed up. But after this episode and knowing that she managed to keep her wits about her, I realized just how brave she truly was.

The Frenches, a Mormon family who owned horses and a cattle farm a couple of miles away from us, befriended Mom and Reggie. On some occasions Mrs. French would visit and bring milk from their cow or freshly baked bread. She was also the one who introduced us to "bars," the cake-like cookies baked in a pan and cut into rectangles. We didn't have "bars" in Chicago. Reggie went to school with their son Jason, and they became best friends. Marty, the oldest daughter, taught me how to ride and train horses during my summer vacation. Eventually Daddy bought a couple of horses from Mrs. French and bred them so each of us had our own.

Anna Mae Hooks and Mom became best friends, and Anna made sure that Mom was kept plenty busy while Reggie was in school. They went shopping in Brainerd or Pequot Lakes or Aitkin, and sometimes they would just go to one of the local cafés for lunch. Anna always had fascinating stories to share about her life growing up and living in Chicago. She also introduced Mom to some of the other women in the area.

While in Chicago, Mom had studied organ and bought a Wurlitzer with a synthesizer and foot pedals. Both the organ and our spinet piano were in the old house, and she practiced daily. To show off the capabilities of her organ, she played one of her favorite pieces, "Satin Doll." She performed with a bounce and rhythm that made you want to get up and dance. Once word got out that she played the organ, the pastor from the Lutheran church in Outing, two miles away, came to visit and persuaded Mom to become the church organist. Thus began a new career for the teacher from Chicago. Mom held that position at Our Savior's Lutheran Church for over twenty years.

Word had also circulated that a dentist had moved into the area. The town of Aitkin was losing their one-and-only dentist, so they approached

Mom and asked her if Dad would consider practicing there. She told them she would talk to him about it and he would get back to them. They talked, and Daddy agreed to work in Aitkin once he closed out things in Chicago.

As soon as the ground thawed, work began on the new house. It began as an A-frame cabin, but we had a family discussion and the cabin became a home with over 3,000 square feet: five bedrooms, four bathrooms (three with tubs!), a living room, a family room, a sunken dining room, a galley kitchen, an art studio for Mom, and a library. There was also a laundry area and space for a small dental office, complete with consultation office, examination room, and a darkroom for developing x-rays. Within a few months, the house was almost completed, and we moved in.

Dad worked on getting the office in Aitkin together, and at his request, Mom painted a mural of Reggie fishing with our dog Nugget on one of the exam room walls. Within days it was time to open the doors for business. So far our experience in Minnesota had been much better than expected, excluding the tree-bearing neighbor. Most people seemed warm and welcoming, but the real question was, would an African American dentist survive in rural Minnesota?

Daddy decided it would be a good move to keep the assistant who had previously been working there. At least that way, patients would see a familiar face. I was the receptionist. The first day, only two people came. The second day, three people came. However, the third day, eighteen people showed up for appointments, and for the next twenty-some years, Dad seldom had fewer than that. He had patients from all over, including a judge from St. Cloud, many of the regional state patrol officers, and even former patients from Chicago who really didn't want to lose him as a dentist. One of his former patients flew in from New York until Dad talked her into saving her money and finding a local dentist she could trust.

Emily, Minnesota, was now home to us. When people needed an organist to fill in for church service, or play for a wedding or funeral, they called Mom, because her playing was expressive. When people needed dental work, they called Dad, because he was the gentlest and most patient dentist anyone had ever experienced.

Growing up in Chicago, I always wanted three things: a horse, a guitar, and a home by the lake. Providence smiled on me and gave me what I wanted. I felt at home here in the woods by the lake. I never understood why Minnesota always felt more like home than Chicago, but it always did.

Years later, I worked at Wilder Forest, the Wilder Foundation's conference and retreat center near Marine on St. Croix, and I had an opportunity to participate in their Dialogues on Diversity. People from every race attended these events, and workshops were geared toward bringing people together to a better place of understanding and acceptance. One workshop that I attended began with a visualization exercise. We were told to close our eyes and move back in time through our mother, her mother, and hers, through many generations. Then we were to notice where we were and what was going on there. I fully expected to be someplace in Africa, listening to the drums. Instead, I found myself by a lake, listening to drums—but they were Ojibwe drums, and the woods around me looked like the woods around Lake Roosevelt. I was surprised, and yet a part of me knew that yes, this was my home.

Anybody But Me on Grand Avenue

If I were the blonde passing the corner in
chain-printed silk shorts—a beautiful teal blue with gold—
curving leg exposed from crotch to her high-wedged shoes
if I were twenty-nine again like her
if my short jacket grazed my hip bones like hers,
I would rush through this sunlight into my car
settle my bare thighs on the seat, put the key in the ignition
and get the hell out of here in a roar. Top down.

If I were the gray haired woman with her slender jeans-wearing daughter
and her afflicted daughter in the red coat,
the one with braces and a screech on repeat
too high for a public place,
I'd be praying for sustenance and the patience to stay loving
through one more hour, one more day.

If I were the brown-skinned man
with stroller and toddler in a white coat
I would keep talking to her as I lifted her onto our bench
I would turn to get the promised cookie inside
forgetting danger, then turn back alert
to hold her in my arms
even if we had to abandon the awning's shade
and start over.

If I were the woman in the yellow silk blouse, her pen caressing
the notebook paper, writing without a doubt
my missed poem about the spit of land at La Fortaleza
me, nineteen and out of the country for the first time

the sky doming dark-light above around beside me,
the thrashing ocean, how small I felt in the world
hardly big enough to contain this thudding heart,
I would walk over and rip the paper from her hands
hold it next to my heart
because she can stop now
she's got it all down.

Afrika

i think of you often now
dream you like a dense forest
in which is buried my Birth string,
    miss your tenderness
    the softness of your desires

i am more a stranger now than i ever was
foreign in every city
home, a moon to which my mother sings
home, my heart pulsing at midnight
i stand outside of time looking at myself
i stand outside of myself looking at time
and how far we have strayed
we children of forgotten gods
dancing for the stars' forgiveness
unable to remember the rhythms
borne of communion with God
unable to see the river which bears our name
which flows like the water from our mother's womb

how will i sing your memory
how will i speak your pain
am i strong enough to love you
with the love you deserve?

Kenwood 1964

When I was eight, my mother embarrassed me by coaxing my father from the religious depths of a bag of potato chips and a cold stunted tumbler of whiskey—the Body of Christ, the Blood of Christ, existential morsels savored each night at High Mass, the Johnny Carson Show. She called him to the kitchen for what had become a weekly ritual since the day we broke the housing barrier in the all-white enclave of Kenwood.

"Frank, come into the kitchen!"

A rabbit's foot thumped against my lung as I sat on a stool before her and imagined my father in the living room groaning on bended knee like a bishop breaking genuflection. Shortly after the sandpaper growl of his slippers on linoleum, he appeared, tall, gaunt, bleary-eyed, and whiskered, beneath the kitchen's white trumpets of neon.

"It's time to cut the boy's hair. You should have done it hours ago. He's reciting 'Gunga Din' tomorrow in the talent show, or have you forgotten?" She looked at his eyes. He turned away. If not for the exigencies of keeping me still on the stool, holding me down as the hum of clippers dive-bombed for me like a river of bees, she would have added, "and don't ask for my liver when liquor pickles yours." Instead she reminded him of more pressing matters. "We don't need these people to think we're raising a long-haired militant."

My father was quiet during these proceedings, unless I squirmed or cried out. Then he'd *whack* me several times across my thigh with the comb and *whack* me again if I whimpered. How could he hear Johnny Carson in the living room if I was crying? The razor dragged swiftly and painfully over my scalp like the blade, now the back, of a shovel digging through gravel. By the end, I was tired and in tears.

"Now don't we look like the moon?" Mom laughed. "Needs a touch of shine." She rubbed baby oil all over my scalp, forehead, and face, stood back and winced, put her hand to her forehead like a visor, "Oh no! The glare is too much for me. Off to bed before you blind me."

Teary-eyed and vengeful, I climbed the back stairs on my way to bed. The front stairs, soft and bouncy with two layers of wine-and-revolver red carpet and the balustrade of mahogany gleaming obsidian over white hand-carved balusters, were not to be used by my two younger sisters and me, just as the "antique" chairs in the living room were not for us to sit on. The front part of the house, kept spotless, was for company, whenever company came, or for show during the long dry seasons when they didn't come, or to remind us that indeed they *were* coming; that "company," our code word for white people, had, at that very moment, packed their bags and taken the high road to hobnob with Mom and Dad.

"Remember your lines?" she asked, marching halfway up the stairs behind me. "Or should we go over them one more time?"

Her words barely registered. I was a million miles away at a gun store, fondling a pistol, counting the bullets I would pump into her chest.

"I know you hear me talkin' to you, boy." Her New Orleans drawl was upon me, a bad sign indeed, a portent of the yardstick, the strap, the shoe, the hand, or whatever's handy, prophecy on the wings of dialect. *One day I'm riding into town with my posse, Mother, gonna deputize all my friends, gonna hang you from the highest tree.* Then it struck me that I had no friends. The whole school, every student save my sister and me, was white. They could hardly be called my friends. By third grade, the year in which they shook themselves of the notion that my black skin was a new form of leprosy, they'd begun to warm to me the way one warms to furry, but caged, zoo creatures. Not with the most elastic stretch of the imagination could I call them friends. My posse vaporized on the high chaparral.

"I said Ah know you hear me talkin' to you!"

"No, I don't need to recite the poem again," I sniffled.

"No, who?"

"No, Mom."

It is a curious twist in the Black male psyche, or the way this gender is socialized, that I did not have nearly as much rage toward my father as I did toward my mother in those early days of traveling incognegro. Even now, it's hard for me to unravel skein upon skein of memory and understand why. All I can do is take the plunge and write it all down. Mom was a rage-junkie. Dad was a somnambulant dragon who could slash and quarter me with his tail as his eyes rolled the sea of a drunken stupor. I never knew what infraction, however small, would incur his fire-breathing wrath. Sometimes a smart remark would send me hurtling before him down the basement stairs to a whipping in the woodshed; sometimes it would conjure no more than a sullen look. Unlike Mom, who criticized every third move I made and thus unfurled the text of what was and was not permissible, daily, hourly, minutely. (Three years later, I would earn some slaps and flogging around the head and shoulders from her—in response to one of her tedious monologues on how hard she worked to put clothes on my back and food on the table, I had looked up from my scrumptious bowl of Cheerios, bored and disinterested, and replied, "What can I say, Ida-Lorraine, that's your job.")

On the morning of the talent show, I was nauseous. Each spoonful of oatmeal had a life of its own, wanting to come up. For a kid who normally yakked to the point of driving people from a room, I was remarkably quiet. At eight, memorizing "Gunga Din" was not my idea of a good time. The thought of reciting it to the whole school was even less appealing.

Two years back, in 1962, the people of Kenwood had humiliated Mom and Dad: five hundred households, not families, but households, in the posh enclave on the hill overlooking downtown Minneapolis, had signed a petition to keep us out. The man who owned the house was selling it for the going rate of thirty-five thousand dollars. The problem was simple: he'd love to sell it to us—he was moving to Seattle—but "you do realize, don't you, that I'll have a black mark against me forever, that I can never come back to Kenwood, they'll turn a cold shoulder to me. You do realize that, don't you? However, if you can get a loan, we'll see what we can do."

In the end, we moved into the white stucco mansion on the hill, not with a bank loan, but with every cent of our insurance policy. My father cashed it in and made a heretofore unheard of down payment of fifty percent. For the other half, he and the owner came to terms on a note. How long did we go without insurance? The rest of first grade? Part of second grade— third grade? I don't know. But I need no help recalling the symptoms of being uninsured in a place where you're not wanted. Dad sunk deeper into drink. Mom blitzkrieged antique shops, buying Greco-Latin statues; a small fountain (boy on a dolphin: dolphin spitting water); and antique furniture, which she drew tape across, arm-to-arm, in case one of us kids wasn't wrapped too tight and got a notion that the living room was a place for us to sit down in. The walls were re-papered with eighteenth-century landscapes replete with the landed gentry striking poses like bargains. She was waiting for the day when the neighbors would finally creep through our front door to see what they could see. She set up this grand display of culture with the cheery enthusiasm of Charlie the Tuna. At all costs she would prove Starkist wrong, providing a desperate rebuttal to the tag line, "Sorry, Charlie, Starkist doesn't want tuna with good taste. Starkist wants tuna that tastes good." And I was scalped on a weekly basis and made to memorize long classic poems, the longer the better, and recite them at the end of each month, when all I really wanted was to eat tutti-fruity ice cream, sing a Chubby Checker song, and do the Twist.

It was then, somewhere between the winter of '63 and the winter of Jack Kennedy's death, when my parents decided that in order to keep the teachers from treating me the way my classmates treated me (the girls wouldn't touch me; the boys called me "nigger" and gave me "snuggies"—two boys hold you down, while one boy pulls the back of your drawers high up your back, thus crushing your testicles against your pelvis, while still another boy mashes your face into the snow) was to insure that I was more *verbal* than anyone else. Verbal people, they surmised, are intelligent people; and intelligent people are well liked. It was B. F. Skinner's S-R psychology taken to a whole new level. "Verbal" was the stimulus, "well-liked" was the response. They were, in fact, both clinical psychologists.

"The oatmeal makes me sick," I told her.

"Same oatmeal you had yesterday." She pushed the bowl back in front of me.

"Mom, do I have to? I feel sick."

"It's thirty below outside. Oatmeal sticks to your ribs."

Dad stopped on his way out the door. "If you're sick go to sickbay," he bellowed, "Don't droop in front of everyone at the kitchen table."

"Can't go to sickbay today," Mom said, "he's reciting 'Gunga Din' in the talent show." Then she looked at my bald head and laughed, "My, my, the moon in the morning."

C'mon posse! Ride into town. Dig in those spurs. We got us a live one here.

Four hours later, on knees of rubber, I took the stage. The hush in the auditorium made me seasick. My head was empty. I forgot why I was up there. The lights, the sharp stab of glare, dug into my eyes. I started to leave when I caught another glare, the glare of Mom's eyes from the back of the auditorium. It jogged my memory.

"My name is Frank B. Wilderson, III. I'm in third grade, Miss Johnson's class, PT [portable classroom] number two. I'm going to recite 'Gunga Din,' by Kipling." Again, Mom's sharp swift glare. I corrected myself. "By *Rudyard* Kipling. A turn of the . . . turn of the . . ." I forgot, and then remembered. "A turn-of-the-century British writer."

> You may talk o' gin and beer
> When you're quartered safe out 'ere,
> An' you're sent to penny-fights an' Aldershot it;
> But when it comes to slaughter
> You will do your work on water,
> An' you'll lick the bloomin' boots of 'im that's got it.

> Now in Injia's sunny clime,
> Where I used to spend my time
> A-servin' of 'Er Majesty the Queen,
> Of all them black-faced crew . . .

I was dumbstruck; blank again. I had said, "Of all them blackfaced crew" at least three times. I caught Mom's eyes. She shifted nervously in her chair, she looked around to see who, if anyone, was looking at her. We were both naked. The murmuring in the auditorium brought me back. I remembered the next line and clothed us. I pushed on.

> Of all them black-faced crew
> The finest man I knew
> Was our regimental *bhisti*, Gunga Din.
> He was "Din! Din! Din!
> You limpin' lump o' brick-dust, Gunga Din!
> Hi! *slippery hitherao!*
> Water, get it! *Panee lao!*
> You squidgy-nosed old idol, Gunga Din!"
> . . .
> 'E would dot an' carry one
> Till the longest day was done,
> An' 'e didn't seem to know the use o' fear.
> If we charged or broke or cut,
> You could bet your bloomin' nut,
> 'E'd be waitin' fifty paces right flank rear.

The recitation went well from that point on, although I spoke a little too swiftly, if memory serves me well. But it may have been because each pause caused the din of silence to roar in my ears and I had to avoid the silent spaces at all costs. Then another line seized me by the throat.

> An' for all 'is dirty 'ide
> 'E was white, clear white, inside . . .

Again, I stopped. I'd done my best, there was no way I could remember the ending. All it took was one half-step toward stage left for me to visualize the beating I would get for giving up. My posse rode into town with the poem's ending in their saddlebags.

An' for all 'is dirty 'ide
'E was white, clear white, inside
When 'e went to tend the wounded under fire . . .
. . .

Din! Din! Din!
You Lazarushian-leather Gunga Din!
Though I've belted you and flayed you,
By the livin' Gawd that made you,
You're a better man than I am, Gunga Din!

The applause was deafening. I had no idea for whom. When I reached the back of the room, not so much as a hug, nor the promise of a tutti-fruity ice cream cone.

"That was good," she said, "but why did you stop so many times?"

After a snowstorm, if there is no wind, the drifts peak high as ocean breakers. And when the shovels are laid to rest, white walls of snow, tall as a twelve-year-old, line the sidewalks. If you're seven or eight, there's no seeing over them. Only your memory can guide you through the white labyrinth to school. More often than not, I was late. Being late through the labyrinth meant staying after and writing on the blackboard, "I will not be late for school," over and over and over again. Sometimes, I had the option of writing one long paragraph beginning with, "The most important thing I learned today was . . ." But I had no way of knowing what the most important thing was and, because I was Roman Catholic and did not want to lie—not because lying was disdainful to me, but because the confessional smelled of dust and decay—I chose line after line of *I will not be late.*

Remembered

God's Chosen People

After the death of his mother, Lloyd Brown lived from 1918 to 1920 at the Crispus Attucks Home, a combined orphanage and old folks' home in St. Paul that was run by and for African Americans.

It was a fine hill for sliding down in the wintertime. Five blocks long, and steep. You didn't need a Blue Streak or a Flexible Flyer; a cardboard carton was just as good after the snow got icy. And when you found a big piece of tin—it was a beer sign that was going to fall off the fence pretty soon anyway—you curled up one end and went bellyflop, just like anybody else.

The big wooden house was on top of the hill and none of the other houses on the street were as fine and fancy. That's where you lived. You and your two little sisters and Georgie and Doug and Jewell and Annie Mae and the rest of the kids and the old folks too and Mrs. Henderson. Your sisters and the other young ones were too little to go sliding, or to school either.

There was a low block of granite near the curb before you went up the steps to the front door. Carved on its street side was one word: SCHUSTER. It looked just like a graveyard stone and the kids across the street said maybe somebody was buried there, and they wouldn't ever step on it. Mrs. Henderson said that the Schusters used to own the big house. That was a long time ago, long before the Society took the place over. Old Man Schuster owned half the timber in northern Minnesota at one time, she said, and when they lived here it was the only house on the hill. Richest folks in town. And now us—and she'd laugh.

Standing right next to the stone was a little black man in boots. That was Jim. He looked real, but he wasn't; he was made out of iron. He stood there all the time with one hand up holding a big ring in it, and he was bowing toward the street. Sometimes after a hard snow, and after the snowplow went by, all you could see was his hand with the ring sticking up. In the summertime, when the waterwagon rolled down with the big gray horses holding back hard, their hoofs braced in the dusty road and their straw bonnets bobbing up and down as they tucked in their jaws, the sprinkler would get Jim all wet and he'd be shinier and blacker than ever. And when it stormed at night and the thunder rolled low and the rain slashed at the shingles you could look out of your window under the roof and see him way down below, a tiny little man standing under the gaslamp. All by himself, but he wasn't afraid.

When you ran down in the morning you said, Goodbye, Jim, I'm going to school, and when you came home you said, Hi, Jim, here I am again. Not all the time, though. Like that day you didn't want to talk to anybody—not even Jim. You ran all the way up the hill and up the steps and around to the back and into the carriage house where nobody could ever find you or ask you what's the matter. There weren't any carriages in the place—just a lot of broken chairs and beds and a cracked pisspot with roses on the lid and some rakes and a lawnmower and a horsecollar on the wall with straw sticking out of it.

Funny how it was. First it was just singing—all the kids in the auditorium singing I'm Forever Blowing Bubbles and Over There and Tipperary. That was after the pledge-allegiance part, with Mr. Olson standing on the stage in his khaki Home Guard uniform holding the American flag. He was the janitor. Then they had to go and sing that Li'l Liza Jane song and they sang the words funny and looked at you funny and smiled to themselves—all of them. Every one of them. Even Theresa Margiotti who was your friend, she giggled too.

You told Jim the next day you were sorry you didn't say hello but you didn't tell him why. You didn't tell Mrs. Henderson either. One time when she saw you running home like that and you told her about how Terry O'Brien called you chocolate drop and the girls all started singing it like a song—like that song they sing when they're jumping rope: *choc'lit drop, choc'lit drop, hi ho a leary ho, choc'lit drop . . .* she washed your face and said next time you just call them po' white trash, that's all, you just call them that—po' white trash! Then she held you close like she did the little ones and you felt worse than ever and wished you were back in your secret place where no one could see you.

It was a big, fancy house all right. Three stories tall and there was an attic and on top there was a little tower that looked like the wedding cake at the Bon Ton Bakery. And on top of that there was a weathervane. The horse's head was broken off. Sometimes at night when you were in bed you could hear him squeaking when he turned around in the wind. Because you were big you had a room all by yourself in the attic. It was a little room but it was very nice and Mrs. Henderson had pasted up a picture of Black Beauty on the sloping wall. There was an iron bed, painted white, with tin cans filled with kerosene under each leg. That was to keep the bedbugs from crawling up. There were a lot of them and the wallpaper was streaked where you squashed them. Like shooting stars.

In front of the house there was a wide porch; it had railings with a lot of little knobs on them like the ones on the big brass bed that Mrs. Henderson slept in. All the way down in the street you could see the sign over the porch: PETER SALEM HOME FOR THE AGED. It was gold lettering and even though some of the words were faded you could read them all. And you knew who Peter Salem was, too—the black man who fought at Bunker Hill; Mrs. Henderson told you. She knew a lot of things the teacher didn't know. Miss Regan didn't know about Peter Salem for one thing.

You were seven—nearly eight—and you had started going to school the same year they brought you to the Home. It was funny at first, you and your sisters being in this place with all the real old people. But after a while some more children came, but they were little kids and you wished the Charities would bring some that were big. Mrs. Henderson said it ought to be just for old folks and they ought to start a home for colored orphans, too. But she was glad to have you just the same.

She was a nice lady, the matron, and when you had the whooping cough she made onion tea and brought it all the way up to your room even though she said the steps were killing her and it's high time they were giving her some help. She was round and fat and laughed a lot. Sometimes she would laugh so hard she'd sit down in her rocking chair and shake all over and the tears would roll down on her apron and she'd say, Law, chile, what won't you be thinkin' 'bout next—you'll be the death of me sure! And she'd give you a piece of bread smeared with lard, sometimes with sugar sprinkled on it.

But mostly she was too busy cleaning and cooking and taking care of the sick ones like Mr. Thigpen to talk to you or the young ones much. Mr. Thigpen must have been the oldest one in the Home. His hair was white and frizzy like the top of a dandelion and he never got out of bed. He just lay there all day and never moved except to spit into the slop jar by the bed after a coughing spell. But he liked to have you come in and tell what you learned at school. And when you told him he'd want you to tell him more things. He hated everybody else and when the matron came in he'd close his eyes and pretend to be asleep. She said he was the evilest old man she ever laid eyes on—wouldn't even let Reverend Bixby come into his room when he came to call. Cuss him out something awful.

One day after school he wasn't there—he went away to his father's house. Doug—he was only five—said that Mr. Thigpen's father must be older than anybody in the world and Mrs. Henderson said that he was. Older than anybody.

· · ·

The old people didn't go out much. Mostly they sat around in the parlor where the children weren't allowed. But you could go in to take out the ashes from the big coal stove in the middle of the room and to fill up the scuttle. It had a different smell from the rest of the house, a dry brown smell like old people and old wallpaper and moldy carpets and curtains and old tobacco pipes. Sometimes they talked, but Miss Rose never talked to anybody. Just sat in a rocking chair by the stained-glass bay window and rocked back and forth and hummed. She chewed snuff. Then there was Miss Redpath and Miss Rainey and little Miss Fowler and Mr. Rixey and Mr. Campbell and Mr. Cherry and some more too. Mr. Campbell wasn't like the others.

He had whiskers like one of the prophets and liked to sit outside whenever it was nice. He could go to sleep sitting on the porch in the summertime and not wake up when a fly walked on his nose. Mr. Campbell carried a potato in his hip pocket for the rheumatism and he could tell you stories about working on the riverboats that used to come all the way up from N'Awlins. There's no more boats nowadays, he'd say, but one of these days, son, I'm going to pack up and take a railroad train all the way back. All the way back to Hannibal and to St. Louis and to Cairo and Memphis, and to Greenville and Vicksburg and Natchez, all the way down—plumb into N'Awlins. He'd say those names over and over like it was a song and pat his carpet slipper keeping time. And he'd blow through his hands like a train whistle: *Whoo-oo-whoo! Hannibal and St. Louis, Cairo and Memphis, Greenville and Vicksburg, Natchez and N'Awlins—whoo-oo! Yes, Miss Lindy, yes, Miss Lou, I'm a-comin' through . . .*

I warn't one of them roustabouts neither, son, he'd say, a riverboat pilot I was—or same as one. Me 'n Cap'n Bob could take you anywheres you wanted to go and didn't need much water neither. Mind the time we went clean up to Fletcher's Landing 'fore we found out that the old river'd doubled back and cut a brand-new channel five miles on the other side! Yessiree, and that's the gospel truth. That was *something*, let me tell you.

Mr. Campbell was a good singer and could sing louder than anybody those nights in the parlor. Sunday nights they were.

The singing was nice but you liked the stories better. They would open the Bible on the little round table first, but nobody would do much reading from it. Mostly they told the stories, a whole lot better ones than those Miss Regan told or the ones in Elson's Second Reader. At first the matron used to make you go upstairs to bed like the little ones, but after a while you found out that if you sat over on the corner stairs where it was dark Mrs. Henderson wouldn't notice you. Or at least she wouldn't say anything.

They'd turn the gaslight down low and when the stove was going good they'd turn it off altogether. The light came through the little isinglass windows and jumped up and down on their old brown faces and their eyes would shine and their shadows on the walls nodded and moved back and forth. Every once in a while Mr. Campbell would chunk up the stove with the poker and when nobody was looking he'd spit into the scuttle. Chewing wasn't allowed at prayer meeting time but he always did except when Reverend Bixby came around. He knew you were back there in the dark on the stairs and sometimes he'd look around and wink at you.

The stories were mostly about the old times when there was slavery and the children of Israel were in Egypt. Some of the words were hard to understand. Like "begat." Abraham begat Isaac and Isaac begat Jacob and Jacob begat twelve sons. There were other things that were hard to figure out, too. If they weren't really children—and some of them were old men like Abraham—why were they called the children of Israel? And why were the colored people in those days called Israelites? Some of the stories were about children and they were good ones, too. Except the one about the little boys who laughed at the old prophet Elisha and called him an old baldhead and God sent two bears out of the woods and the bears ate them up. But there was the one about little King David who took his slingshot and killed the giant. In those days the old people weren't always telling you that you couldn't have a slingshot, you might put somebody's eye out with it.

Then there was Joshua—he was a *fighting* man—and Moses and Aaron and how they ran away from Old Pharaoh and got across the river just in time and the white men and all their hound dogs were drowned when the waters rolled down. And God showed them the way to go with a cloud in the daytime and a pillar of fire at night. Except for Harriet Tubman. Then there was nothing but a star that they followed and they didn't go by day at all. But they got away just the same.

That Harriet Tubman. Black as night and tall as a pine and strong as Samson and her eyes were like lightning and no man living could stare her down. Yessir, and she carried a pistol as long as that poker and when you looked down the barrel you could see Kingdom Come. But she didn't need no weapons. If a man got scared and wanted to turn back, all she had to do was ball up her fist, r'ar back and *wham!*—they'd throw him in the wagon like he was dead. Never knowed when she was comin' but when she said *git*, brother, you *got!* Never been nobody like her.

But even when they ran away from Old Pharaoh there was always somebody else to fight. There was always some old king and the Babylonians and Philistines and Assyrians and Persians who put the children of Israel back into bondage. Then there was another lady—not Harriet Tubman but another one—who set the people free by killing the general who was leading the soldiers after them. She took the general into her tent and gave him buttermilk to drink. (You didn't like buttermilk but Mr. Campbell did.) Anyway, when the general went to sleep the lady took a hammer and a nail and hammered the nail plumb through his head and killed him and all the Israelites got away—across the river. There was always a river: the Jordan and the Ohio and some more.

But they didn't all live in tents like in that story. Those that lived in the desert—before they got to Canaan—lived in tents and ate manna that God dropped down. But the others lived in little cabins and ate hoecake, and fatback when they were issued it. Sometimes they would find a hog that got lost and it wasn't in a desert because they'd go off in the woods to barbecue it over a fire. And they used to snare wild turkeys in the woods and eat them, too. And 'possums. (Like Mr. Campbell said, folks down there will eat a 'possum quicker'n a goose will go barefoot.)

Miss Fowler told about the cabins. When she was a little girl, a long time ago when there was slavery, she lived in one of them with her mother. It wasn't much of a place to live, without any floor or a fine big stove like this one. They made a fire on the floor and the smoke went up through a hole in the roof. You could see the stars through there, too, and Miss Fowler's mother told her that maybe someday they would see the star you could follow clear through to Freedom.

But it was a long time a-coming and when it did and the others went away Miss Fowler's mother couldn't go—she was in the family way. Colonel Alcorn and the other white men went after the slaves on horseback and with their dogs. They caught some of them. Frederick was killed out in the swamp and they cut off the ears of Ephraim—that was Miss Fowler's uncle. The rest of the ones they caught just got beat. But most of the runaways never were found, and Miss Fowler said praise the Lord for that and Miss Redpath said Amen.

One night after the old people had talked about how the children of Israel were put into bondage again, this time by the Babylonians, Mrs. Henderson said God's chosen people sure had a hard way to go, didn't they? And Mr. Campbell said yes, and it's still a hard road, a long hard road. Miss Redpath said Amen and everybody else nodded and said it's the truth, Lord knows it's the truth.

Apology for Apostasy?

Soft songs, like birds, die in poison air
So my song cannot now be candy.
Anger rots the oak and elm; roses are rare,
Seldom seen through blind despair.

And my murmur cannot be heard
Above the din and damn. The night is full
Of buggers and bastards; no moon or stars
Light the sky. And my candy is deferred

Till peacetime, when my voice shall be light,
Like down, lilting in the air; then shall I
Sing of beaches, white in the magic sun,
And of moons and maidens at midnight.

from Swallow the Fish

after this you will love me
I live in a cold place.
This is as good an answer as any
when people ask me: "Why performance art?"
I arrived to Minnesota, young, gifted and black,
to teach at a women's college.
I arrived to Minnesota, more beautiful
than I knew at the time.
I look back and see shining,
radiance exuding through brown skin,
twinkle of excitement, flush of expectation,
desire for the first day of school,
those burst capillaries the night before,
gleaming hope for love affairs.
And as happens, perhaps, for every girlchild,
for every woman in the world,
those deemed beautiful and those not,
it didn't happen the way that I thought.
("and my sexual growth and development as a woman
which all women know about")
It matters too that I was dark and brown and plump,
although these are not tautological distinctions.
The world I was moving in was white and cold.
My body covered up in sweaters and coats and gloves
whose mates I kept losing.
I wanted what I felt was my glorious destiny,
("New York and Paris and love"),
what I expected to be, if not effortless, then seamless, organic,
the natural process of life. ("there's no such thing as natural."
My mother had to roll her Afro in the sixties.
For me, also artifice, fabrications, concoctions.)
In Minnesota, I felt invisible, ignored, sexually bereft.
I wanted attention, affection, for once to be seen,

to be visible and undeniable
as beautiful as poetry as intelligence
as image as a way to transform my life
and the way I felt in it, in my body,
to gain presence, to be fully there in space and time,
to contradict one kind of present,
to stop waiting for another future and manifest it myself.
Love. (Is this what the Venus Hottentot wanted?
Or Josephine shaking her banana tail?)
It's difficult but important for me to confess this wanting
as a part of my performance impulse.
In so many of my early pieces, it's painfully clear
in my yearning, frustration, isolation,
dejection, desperation and wry, resilient desire.
This flush of heat through cold, this opacity made transparent.
To keep a sense of humor about my quasi-pathetic quest for love,
to push through shame or embarrassment or pride
into something aesthetically to mine.

Migrations

The diesel truck grunts to pick up the house, to
ease the residence onto its broad back, to haul 1619

whole down the highway. The home——wobbles
without foundation, trembles by sudden movement,

by turbulence and blurring trees, is disturbed
by groundlessness. It wavers and hiccups,

reduced to numbers on a flapping door, growing pains
without Little Africa or Creek Center claiming its walls.

After this crossing from South to Minnesota, will
wooden floors hold when the truck settles them?

Will walls endure after being upswept, or will
the house crack and crumble? What of the father

driving the Buick, the mother unwrapping
sandwiches, the three children in the backseat singing?

Glitter Lions

from A Star in the Face of the Sky

Daniel bustles in the cupboards and drawers, pulling out tape and scissors and ancient markers, which he tests on the paper bag that he loads the art supplies into. Every other marker works, and he wisely dumps the dead ones right in the garbage—something she herself has never able to do. Most of them are older than he is by half, from a short-lived pep squad phase that his mother had immersed herself in, one of so many whims that Janet cannot even remember them all.

"Doing a little housework, are we?" she asks, untangling herself from a hug from her grandson that she had neither initiated nor expected. Rare, they were the best kind, really.

"Something like that," Daniel mumbles, taking another sip of the coffee he's brewed. He's disinclined to reveal his actual purposes. She herself could use a cup or three of that coffee, and the boy makes it strong. She knows how soundly he sleeps and the pick-me-up will do them both good.

He pulls out a pack of glitter markers with see-through tubes that Keisha used to love to shake in order to watch the silver and gold flecks dance. (Simple pleasures for a simple mind.) He dips the ends into a cup of water to see if they can be revived. So damn messy: the markers and Keisha both. She and that friend of hers would sit here and color in posters encouraging the Lions to GO! and for days after Janet would find the dried confetti remains of those markers stuck to the tines of her dinner forks.

The coffee hits her already sour stomach and she thinks it's probably a good idea to get some food inside her.

"Breakfast?" she offers.

He makes the mumbling sound that means he will eat as long as someone else is cooking. At least this one won't care what she serves him. Keisha would have been shouting out her order as if this were some damn truck stop.

Miraculously Daniel revives the glitter markers, which Janet can hardly believe. (Who said things weren't made to last?) She must have spent fifty dollars in the craft store on supplies just for the pep squad—say nothing of the "young inventors" phase, or the punk rock phase, or any of the other ephemeral stages that her daughter passed through (thank God the Bible-thumper period mostly came after she left home); and Janet had to admit that for those few months when, for whatever reason, the boy's mother had immersed herself in the mechanics of school spirit, she had allowed herself to entertain just a glimmer of optimism that just maybe something would finally take root with Keisha and that her daughter might stay happy for a while. But that didn't happen. The world wouldn't allow it and neither would Keisha.

The thing with Daniel's mother: she never engaged. With anything. Even during the school spirit phase, Janet would see her there at the table, blocking out letters or pasting down cutouts of lions, and it would seem to her that her daughter was only halfway present.

She'd connected with some girl, another in a series of temporary friendships (Marcy or Marsha or Marty: who could keep track?) and Janet remembers thinking that the two of them were the sorts of girls found in pep clubs in schools across America: Mousy or chunky or plain, nowhere near perfect enough to stand in front of the crowd with the pompoms and lead a cheer, Keisha and Marcy—she had been a Marcy—were the kind of girls that the successful girls taught to scream along with them so that there would at least be a critical mass of voices encouraging the team. Pathetic shills: That's all they'd been.

This had been back in the days when Janet believed that if Keisha could just lose that extra ten pounds she would be the one out there in front, assigning girls such as Marcy to have a half dozen posters ready to hang in the halls on the Wednesday before the big game. She'd come in from work and find the two of them at the kitchen table, vulgarly sincere boy-band music blaring from a music countdown show on the television, the two girls industriously coloring away on those posters like the fate of civilization depended on it. She'd be relieved, of course, Janet would, to find Keisha at home. She prayed daily the prayer that all latchkey parents prayed—that she'd open that door and that her child would be inside, that the rules had been followed, that the child would not blame you for leaving her alone—a class of prayers that it seemed to please God to rebuff, frequently.

She places the bacon between towels in the microwave and breaks eggs into a bowl, a half dozen. No need to ask how many he wants: she's thinking a little more than four for a growing boy. She'll scramble them so it won't look like so much, and then scrape off a small portion for herself.

Daniel drops the last of the markers into the bag then drops two slices of bread into the toaster. He retrieves the butter dish and the orange marmalade he prefers.

"The grape also," she orders. He's wearing, she sees, an older pair of jeans and a white T with some cryptic message on it that she doesn't quite get—the name of some musical group, she presumes. Could be worse, she's sure, and for what it's worth the logo is actually well-designed—and she's a woman who's supervised the design of more than a few corporate logos in her day. It pleases her that he took more care in his appearance these days; this one's mother bounced through fashion periods the way she bounced through all of her fads, sometimes a victim of the latest trends (and God have mercy on anyone suggesting girls her size avoid exposing their belly buttons), sometimes not seeming to care about her appearance at all.

Marcy's father taught physics or some other humorless subject at Washington University, and the family lived in the hilly area west of the campus, full of elegant brick homes and ancient trees. Janet had delivered her home one evening after a poster party, and—responsible parent that she was— had seen the girl to the door.

"It's okay," Marcy had tried to discourage her. "It's not like there's anyone in there."

Janet assumed Marcy meant the monsters under the bed had been subdued, the closets checked for serial killers; but when the door opened and the house was absolutely still, she realized the girl's confidence was actually in the fact that there'd be no one home to receive her.

"They're never here," Marcy had said. And the place was a pigsty—like what you'd expect drunken college students to live in; makeshift bookcases, apparently not for the books that had been strewn everywhere, stacked haphazardly and interleaved with sections of the *New York Times*. Augmenting the décor, a wide range of overflowing ashtrays and half-dead houseplants—leggy ones, layered with dust and gasping for life in the sorts of slapped-together containers that amateur potters sold at the St. Charles Art Fair.

She knows now that for Marcy those afternoons in the Williams' kitchen had been something of a respite from her dreary existence in University Heights—that coming home to this empty house with a friend had been so much better than coming home alone to that wallow of filth that her parents inhabited. And it explained why she would light up when Janet came in the door, bearing treats from the bakery and silly stories about life in American telecom. (She particularly appreciated Janet's theory that the entire wired grid had been held together by chewing gum and duct tape and two guys who Janet knew to be beyond retirement age.) Marcy reminded Janet of nursing home residents, the kind who snagged perfect strangers in the hall, chatted them up, and seemed so grateful for the moment of grace that the anonymous conversation would be.

Keisha couldn't have been more evil about Janet's attention to the poor creature, would steam with rage whenever Janet talked to anyone she brought around—a rare occasion anyway, her having a friend.

"Come on," she'd say, whenever Janet came into the room, dragging whomever it was upstairs to her bedroom or out of the house entirely, and she'd give Janet one of her trademark scowls, her face screwed up in disgust the same way she did if her eggs were too runny.

Keisha's son preferred them tight as well, and so Janet had come to tolerate the rubbery texture herself, had a special non-stick pan she'd purchased at Famous for just this purpose, just because she was sick of ruining her good cookware over a couple of morning eggs. She gives the eggs a final stir: When they're as solid as gum erasers, that's when he'd eat them without fussing.

The toast pops up and Daniel does his usual trick of snatching it hot and flipping it across the room to their plates before his fingers burn— obnoxious, but benign behavior in the overall scheme of things.

At least the pep squad phase had been a wholesome one for the boy's mother. And while all but the most naïve knew that the wholesomeness of the school-spirit brokers was largely a façade—knew what whores certain cheerleaders were, knew the drunken debauches that made up their weekends as well as the rest of their lives—for the Marcys and Keishas of the world, the reality was that they were dismissed before the parties began— time served—sent home to watch HBO in their pajamas, maybe order in a pizza, before getting to work on next week's campaign while the popular girls conducted their popular lives. Even despite the deep-seated ambivalence that any parent would feel knowing that her child was a server instead of one of those served, Janet had savored the period of calm that arrived with the advent of Keisha's pep squad responsibilities. She knew more than she needed to know of some of the other less wholesome stations on her daughter's teenage travails.

Daniel, her sweet Daniel: he'd never even gotten into the game. Neither server nor served, he was the sort who moved seemingly clueless through the high school fray. He didn't join things—sometimes didn't seem to know there were things to be joined. Across the table he curls over the eggs as if guarding them. His expression today reminds her of his mother—a closed-in, wary paranoia; broken here and there with the kind of fake obligatory smile one got at the ticket counter at Lambert Airport. The resemblance troubles her because that expression had always meant trouble, at least whenever it appeared on his mother's face.

"Feeling okay, sweetie?" she asks. She knows he disdained being mothered this way. He shrugs—as if, she thinks, someone else might know better than he does how he's feeling right now. He'd been self-reliant from the start. He never let her dress him or even pick out his clothes, as far as that went. Early on it was as if he had catalogued the tasks that parents do for children and set about learning to do them for himself. When the spirit struck, he made whole meals from scratch—had done so since before junior high. Not just bacon and eggs, but elaborate casseroles, roasted meats with sauces, desserts. He ironed, would mend his own clothes—or she assumed he did. At least he never asked her to repair them. Or maybe he just wore them more carefully than most boys. He'd always had that meticulousness about him.

Keisha: she'd pop a seam daily, and then she'd be in your face, waving it at you and demanding it be fixed immediately. Self reliance had been as alien to that child as whatever language they speak on Mars.

Marcy, by contrast, was competent the same way Daniel is—(perhaps for the same reasons?). It was she, Janet recalls, who would lay out the task and make a plan for how to execute it. Keisha, a girl who if she had any known leadership skills they had escaped Janet's notice, also happened to be bad in the follower-ship department. God, the girl hated to take orders from anyone—would kick and scream and tantrum over simple requests to pick up after herself or to help clear the dinner plates.

Keisha had been only eight when Wallace had died—suddenly and without warning, of a stroke, and only forty-five years old, the dear man—and Janet sometimes wondered if Keisha didn't secretly blame Janet for his loss, because her willful insubordination always had about it this sense of resentment, as if she were saying "You're the reason *my* Daddy's gone, so clean up your own damn dishes."

(But, no, really: Hadn't she always been that way, even when her father was alive?)

Marcy seemed immune to Keisha's high-handedness—to the point that sometimes Janet wondered if the girl had been in some way rather thick. "Since the background will be dark," Marcy would say, "we should cut out letters instead of drawing them in." And immediately Keisha would say, "Okay, here's what we'll do," and then repeat pretty much word for word Marcy's original plan.

Keisha's officiousness bothered Marcy not one iota, by all evidence, and for the most part they spent companionable afternoons those happy few months, coloring and cutting and gossiping, no doubt, about the girls who had ordered their industry. Janet's comment on that gossip had probably been the undoing of this transitory and blessed respite. But while it lasted, there had been a feeling of relief: Relief that someone had busted into the cocoon and found someone inside worth relating to in whatever way.

As for this child, occasionally—rarely—Daniel would turn churlish with her and his voice would take on the derisive quality she'd hear other teenagers assume with their parents out in public. If he were mine I'd slap the shit out of him, she always wants to say to those mothers (always with the mothers, that tone; NEVER with the dads). And her instinct in the moment is to jump up and spin him around and say, Who do you think you're speaking to, young man? A scene she had played with his mother weekly if not every day.

Ironically, her biggest fight with Daniel had been the mirror opposite of many of her fights with Keisha. It would break her heart, the poor boy up in that room, all alone, so with all good intentions she made her suggestion.

"Why don't you get out of here for the evening? Go meet some friends or something. Go to the movies."

He'd shoved back from the dinner table and seethed for a minute before speaking.

"Don't you ever fucking tell me what to do." That's what he had said to her. The words had sliced through her, with all that they implied about their tentative ownership of each other. He went and slammed himself into his room. Didn't come out for two days. And she remembers thinking, so okay, there she is: There's that mother of his. What she'd been waiting for and fearing for almost a decade had finally arrived in all its hate-filled glory.

Over the years she had rehearsed a number of possible scenarios for what she would do when the inevitable happened—and she had never doubted the inevitability of that day. Apples didn't fall too far from trees, after all, and a tree that rotten was bound to produce poison fruit. In her desk at work was a file packed tight with brochures from the kinds of schools that advertised in the back pages of Sunday magazines, schools promising success for "demanding" learners, and more than one of Janet's scenarios included a trip to the bus depot and a one way ticket to Indiana (where for some inexplicable reason many of such schools are based). She would not—could not—survive another Keisha, and so good riddance it would be for the boy.

She'd heard that same tone in his mother's voice so many times, and

Keisha had even said the exact same ugly words to her once. And, oh, how it would enrage Janet when her daughter spoke to her this way. She'd want nothing more than to close her fingers around the wench's neck and squeeze tight and then slap her senseless. It shames her sometimes to remember how often she'd gone there—reared back with her open hand and let the girl have it. And it always seemed to her that doing so was exactly what her daughter had wanted her to do.

She comes up behind Daniel, handing him the juice glasses to rinse. She puts a soft hand on his back. He had a low tolerance for touching, this one. He smiles at her shyly, so she knows he isn't surly. He has never been, really. That one ugly moment with him: she understands now that she had instigated it, reminding him—cruelly if unintentionally—that at that particular moment in his life there were no friends to call—rubbing his face in it, she bet he thought. When after sulking he had emerged from his bedroom, he came down and sat next to her on the sofa in front of the TV. Neither of them said a thing. She knows that each of them was afraid that the other might completely come apart if either of them spoke. So they sat, as they often would do, silently watching the television world pass by in its merry and disordered way.

Keisha, on the other hand, feared nothing. Certainly not her mother's rebuke. Could there ever have lived anyone who took more calculated pleasure at breaking the rules? For a while, post pep squad, she'd briefly taken up smoking, and reformed smoker herself, Janet could tell that her daughter derived no pleasure from the drug, that instead the satisfaction came entirely from the frustration it caused the adults around her—the vice principals who patrolled the girls' lavatories and, in particular, her mother.

But the pep squad days had in fact been a genuine break in the routine, and Janet can even recall a pleasant "Good morning!" or two over breakfast during that time as well as the unbidden offer to help out around the house.

The day it all went wrong, she remembers that at the phone company, she had been moving the St. Louis offices through the apex of yet another reorganization—a necessity any time the senior management shuffled, which was frequently. She'd become expert over the years at redesigning charts and jumbling the office manuals in a way that suggested "organizational transformation" all the while allowing people such as herself the latitude to keep the real work moving forward.

"Afternoon girls," she had said, breezing in the door. Earlier in the day she'd been promoted into the position that would allow her to eventually become queen of human resources, so she had been feeling particularly pleased with herself—had stopped in at the bakery that used to be on Delmar, near North and South, for some éclairs for herself and for her little spirit-pumpers. Typically, Keisha had loaded one onto a plate for herself, leaving Marcy to fend for herself, but this was a fight conceded by Janet years earlier. The child was just rude, plain and simple.

It had been hoops season—toward the end of it—and cleverly Marcy had crumpled rounds of orange tissue paper in order to resemble the mottled surface of the balls. Keisha's job was to black-magic-marker semi-circles on the basketballs in order to complete the effect. Marcy, bless her heart, would discreetly discard the ones that Keisha could not manage to do properly—most of them, if truth be known—and she'd wryly roll her eyes at Janet as she did so, as if to say "What are you gonna do with this kid of yours?"

"How are your parents, Marcy? Busy at the university, no doubt." Marcy's mother ran some sort of ad hoc women's study center that Marcy seemed to know little of and care even less about.

"Same old, same old," Marcy chirped. Girls like Marcy, in Janet's experience, came in two varieties. Bitterly standoffish—which would be your garden variety. You saw them everywhere—in libraries and bookstores, at the solo counter at Starbucks—sucking up their disappointment and staring with disdainful pity at people just like them. Rarer were the Marcy types: deviously and deliciously satirical; insiders, somehow, to the larger, cosmic joke their oppressors would take lifetimes to appreciate.

Keisha had mis-lettered "Friday" (of all things!) and in her good-natured way, Marcy laughed it off.

"It's not like anyone on that team knows the days of the week." She and Janet had laughed, although the joke had passed Keisha by—as did most jokes, for that matter.

"I'm serious, Mrs. Williams. We cheer 'two bits, four bits, six bits,' and I swear half of them count on their fingers."

"Oh, you hush, Marcy. That's too funny." It had been a joy to come home and find Marcy there. A funny-looking little thing, she'd made the most of her pale-skinned and freckled homeliness, dressing herself in ironically childish sweaters and mismatched socks. She had lovely green eyes, Janet recalled—wise and full of sass.

Keisha, of course, had not been charmed and was quickly losing patience with both of them. Had Marcy been sitting there scowling and mocking Janet, Keisha would have been fine, but the harmony between Janet and Marcy had been beyond the evil girl's tolerance.

"You know what else," she interjected. "DJ Simpson's mama is a whore and two other boys on the team gave her fifty dollars and fucked her all night."

Both Janet and Marcy had stayed quiet for a moment—both shocked, Janet knew, at how wrong the girl could be. So typical, though. Not just wrong, but colossally, abysmally, totally inappropriately wrong. And, of course, willfully so.

"Wow," Marcy said, at last breaking the silence.

"Well," Keisha challenged. "It's true. It is."

"Baby, that's not really the point."

"The point is, his mama's a ho, and those boys fucked her for a fifty."

Marcy had hunkered down over her poster the way one does in witness of another family's domestic strife. Some might excuse themselves and quit the premises, but Marcy hadn't owned that brand of spunk. (Janet also suspected she feared becoming victim of some worse behavior should her head be raised.)

For her part Keisha had pushed her markers aside—never, in fact, to return to them.

"This is unbecoming, young lady," Janet had said.

"What? So it's okay for the two of you to make fun of how dumb they are—which some of them aren't, if you want to know something—but it's not okay to say something that I know for a fact because one of them told me."

"Some things are better kept to yourself."

Keisha scoffed. She sat back in the chair and crossed her arms in contempt.

"I guess it just isn't nice," Janet had added, and even at the time she knew she'd gone a bridge too far. Keisha had mocked her, and Janet remembered how hard it had been to not strike her. And though she knew she should leave it alone, there had always been something about her daughter where her need to have the last word would trump her best judgment otherwise. She said, "Marcy, I apologize for my daughter's discourtesy. I'll leave you girls to your work."

Heading toward the stairs she heard Keisha's voice—its ugliest, most disdainful tone:

There.

You see what I mean.

See how she is.

I hate that bitch.

Damn, I hate her.

It would be many long years before Janet saw Marcy again. A year or so back, shopping in the Dierberg's at Brentwood Crossing.

"Mrs. Williams?"

She couldn't recognize the girl that she'd known inside the woman who approached her in the produce aisle. Still not quite pretty, she'd learned the tricks that all smart girls do to work with what God had given her, had styled the mousy brown mess on her head in a way that sent the focus to her best feature—those sparkling green eyes.

And she'd given Janet a hug—which surprised Janet, even as much as it felt wonderful—and told her how good it was to see her and how often she'd thought of her and how much fun those times had been around the table with the bad posters and the sweet treats.

They had not, of course, talked about Keisha. People rarely brought her up. It was better that way.

She was married, Marcy was, living in Ithaca with her math professor husband, and they had two kids and dogs and cats and fish—the whole crazy package, as she'd called it in her classic ironic way. She'd been in town visiting her mother—the father had died—and, guess what? She was taking up tai chi, she and her sons.

Well, good for you, Janet had told her. Good for you, indeed. Here's one who made it through, who proved it was even possible to do so. There might be hope for this boy, who had been at her side on the day she ran into Marcy, to whom she had been unable to explain the rationale for the exuberant bubbly woman in the supermarket. Just someone from the office, she'd lied. Daniel left it alone, as he so often did.

"Are you sure you're feeling all right?" she asks him again as he crumbles into his mouth the last bite of toast.

He raises his eyes to her slowly, takes his time to read her mood.

"I'm fine," he says, not quite flat, not quite defiant. He hands her his dirty dish.

"Of course," she responds. "I'm sure you are." She rubs a hand around the small of his back. There's power coursing through this body. She feels it and it electrifies her.

"Do you need something?" he asks—his way of telling her she's in his space, and Janet counts her blessings, imagining what his mother might have done right about now.

"Who me?" she teases, and rubs his head—another annoyance, she knows.

Hell if she's going to let another teenager get the better of her.

Autobiographia

I had everything and luck: Rings of smoke
blown for me; sunlight safe inside the leaves
of cottonwoods; pure, simple harmonies
of church music, echoes of slave songs; scraps
of candy wrappers—airborne. Everything.
Mother and father, brother, aunts, uncles;
chores and schoolwork and playtime. Everything.
I was given gloves against winter cold.
I was made to wear gloves when I gardened.
I was made to garden; taught to hold forks
in my left hand when cutting, in my right
when bringing food to my mouth. Everything.
I had clothes I was told not to wear outside;
a face you could clean up almost handsome;
I had friends to fight with and secrets, spread
all over the neighborhood; the best teachers,
white and colored. I'm not making this up.
I knew that I had everything. Still do.

Shameless Lutherans

Before we reach the heated pool
we bathing beauties strip
such flesh unequalled
since a Rubens painting
roundness gleaming wet
hanging, poking shapes
that jostle in a sea of pink
cresting in my one brown body.
In this upper midwest locker room
careless as the original graces
we cavort among the showers
flaunt our baby-nakedness from
so many years ago.

St. Peter, Minnesota: Barry Harris

On this warm fall night
jazz mingles with a
steady southern breeze
drifting through all
these dark and deserted
streets. The rustle of
fallen leaves keeps
perfect time with
the light steady tapping
of my feet.
You came on
late
last night
with the warm
end of September
breezes
deep down in
south-central Minnesota
playing your bebop piano
I'll Keep Loving You
And I recognized your nod
To the great Bud Powell.

Granny's Story

At first glance
My heartbeat dropped
Like a cliff
Overlooking my dreams

His hands were calloused in
Places and smooth in others
Strong
His eyes were soft
Almost like a young boy's
Innocent
But brave like my father's
His gaze was hypnotic, just playful enough to tickle
His voice rich
Like the red soil I grew up moving my toes through
On rainy summer days

There was something familiar the first time we met
The way he parted the air
The way reality and time stood immobile
In his presence
Or maybe it was the way he spoke my name
Gentle

It was too good to be true I told myself
A lover who left love notes on my doorstep
Written on the backside of autumn leaves
A lover who sang sonnets into my answering machine
A lover strong enough to allow vulnerability in
To be free and open
Up to me in the most silent hour
Revealing that which is sacred between two people
We laughed, we talked

We danced
We . . .
Smiled . . . softly at the delicate pleasure of private poetry making
Trading secrets and kisses on stolen snatches of memory

It was too good to be true, I told myself
A gorgeous, hardworking, respectful, chivalrous, spiritually grounded,
    humorous,
Intelligent, feedmebreakfastinbed man
Who understood my need for independence
And smooth rounded fingers
That moved scented oil through my hair and across my back

My lover
Before me, on bended knee

I told myself it was too good to be true

But it was . . . true
And yes . . . I was his

Places

from The Slide

A Novel in Progress

If I could kiss you I would. Right now. If you were here, sitting within reach, I'd sweetly and perhaps even artfully reach right out there and gently pull your beautiful face closer to mine. Close enough so that I could lean forward and softly press my lips to yours. A kiss. For you. You need a kiss, don't you? I know. We all need kisses from time to time. I know I do. And touches. And there is no touch as wonderful as a kiss. Maybe there are two reasons I want to kiss you so much right now. The first is that I can't. And the second is that I need that kiss as much or more than you.

I have no idea where you are. There are people here with me. I can see them. They come and go, breaking the lights above me. Sometimes I can see faces, wavering as if between us was a deep pool of clear water. But no one seems willing to immerse themselves so that they can touch me. I can't tell if they want to, I only know that I haven't felt the touch of another for some time. I don't know enough to feel sorry for myself yet. I can't tell yet whether I am embedded in a massive tragedy for which there is no possibility of joy or if this trap will be sprung and I will emerge smiling and whole.

I do know that I miss you. And I miss that kiss. It was promised to me, and I think you know that I'm just a little stubborn. So I want it.

And while time poses for the artist, there is the story.

In James Wright's office, there was a gallery of criminals. Photographs and articles about the men pictured in them were scattered in small stacks all over. There were over a hundred faces, most with attending narratives of their crimes, flashing their shaded and overexposed images about the room. James had tried to contain the ever-growing number of pictures, but they had outrun his ability to keep them organized and in some respectable order. His office had slowly degraded into a warehouse of ghosts and villains. Some were on both chairs that faced his desk. Some were on the green leather couch, on the coffee table, the floor, and of course there were stacks covering his desk. Even his prized model of the USS *Sylvania*, his old navy ship, was partially covered. This, in itself, was unusual, because he'd had to hunt to the ends of the earth to find that kit. Companies didn't make many models of decommissioned supply ships, and until recently it had been the focal point of his office. Now, it was nearly forgotten.

James sat back in his chair, exhaled, and stared at the photocopied picture of two Black men standing together in a courtroom. There were people all around them. But their faces were like two brown planets among a constellation of white stars.

He stared hard. Perhaps he was already too tired, even though the lunch hour hadn't arrived yet. But his eyes were tearing and they burned slightly, as if under strain. Yes. It was strain. He closed his eyes for a moment and then stepped into the picture.

Once there, embedded in an emulsion of anger, he tried to remain perfectly still. His eyes were cool now, rested, and so he opened them again. In an instant he could see the famous lawyer Johnny Cochran trying to mask a stunned but deeply relieved expression. Beside him the equally surprised face of his client, a once great football player, showed a renewed flicker of life.

It wasn't like the images were talking or moving. It wasn't like he'd slipped into some alternate reality. It was still a picture. Two dimensional and flat. But for a moment, James felt a part of it. A third brown face stunned by an unsuspected verdict. Stunned by the sheer power of it all. If O. J. Simpson had in fact murdered his wife and her lover, it was at this precise moment, caught on film, that he heard a court clerk announcing that there would be no punishment for it.

There is only one way for a guilty man to look when he has outfoxed his prosecutors . . . thankful. Surprised and thankful.

And then James, still tucked into the grainy shadows of the photograph, heard a voice: A deep, sonorous voice. The kind that makes your very bones vibrate. And it said, "Another fine example of the Negro race."

James closed his eyes again and left that picture. That wasn't where he wanted to be. He wanted to be in his father's Cadillac, the 1962 white Coupe deVille (when it was new) on a Sunday evening, probably going to get ice cream from Pflaumer's. Now that was a tradition he liked. Pflaumer's was one of the last old-world-type ice cream parlors left in Philadelphia's inner city.

It survived because it was nestled on the edges of Fairmount Park and was still able to serve its white clients, who had long left North Philadelphia but felt safe enough, in the early sixties at least, to dart back into the heart of darkness to get their favorite ice cream. And because the ghetto was steadily becoming the 'hood, Pflaumer's had new beasts to tame. And nothing tames a beast like ice cream. Butter pecan ice cream. For butter pecan, James's father would almost gleefully gather up a group of kids to make the short trip to Pflaumer's.

That was a memory he wanted to have. A place he wanted to be. He wasn't sure why that particular experience asserted itself at this moment. There were others he could explore, to be sure. But he didn't want to see O. J. Simpson's face anymore. And he didn't want to read the neat script across the bottom of that picture. "Another fine example of the Negro race."

Why was this happening to him? Why, suddenly, did each day's mail bring an envelope with at least one picture of a Black man who had been caught doing something illegal? Sometimes the pictures were accompanied by articles. Other times they were just pictures with pithy little statements, like the O. J. one. They were contemporary and historical. Murderers and deadbeat dads. There were pictures of Nat Turner, John Malvo, and Michael Jackson among the hundreds of others. It had been three months, almost to the day, since they started. And the tension they created grew.

It was an expensive hobby for the person who was stalking him. Whoever was doing it had eschewed the use of e-mail or other anonymous forms of delivery and chosen to make high-quality copies of both the articles and the photographs. In addition to the costs of the materials, there was the time involved. Who had time to scour historical records and contemporary news outlets to clip and copy the many accusations and allegations levied against such a wide range of Black men?

James kept each one. At first he found them oddly amusing and somewhat educational. He'd known nothing about Gabriel Prosser or Mumia Abu Jamal. But as the pictures and articles kept coming, some of them taken from right-wing newsletters and publications with their blistering pejorative language, the tension in his body began to rise. He found it harder and harder to put the pictures out of his mind. The days were slowly being colored by the morning mail and the ugliness it contained. Who would do this to him?

He opened his eyes and climbed back into the world. Into the corporate reality that dominated his life. His office was really a wreck. Beyond the hundreds of photographs there were stacks of paper everywhere. Long-resolved complaints and the massive files that they created were piled up in uneven columns. And even though he had a computer, most of his work was hopelessly paper based. It didn't matter anyway, he hated the computer, too. His e-mail box was fairly pulsating with unread messages. He knew he was careening precariously close to the edge of ineffectiveness. And that made him even more anxious.

He found himself wondering whether *they* noticed he was slipping. He shifted the long lean angle of his body. This wasn't what he'd wanted for himself. He once had hoped for a life of letters and poetry. When he was in the navy, he expected he'd get his degree in literature or creative writing, write a few books, be celebrated, and end up a respected professor at a small college somewhere. A place where he could wear tweed jackets with elbow patches. Where he might sit in repose, absorbed in deep thought about important matters of the mind. But instead, here he was, sealed in a small office, surrounded by pillars of paper, feeling inadequate and incompetent.

James turned his chair to face the window. Out there, somewhere was home. Out there, somewhere was peace. It definitely wasn't in the room with him. It wasn't in the paper scattered about his office. It wasn't on his calendar. Peace was nowhere within eyesight or memory. It was, actually, just a hope.

That—this belief in the idea of hope—was probably the biggest gift he'd been given by his mother and father. He had never caught even the slightest whiff of defeat or quit in either of them. They hardly ever complained. Now, as he began shuffling through the files on his desk, he found it astounding that they never seemed overwhelmed by life.

How could two African descendants, who loved each other in America, not feel doomed? He knew they didn't. But how did they manage that? Here he was, in the eyes of a lot people, practically at the pinnacle of his career, and he was beset by all manner of discomforts. Would the company promote him into a dynamic new executive position? Why was some asshole racist harassing him? Could his own marriage survive this period of desire and change? Or would the world around him simply implode before he got the chance to feel whole? That was what he was searching for, a sense of wholeness.

Maybe his parents had felt the same type of pressures but had chosen not to share them with him. Maybe late at night, as they lay in bed together, his father had complained about how his white boss treated him. Or perhaps his mother would quietly, maybe even tearfully, confess her fears about their capacity to pay their bills. Or, perhaps she had vented about the difficulties of being a young mother and having to leave her child at a nursery run by white women while she went off to work at the navy shipyard. They must have done that. They must have felt the weight of race sitting on them.

But James turned a wry smile as he considered this. They must have felt it and even talked about it, but they never did it in front of him. The only stress present when he was around was the lack of money. And even then, his mother's resurrecting energy always punctuated any moment of rising despair.

There was a sense, in the gift of hope his parents had given him, that if you keep moving forward toward wherever it is you're trying to get to— "put one foot in front of the other," as his mother would say, and "stand up to the wind that blows in your face"—you will slowly make progress. "And that is good. Progress, however slight, is cumulative, and that is what makes it good." His mother was a philosopher in a way known only to Black women. Sage, stinging, smooth. Part scholar, part witch.

But his parents had failed in some way, too. They had pushed him just hard enough that he'd fallen out of phase, so to speak. At least that's how he thought of it. Somewhere along his life he'd slipped. And now there seemed no place he could find that felt like home. No, not a place that "felt" like home, because sometimes he actually did "feel" at home. But the truth was that he hadn't *found* a home since he'd left theirs.

It certainly wasn't in his office, the office of the Assistant VP for Equal Employment Opportunity, as was his official title at PowerTech. James turned back to the window. He'd almost gotten used to the dramatic scene it framed. He could see the last of the falling leaves flutter to the ground forming a Faith Ringgold quilt of muted brilliance on the hardening ground.

He was interrupted by a soft tapping on the open door of his office. He turned into the forced smile of his assistant.

"What's up, Doris?" His voice was lifeless. James knew he could recover its power. But he also knew he didn't have to fake it for Doris.

"This is past getting old, James. I don't even want to open the mail anymore." She sighed and handed him an opened eight-by-ten brown envelope.

"Who is it today? Idi Amin? Papa Doc Duvalier?"

"It doesn't matter, does it? They're all starting to run together in my head." Doris moved the papers and photographs from one of the two leather chairs that faced his desk and sat down. "How long do you think this is going to go on?"

James shrugged sympathetically, "I don't have a clue." And now *he* sighed. Doris calmed him.

"But what does it mean? Why is this happening now? This country is on the brink of war and somebody takes their precious time and money to do this. Why?"

James had opened his eyes for the past ninety days asking that very same question. "I don't have a good answer for you. I wish I did. It's not like I haven't been trying to figure it out. I mean, I think I understand what it means, in a way. It's a message, I guess. You know, like 'Don't get comfortable. I'm watching you. You're no different from the men in these pictures,' I guess . . ." He stopped and then for punctuation said, "I don't know exactly."

"And you still won't call security or the police or tell someone? The world is spinning out of control right now. You don't even know what this is all about. You could be in real danger."

James fiddled with his St. Laurent tie as Doris talked. This was the first time in over a month that she'd expressed concern. But he knew that if he was feeling the pressure, she had to be as well. She loved him. He knew that.

And that was perhaps the most astounding thing about Doris Stone. She loved him. Not a physical, consummated love, but love nonetheless. In the beginning it had baffled him. Doris was an attractive, Minnesota born, Lutheran, Scandinavian woman, some ten to twelve years older than his wizened thirty-four years. It was indeed odd that a veteran executive assistant like Doris would hitch her wagon to a Black middle manager, even if he did have potential.

She'd proven her loyalty to James over the past five years in countless ways. Indeed, she'd chosen to remain his assistant when better opportunities had come her way. And even though he was Assistant Vice President of Equal Opportunity it wasn't like such a thing as that—equal opportunity, that is—actually existed at PowerTech, a Fortune 500 corporation with thousands of employees and thirty-six stories of black-glassed, money-making energy.

Doris knew how ambitious James was and how determined he was to climb the slippery corporate ladder. But she wasn't blind. She knew that his chances were slim. Yes, he had become increasingly careless over the past three months, who wouldn't under the pressures he'd been under? But she knew how hard he worked. How much he cared about the people who depended on him. She never saw a break in the veneer of self-confidence that sealed his body. She loved that about him. How resolute and committed he was to his life, his job and her. But the fact remained that there were no Black vice presidents of any other departments other than that of EEO/Affirmative Action. And this spoke more clearly than James's desire.

She knew that. And still she stayed with him, helping him to solidify his career. James hadn't had the benefit of the typical corporate mentor. His only guide was Doris, who had already been at PowerTech for ten years before he got there.

His co-workers often teased, calling her his "godmother." "What did *godmother* give you for Christmas?" "Saw you and *godmother* eating lunch together." Stuff like that. She tolerated it.

James had to admit that he allowed the teasing because it provided a cover for the underlying discomfort their relationship obviously caused. There were many executives who had tried to woo her away and her stead-fast commitment to him was perplexing. If it wasn't "godmother" it would have been something much more damaging. He was sure of that.

Doris crossed her legs revealing just the slight line of whiteness under the blue skirt of her business suit. Her Anne Klein working girl pumps were immaculate.

"I keep thinking it's going to stop," he said.

"But it hasn't, and frankly, it's really starting to get to me."

"I know. Listen, if it doesn't stop soon, I'll talk to the head of security. Get his advice about what to do. Okay?"

Doris rose slowly and after looking for a place to put the photos and papers she was still holding in her hands, she placed them back on the chair and headed for the door. "James, take care of this. Don't blow it off. It's been unrelenting. I thought whoever was doing it would have stopped by now. I mean, really. Every single freaking day? It doesn't make sense." At the door she turned back to him, "I've got a bad feeling about this."

"Doris, I have so many bad feelings these days, if I responded to each one, I'd never leave my bed."

"Still . . ."

"Still. I understand. Let's give it a day or so." He knew what he was saying made no sense. And he knew she was thinking the same thing. Whoever was sending the pictures wouldn't stop.

"I almost forgot. You have that Sandra Foxworth meeting this afternoon. The files are on the top there," she pointed at a stack of manila folders that sat on the corner of his desk. "Have you read it? I almost don't believe what happened to her."

James had read the file and wasn't looking forward to the upcoming meeting. It was like the rafters were coming down. Like there was a storm, a huge swirling chunk of sky hurling itself at his little cabin in the lonely world, and even though the storm was still off in the distance, the walls were shaking. Pictures were falling from the walls. Silverware was rattling.

Doris recognized the look on his face. And she wanted to comfort him but she could barely staunch the rising sadness in her own body.

"Oh, and one more thing, Mr. Kearney called and said he'd be down to see you. His office is being painted so he'll come here instead."

James had almost forgotten about the Kearney meeting. It promised a break in the bleakness that was foreground.

After she'd gone, closing the door behind her, he emptied the contents of the envelope. Three photocopied pages slid out. James recognized the new face immediately. The much hated Wayne Williams, convicted killer of ten Black children in Atlanta, Georgia. He felt a scream rising in his body. Instead he swept the papers on to the floor and reached for the Foxworth file. Life was a lurch from joy to drama to who could guess what.

As a college student, James had read Richard Wright's *The Outsider* in a course entitled "The Hero as Maker in the Black Novel." It was the first time anyone had ever explained the feeling of fear and uncertainty that he'd always held in his breast. Wright had called it "dread." A sense that failure was inevitable. And he understood it as something that had been put on him. Given to him by the society he'd grown up in. Injected into him like a serum. Mixed into his blood; coursing through his body. Giving him, on the one hand, hope, and on the other, dread.

Even now, he felt his breath coming shallow and rapid. Maybe it was the talk of war that permeated the outside world. Iraq stood in stupid defiance, threatening. The United States, wounded and angry, floundered in the clutches of some almost invisible force that was dragging it into oblivion. And he was supposed to go about his day, dealing with equal employment issues at PowerTech as if in days there wouldn't be children dying from bombs. And he was supposed to go about his day, dealing with the knowledge that someone was out there haunting him with images of Black men who had committed crimes. And he was . . .

It all suddenly seemed frightening. The only flicker of light in the middle of this dark day, James hoped, was the possibility that Bill Kearney had asked for a meeting with him to announce a promotion.

That news would be the sunlight, the shine that would erase all the dinginess that pervaded. A promotion would take him out of EEO, away from the Foxworth cases, maybe even away from those damnable pictures.

James tried to still himself. This was the big trick of life, was it not? Trying to live and breathe and eat and sleep and be normal in an absurd world. That was the trick. Take meetings. Write memos. Go home. Kiss the wife. Watch TV. Be normal with bombs and bullets flying everywhere.

I can't help but wonder if you even think about me now. If you are somewhere guessing what I might be doing. Although, obviously, I'm not doing anything. Maybe you already know that. Maybe you already know that I am gone. Disappeared. Erased.

This would all be easier if I wasn't able to remember. After all that has happened, about the only thing that has survived, to my consternation, is memory. Memory persists. I wish I could elude its embrace. Really. You might think this is an illusion, some magic or trickery I've conceived to make myself larger in the landscape you breathe in. But I swear to you, I swear that this is simply the moisture that gathers around the place I sit. Stand. That is all there is. Memory.

And memory refuses to go unused. Memory practices its own truth. I am a devotee of it, now. I bow down to it, now. When once it was something once lived, once expressed, once seen; I didn't care about it. It was something more or less unnecessary to the flow of forward. Now I wallow, like a little sparrow in pretty dirt. Shaking my tail. Fluttering. Ha. Now I understand why people walk around as if the world was spinning on an edge. Memory. It hurts you. The good things. The good things hurt you. The bad, well, they are simply heavy. Hurt and heaviness abound within the sturdy walls of memory.

I miss you. I will always miss you. I cherish these moments when I can simply forget everything but the things I don't want to forget. The good things. You. Heavy. But when there is an opening I try to make myself small, tiny; and race toward the trace of space there. I am too slow, of course, to make it all the way through the threshold of the opening. But there are moments, like now, when there is a flash of light, and I am able to grab an image of you, hear a word you've said, see something you described as if what you were describing would actually and truly be seen and understood by me in precisely the same way you saw and understood it. When that happens I am able to say that if I could kiss you, I would.

Our Grandmothers

Thula, thula mama, thula mama
Som ta ta, som begga eh kay ya
Wa suga wa kaya wati ma buy ye

My grandmama would sing this song,
She said
And the earth would stand still on its axis
She would close her eyes and part her lips
And sing *Som ta ta som begga eh kay ya*
Wa suga wa kaya, wati ma buy ye

Slow and peaceful as if no one was watching

Hands, dried and cracked twice over
Imprints of wooden handles and barbed wire
Nothing like rotted pine or thirsty moss
But smooth like sanded Berber wood or daisy petals

Split between African tongue and Canadian rum
She would open her mouth and belt smoky words with lazy rhythm
So soothing and melodic the gunfire would silence
On those days I would fall asleep in her lap
She said

One day, its gon be our day
And on that day
I'm gon be ready

My grandmama would sing this song
I said
And the earth would stand still on its axis
She would close her eyes with bent smile and bare gums
And sing

One day, its gon be our day
And on that day
I'm gon be ready

Tranquil and serene as if no one was watching
Forehead, shiny like polished magnolia leaves
Touched softly with olive oil and coco butter
Skin slightly wrinkled and twice baked
The color, nothing like chestnut or mahogany
But caramel butter mixed with maple syrup

Split between African tongue and Mississippi rum
She would open her mouth and blow out Red, Black, and Green words
So soothing and melodic, the smell of burning flesh would dissipate
On those days I would fall asleep in her lap, I said

One day,
its gonna be our day,
And on that day
I'm gon be ready

Our grandmothers
Would sing these songs, we said
And on these days nothing else mattered.

Tongue Swallow

This thang do me like
I don't belong
This thang hang around
Like weather fronts and stall
Above me making it snow
Rain and storm
Making rivers
Lakes and seas rise up and rebel
Against land and everything
And everybody on it
This thang like climate change
Got so many names
We can't point a finger at it
And identify it well enough
To get help putting it down
Duke Ellington found a name for it
The miasma of the oppressive culture
Is known as Transbluesency
Defined as *A blue fog you can almost see through*
We live our lives in that fog
Imamu Amiri Baraka says in *Funklore,*
That's why our spirit make us the blues
We is ourselves the blues
Fred Moten author of *In the Break: The Aesthetics*
Of the Black Radical Tradition called it
Resistance of the object
A conscious intention to resist as well as
Unconscious resistance to dominant cultural ways of being
And knowing
Simply because they are values of the oppressive culture
I struggle to reclaim
My tongue and attach it

In my mouth so I can speak
My language
Sometimes I'm too angry to write
But I try everyday
Too often my words won't dance into
Something that feels like grace
So I suffer with passages
On a page that can't be shared
I write and recant
Because I don't want to leave records
Holding only rage
I don't want writing that's too raw
To escape and misrepresent me
I made space to write and now
Time and space betray me
Put out my shingle announcing
My intentions
Now what
Who is this man masquerading as me
Who can't write his way out of rage
Out of this thang
And an identity crisis
An invisible foot is kicking my butt
And when I turn around there's only his story
His values
Her domination and none of them are visible
Anymore
They've disappeared behind time
Institutions and traditions
As if they were never there
It used to be I who was out of sight
Now I'm a target for long-range weapons
Unmanned drones
Some drink to forget
Others drink to remember
I drink to lubricate mouth parts
Too dry
Clinched
Jaws too tight

Christmas Tale

He filled the bowl with hot water and soap, then dipped the dishes and cups into it. Instead of rinsing them in a water-catch he held them under the faucet. He knew that it was wasteful. The dishwasher was loaded and when the sink was cleared he attached the hose and turned on the controls. He let the dishes that he had handwashed dry upon the counter. Now he carried the litterbag out back and dropped it into a can. He heard glass tinkle as the sack fell. He had broken two wine glasses in the sink. A few days before that a wine glass shattered as he polished it. So thin.

There were guests three consecutive evenings and he had tidied the house each day. Dinner, card party, party. Ruth washed clothes, cooked. The understanding was that he monitored dishes. The arrangement worked.

He was disturbed at himself. The first night he stayed up late cleaning. He put bowls in the cupboard, crackers in the bin, glasses and dishes in the pantry. Heavy mugs sat on an oak counter awaiting their turn. As he picked them up with his fingers serving as hooks, he noticed a water stain. One bottom hadn't dried and a towel was of no help.

Two days later he did the same. Ruth left a note: There are more rings. Have a nice day. I love you.

He looked on the dressers. Upstairs had nine of them. He searched his over-coat pockets, jean jacket, workshirt. Not on the bathroom sink, the counter, nor at bedside. He was certain that he had worn the Seiko that morning. When he jogged he timed the 2.8 miles around the lake. Twenty eight minutes. He sighed concession and felt his wrist. There it was.

The tree was exotic. Tiny beads of red and pink, green and yellow. Before Ruth returned he placed three presents beneath it. He couldn't wrap well but enjoyed plastering tape over paper. Other packages were done by Macy's Gift wrap. The middle-aged woman remembered him from the year before. She beamed at the soft coat that he had purchased.

When he slid the brown package close to the base the tree tilted forward. He caught a center limb and worked it upright. They had cut the pine on Sunday. Drove fifty miles in mild weather. Gas was expensive and the tree was only six dollars.

That evening Ruth watered the treestand and the pine tilted again. He held it steady as she tightened the stays. They snapped at each other as they hovered over the gifts.

At night the tree filled the house with reflections. The bookcase threw a muted collage into the den. The sunroom bent the colors around the north corner. Before company arrived he jogged the lake and cried at the beauty that spilled onto the east shore. The sky fanned pink, clung like a half-shell onto the receded sun and dabbed the water not yet frozen. Quiet country. His breath jumped at each pace. He recalled Ruth's description of her jog over this same path during the first snowfall. The light flakes fell into her eyes and her legs danced through the showers. Then she had witnessed a sunset from the car, over the river, a fall of amber above South Dakota. It stayed with her. Both of them were stocking up on majestic sights.

When Tara looked up he was pushing the door open. "Daddy." She was four. He panted into the living room. The tree was there. She was coloring a paper and stopped to smile. He was stunned by her eyes. He crouched next to her and said, "let me see." The green in her face radiated and he shook his head. "Where's the brown? It's gone." She lowered her eyes to the colors and whispered, "Daddy."

He caught his breath and began to sing. "Chestnuts roasting in an open fire."

"Stop, Daddy."

"Why? Did I get the wrong words again?"

"Stop."

"Do you love me?"

"Yes but—I get a heachache when you sing."

The company enjoyed the evening. One guest sat alone for a time. He wore strong black shoes and long underwear hugged above them. His face was sturdy and good and his fingers were thick like the kindling wood in the shed. He said he worked for the Park Department. In all his years he had never had a week like this one. "Kids vandalized the warmin' house. Tore out boards. Mus' a been a crowbar. Tire iron maybe. Windows were burst proof and they knew it. Broke into the room and burnt them. That's one thing them windows aint. They can catch fire. Sure can."

Tim had a full plate. Rice, sticks of meat, pink salad. He had been called by a California pollster for the Gallup people. They interviewed him for 45 minutes about Lebanon. "I used to wonder who those people were that they called. Never matched my views. Now here I am—interviewed. I took ten pages of notes so that I could review what they asked."

Alex had a 16 year old Egyptian lad at his place. He was proud of the experience. His foot was heavy and it brushed up and down to a branch of the tree as he beamed with each story. "Hard adjustment. Women are regarded in a different manner. Calls me dad. His own father means so much to him. Before Sadat was killed he'd see him on television and sit bolt upright. They loved Sadat."

Tara played upstairs with Shawn. Shawn's parents attempted to put him to sleep, but music from the Nutcracker Suite interfered. More than that Tara would not cooperate. Shawn's dad was exhausted from the tribulation and Ruth was upset with their daughter.

He looked at the windows behind the sofa. His company bobbed their heads over white cups of coffee. The windows glowed. He had washed them from the outside that morning. Washed windows in the winter. It seemed silly to him, but on the ladder he saw a white squirrel. It was a fine omen.

When the last friend kissed them goodnight, Ruth got into her night-gown and climbed under the comforter. He picked up napkins and shook crumbs, scraped and poured dregs, nibbled at peanut brittle and loaded the washer. He returned wine to the basement, restored the antique chairs to their places, failed at fitting a wing to the dining room table. He closed the damper in the fireplace but it was premature. The room filled with the smell of ashes. Outdoors on the walkway he pondered over 25 sacks that had votive candles anchored in sprinkles of sand. He decided to allow them the night. They were elegant and added a fairy tale dimension to the street. Inside he paused a few moments at the tree, the gifts under it. Then he touched the light switch and climbed the stairs to Ruth and Tara.

He spread sliced meats upon blue and white plates, slabs of cheese, Coors beer, pumpernickel, ginger cookies and spiced mustard. The card game halted as the six men prepared their plates. They sat by the tree and talked of peers, retired professors and the state of affairs. He loved them, but all he could offer (and it came as an announcement)—"what a fine group we are."

When the game resumed he concentrated on a diamond flush. The men were exchanging jokes and he warmed at the laughter. He concentrated so hard on his hand that he heard only snatches;—

"Cast the first stone . . ."

"Life lies in the breast of pheasants . . ."

". . . and the pope said, 'the immorality of divorce' . . ."

When they departed, Arthur lingered at the door. "Want you over. We'll ski. Do a few things." They were close. Very close.

When he crawled into the comforter he felt a numb pain in his testes. Two years ago his doctor had examined him there and had told him that one day he'd have trouble. He thought of that now. Curiously enough he also thought of the rust stain in the large English bathtub, the church bells that rang out earlier. What church was it? He thought of Tara's grandmother and her struggle to comb a ponytail. He thought of lox and cream cheese, failing vision, Ruth calling from the bedroom as he descended the stairs; "I love you." He noticed that she emphasized each word as if to be certain that he understood.

Santa hung from the limb of the pine tree. A donkey. A clown. A giraffe. A crimson heart. He switched it off.

Creating Change

I

You just can't ignore this one, hanging on the walls
Of the Walker Art Center
Brows thicker than caramel syrup
Eyes that stare a hole right through to your soul
And those juicy fruit lips.

You can call her when the
Sun goes down
and the lights go out
Down low lover, it's
gon' be alright
Everybody gonna ride the train
To the end of the line, one day.

There are rituals
That she observed
On days like these
We call on the ancestors—those
Blues singers and griots

II

Travel this path forever
Through space and Through time
Through light and Through sound

Tried to do it all at once—
Failed at everything
She awoke to a purple tinged sunrise
Still trying to get to the bottom of things
This was lust lurking behind

Her hypnotic eyes
Saying, "you sure wanna do this?"

Everybody lined up to pay their respects
The preacher proclaimed hip-hop died this morning
Said they were creating change

She goes to art openings
and poetry readings 'n shit now.
This whole church thing was sounding like fairy tales.

III
She wanted to revive the magic
Of Jean Michel Basquiat, Romare Bearden,
And Buford Delaney to compose a postmodern
Work of art in a time of need

You can't imagine what it was like last Wednesday
Thick blues rolled down like a full bodied
Syrah—they covered everything and everybody
When the fog lifted

The Magnolias took on
A whole new life
Velvety petals—spiky stems
Lining her imagination
Leading to a place
Beyond the bounds of discipline

IIII
She thought it was all about
The ofrenda over the bookcase
The faded photographs
With a cigarette in one hand
and tequila in the other
The King James Version of the Bible
Opened to the 23rd Psalm
The Lord is my Shepherd

The artist has to struggle
With the darkest recesses
Of interior landscapes
Abstract sploshes of Muted oranges
Powdery blues and sublime greens
Midnights blacks.

She called this duende.

All the Information We Have

1-30-75

Shannon Elaine was born on January 30, 1975, at 6:12 AM in Ann Arbor, Michigan. Birth weight, 5 pounds 15 ounces, birth height, 19 inches, head circumference, 33 centimeters.

The pregnancy was full term with an elective forceps delivery. Born with the bud of her daughter inside her, born of an unfinished idea. Something you never said.

2-28-75

She has gained a normal amount of weight but is very small in size and a delicate looking infant (shape of small troubles to come, big voices in her eardrum). She is on Enfamil only and it was noted that she had a lot of arm tremors. Says things sometimes we cannot hear, but almost see. Tells herself often that the world knows she is here.

4-29-75

Everything is normal, except the doctor noted a malevolent infection behind the eyes. Some kind of apology for the absence of her father, locked up mother. The reason why whiteness is everywhere in the hospital—and everywhere else—and also the reason why we must call her *black.*

5-30-75

An injection to the eye was given. All else was normal as per child's development, feeding, etc. She is beginning to reach and follow objects 180 degrees. She is growing accustomed to lying in the crib alone, yearning for these white arms.

New Health History

Shannon Elaine Gibney is pregnant at 34. Still fighting with white adoptive parents over the nature of reality. Will not eat liver or melon popsicles. Continues to deride white people daily—often around whites themselves.

Baby is half-African. Father is 26-year-old accounting student at the

University of Liberia. Thinks of the baby coalescing into something in her belly, and sometimes feels trapped that the only way for it to go now is *out*.

Angry. Easily excitable. Writes songs to herself in her sleep.

Occasionally suffers from pain in her hair; the weight of a brain that will not turn off. Bumps on her body come and go. Often, they have no story. She frets, and the worry makes them go away.

Believes her house talks to her in the speech of *silence* when she is alone there. *When we die, we go back to where we came from,* it says. *And that is nothing we can ever know until we are it.*

Takes a drug to make her not so sad, but it still comes, sometimes. Doesn't think the world will ever end, nor her children, nor their children in it. The line will keep on laying down. Down, down, down.

from I Believe I'll Run On . . .
and See What the End's Gonna Be

I wrote this play in the late 1990s, in response to Minneapolis being sarcastically called "Murderapolis." My city didn't have the numbers of homicides that were seen in places like Chicago or Detroit, but we were quickly on our way.

This play touches on many things that violence within a community brings about. There are the many factors changed for the worse within the family: family dynamics, culture, and relationships. However, there are the issues of physical and mental health and safety . . . and, not to be minimized, spiritual health, too.

Violence affects the community on a large scale as well—quality of life, lower property values, etc. One of the worst things is the breakdown of connections between generations and the extinction of extended families. Identity, values, history, and information is lost, not passed on. All of this loss helps to put our youth into a state of "damaged goods"—and it's so hard to turn your life around if that is the only way you see yourself.

Synopsis: The play takes place in the present time.

Teenagers Donny and NeeCee live with their grandmother, because of their mother's drug use.

NeeCee aspires to graduate from high school and go on to college. Donny gets involved with a gang. Almost killed, Donny is relegated to a wheelchair due to a spinal injury and seizures.

When Donny has his seizures, he finds himself in a desert at a bus stop talking with six-hundred-year-old Queen Esther, the keeper of history of all of the Black people born in America (descendants of the original Africans kidnapped from their homeland), and Uncle Best, who has spent his life searching "for the right home." The pair seeks a member of a younger generation to whom they can pass down the legacy of the Black race. This is the second time that Donny has met up with this pair. This conversation focuses on the bus (activism) and what the Black community was like before it became a "desert."

SCENE 4

(It is the desert once again. The bus bench is present, but now there is a large boulder that is situated just a little upstage of the bench. Uncle Best is sitting on the bench looking through his binoculars singing.)

UNCLE BEST:
(singing)

"This little light of mine, I'm gonna let it shine . . . this little light of mine . . . I'm gonna let it shine. This little light of mine, I'm gonna let it shine . . ."

(Donny walks in from a distance. He seems confused and not sure of where he is or where he is going.)

"Let it shine, let it shine, let it shine . . ."

(speaks)

I knew you'd be back.

(He stops speaking, puts his binoculars up to watch Donny walk past.)

Where are you going?

DONNY:

I don't know . . . I thought I was—

UNCLE BEST:
(cutting him off)

Yeah, well—so did a lot of other people. Well, sit down.

(Donny sits.)

Where did you go off to?

DONNY:
(confused)

I was—I was—

UNCLE BEST:

Well—wherever you "was," you done missed the bus again.

DONNY:
(walks past Uncle Best)

The bus?

UNCLE BEST:

Yep, it was here. But it left. Couldn't stop and wait for you. I guess
you'll have to catch the next one when it comes . . . there ain't no regular
schedule.

DONNY:

What kind of bus, ain't got no regular schedule?

UNCLE BEST:

The kind of bus, what had no regular passengers in a real long time.

DONNY:

Well—how do you know if it's coming back?

UNCLE BEST:

Oh—it's coming back, all right . . . knowing the times we're living in right
now . . . it'll be back sooner than anyone dares to speculate. I've seen it
come and go over the years.
　　　(a long sigh)
Yep—I remember back in the mid-60s . . . it ran on time—just like the
trains.
　　　(smiling)
It was a big old green, black, and yellow bus. Slightly dilapidated,
but running tip top. A big old handsome thing, complete with air
conditioning.
　　　(turns to Donny)
I gave up my seat to somebody who was trying to get someplace real fast.
Don't know if they ever got there. Then somewhere around the mid-70s,
it broke down and needed some fixin'. It started running off schedule
around that time. I remember getting off to help check the tires and then
sat down here to rest a spell and when I turned around, it was gone. Now,
it only seems to come when it wants to . . . not ever when you need for
it to.

DONNY:

Yeah—well, I hope it comes soon. I've got to get back to—

UNCLE BEST:

　　　(quickly)
Where?

DONNY:

What?

UNCLE BEST:

Where do you have to get back to?

DONNY:

(confused)
I'm not sure. I don't know . . .
(He looks off into the distance.)

UNCLE BEST:

(sighs)
Yeah—well a lot of people have been waiting for that bus to show up.
(pointing outward)
Ohhhhh, they're all up and down the road . . .
(He sees something and quickly picks up his binoculars to get a better look.)
Ahhhh—there goes another one . . .

DONNY:

(trying to see what Uncle Best sees)
What people are you talking about? I was out there walking and there wasn't anybody else out there.

UNCLE BEST:

I don't know how you could've missed 'em. You'd run right into them, there's so many folks out there. Unless . . . unless you didn't see 'em. Yep—then I could understand you not noticing 'em.

DONNY:

(confused)
I don't know what you're talking about. I came up that road over there and there wasn't nobody along the way.

UNCLE BEST:

That's all right. Many of us think we're on that road all by ourselves, 'til we look back and see all them bodies.
(focusing on a view through his binoculars)

Humpf! They're gonna pick off his narrow behind real soon . . . real soon.
He can't make too many more mistakes and they're gonna pick him off
just like a duck picking off a June bug.

DONNY:
(tries to see what Uncle Bet sees, but can't)
Who are you talking about?

UNCLE BEST:
If I could just find that damn recipe!
(turning to Donny)
Sorry . . . didn't mean to curse in your presence.

DONNY:
Shit—I don't care.

UNCLE BEST:
It's called respect. My intent was to be respectful.

DONNY:
Yeah—well if I had felt that you were dissing me, I would've told you.
(beat)
I don't like people dissing me—but I'm good about cuttin' folks slack.
I mean don't get me wrong. I ain't no punk or nothing . . .
(Uncle Best takes something from his bag to eat. He offers some
to Donny who looks at the food, smells it then decides to take a
bite. They are silent as they eat.)

UNCLE BEST:
I bet you're thirsty! I've got some water here.
(He pulls a bottle of water from the bag.)

DONNY:
No, I don't want to drink up your water, old man.

UNCLE BEST:
Don't be a fool! When somebody offers you some life-sustaining
refreshment, have sense enough to take a sip. It just may save your life.
(Donny hesitates.)

QUEEN ESTHER: (O.S.)
Take it! You're in a desert—or haven't you noticed?
(*What was seen as the boulder is actually Queen Esther.*
She moves to standing position.)
Give him the water, Best.
(*She looks up at the sky as Best offers Donny his water bottle.*)
Every day the sun gets hotter and hotter. This ain't no kind of place to be
with no water on you.
(*Donny takes sips and looks at Uncle Best for a moment as*
Queen Esther shakes her head.)
My job was so much easier way back when. And this place . . .

UNCLE BEST:
(*interrupts*)
Oh . . . now . . . Esther . . . it might have been different, but I don't think it
was all that much easier.

QUEEN ESTHER:
(*shakes her head*)
It surely ain't like in the old days when this wasn't a desert.

DONNY:
What was this place before?

QUEEN ESTHER:
This place was the prettiest sight you'd ever want to lay your eyes on in
your life. Green—everywhere . . .
(*turning to Uncle Best*)
Ain't that right, Best?

UNCLE BEST:
(*turning to Donny*)
It was way different. Everywhere you looked there were gardens and birds
and flowers . . .

QUEEN ESTHER:
(*cuts him off*)
And people smiling and singing . . . Ohhh the sounds! You haven't heard
them kinds of sounds. Humpf! You're too young and you're living in a
different time.

UNCLE BEST:

Not even in your mind's eye could you dream up anything that comes close.

QUEEN ESTHER:

I think back to when I could hear that music every day or whenever I needed to hear it . . .
> (*starts to get emotional*)

I get a lump in my throat just thinking about it. I can barely breathe . . .

QUEEN ESTHER:	**UNCLE BEST:**
. . . let alone swallow . . . and my heart aches so bad . . . like my soul's being ripped right out of me . . .	(*whispering*) Breathe . . . Take a breath . . . Breathe . . . Take a breath . . . Breathe . . .
(She trails off, trying to control her tears.)	*(Inhales and exhales)* Hahhhhhhhhhhhhhhhh!
Did I tell you about the fountains? They were all over the place . . . the pools pouring forth water like—	

DONNY:

> (*impatiently cuts her off*)

So, what happened?

UNCLE BEST:

Everything just dried up. Just like a mama's titty when the baby takes to solid food.

QUEEN ESTHER:

> (*looking round*)

Gone . . . everything . . . gone . . .
> (*She trails off.*)

UNCLE BEST:

> (*abruptly*)

Didn't nobody want to take care of it. They all wanted to stay here. They all wanted to receive, but nobody wanted to give.

QUEEN ESTHER:

I could see it coming.

UNCLE BEST:

Hell—we could all see it coming, but nobody wanted to believe it was happening. It started with the flowers. Seedlings'd come up and grow a little bit . . . but there wasn't nobody to weed . . . and after a while there wasn't enough water to keep them going. Soil started turning bad. Pretty soon the rich black dirt turned to a yellowish white sand.
(shakes his head)
Can't grow nothing worthwhile in that.

QUEEN ESTHER:
(face shows no emotion)
Birds stopped coming around. Folks started dying out. No more singing . . . no—couldn't hear no voices at all . . . not even so much as a . . . mumbling word . . .
(She trails off, lost in some vision. The silence is broken as Queen Esther lets out a wail.)
Man! Man! Best Man!

UNCLE BEST:
I know . . . I know . . . Esther . . . I know . . .

QUEEN ESTHER:
What are we gonna do?

UNCLE BEST:
I've been looking . . .

QUEEN ESTHER:
You promised me . . .

UNCLE BEST:
Well, it hasn't been easy . . .
(He looks through his binoculars.)

QUEEN ESTHER:

I told you it wasn't gonna be easy. I told you that. But you don't listen
to me—

UNCLE BEST:

I listen to you—

QUEEN ESTHER:

You don't listen to me!

DONNY:

What's going on? What are you looking for?

QUEEN ESTHER:

(to Uncle Best)
I'd like to see the history move on with some pride and dignity. Then I
could think about moving on . . .

DONNY:

(to Uncle Best)
What is she talking about?

QUEEN ESTHER:

I've got to go . . . I'm getting old . . .

DONNY:

Got to go? Got to go where?

QUEEN ESTHER:

I've got to run on and see what the end's gonna be. Forge ahead and see
our future. I'm over six hundred years old. And I want to go, now. But
I can't 'til I know that we're gonna move forward. Then I'd feel better, a
whole lot better.

UNCLE BEST:

Well, don't pack your bags just yet. 'Cause I just can't seem to get a clear
picture. But then they ain't ready . . . these young ones just ain't ready!

DONNY:

Ready for what?

UNCLE BEST:

Boy—haven't you been listening? Y'all ain't ready! You ain't ready for to take on your birthright—

QUEEN ESTHER:

Your heritage . . .

UNCLE BEST:

Your legacy . . .

DONNY:

I don't know what the hell you talkin' about—

QUEEN ESTHER:

See—just what I was saying . . .

UNCLE BEST:

And you don't know enough to be cursing me, boy.

DONNY:

I'm—I'm sorry. Sir.

UNCLE BEST:

That's more like it! Respect is the key to so many things . . . and it ain't about tennis shoes and funny looking signs made with your fingers.
 (taking a quick look at Donny's hands)
And you need to *clean* them nails . . . acting like nobody's ever told you how to—
 (he sits and shakes his head)
Now, you're making me lose sight of what I'm looking for . . .

DONNY:

 (accommodating)
Look, what do you need? Huh? I've got what you need . . . and if I ain't got it, I can get it. See—no need to fret, 'cause I've got your back.

QUEEN ESTHER:

Boy—you haven't got his back or my back or anybody else's back! I think you better sit yourself down!

(moving away from Donny, shaking her head)

Lord, I'm weary! Lord, I am weary!

(starts to sing)

"I've been 'buked down here . . . and I've been scorned! I've been talked about just as sure as you're born . . ."

(starts to wail)

Man! Best Man!

UNCLE BEST:

Yes, Esther—

QUEEN ESTHER:

I'm tired. I'm real tired . . .

DONNY:

Y'all don't understand—

QUEEN ESTHER:

(cuts him off)

No! You're the one who doesn't understand . . .

(to Best)

You had to pick this one. I told you I had my doubts. The turnaround time just may be too short. I may be writing his name down in the book before we've had any time to work with him.

UNCLE BEST:

He'll be lost to us—

QUEEN ESTHER:

And we'll just have to start all over and try to find another one . . .

UNCLE BEST:

(agitated, whips around and faces Donny)

Boy, do you understand that you ain't got much time?

DONNY:
I ain't got much time?!

UNCLE BEST:
(pointing to his watch)
You're gonna have to make up your mind, boy. You've been sitting up on fool's hill for a long time. The clock's working against you, for sure. So what's it gonna be? Huh?! What's it gonna be?

QUEEN ESTHER:
Better think fast, 'cause right now you ain't no where and that's a bad place to be.

In his waking hours, Donny lives in anger over the changes in his life and tries to figure out who should pay for his physical injuries.

Stakes are heightened when Donny's grandmother makes up her mind to put her grandson in a spinal cord medical trial, which requires that she put her house and café up for sale. However, Donny has no idea of her selfless plans, and the grandmother doesn't know that Donny has decided to seek revenge on a rival gang, thus putting his whole family in danger.

Donny's journey has him questioning his decisions in regards to his need for revenge, the use of violence, and how his actions not only affect his family but have added to the list of problems within his community, as well.

Queen Esther and Uncle Best convince Donny that he has everything he needs from the past to inform him and guide him. Donny is chosen to carry the legacy of the Black people into the future.

As You Leave Me

Shiny record albums scattered over
the living room floor, reflecting light
from the lamp, sharp reflections that hurt
my eyes as I watch you, squatting among the platters,
the beer foam making mustaches on your lips.

And, too,
the shadows on your cheeks from your long lashes
fascinate me—almost as much as the dimples
in your cheeks, your arms and your legs.

You
hum along with Mathis—how you love Mathis!
with his burnished hair and quicksilver voice that dances
among the stars and whirls through canyons
like windblown snow, sometimes I think that Mathis
could take you from me if you could be complete
without me. I glance at my watch. It is now time.

You rise,
silently, and to the bedroom and the paint;
on the lips red, on the eyes black,
and I lean in the doorway and smoke, and see you
grow old before my eyes, and smoke, why do you
chatter while you dress? and smile when you grab
your large leather purse? don't you know that when you leave me
I walk to the window and watch you? and light
a reefer as I watch you? and I die as I watch you
disappear in the dark streets
to whistle and smile at the johns

Home Delivery

I used to deliver newspapers in Minneapolis. It was a lousy way to make a buck, but the task itself wasn't always unpleasant, although cold precipitation could make it so. I got to the route before dawn, my favorite time, and at least it was always quiet and peaceful, except after a blizzard when the plows were out.

I got nineteen cents for every copy of the *Star Tribune* I delivered. It didn't matter whether I stood outside the fence and flipped it onto a big, wide porch or had to struggle up your dark, icy, broken steps and put it in the door. It was nineteen cents to me.

I liked the throwing. At home I wanted my paper to be close enough to the front door for me to get it without going outside. In Minnesota there are a lot of days when going outside is to be avoided.

So out on my route my bull's-eye was a spot beneath the front door opposite the hinges. I was usually satisfied with the top step, but I wanted that spot.

Monday and Tuesday meant a light paper that was difficult to throw accurately. They were like Whiffle balls—I never knew where they'd end up. They could catch the slightest breeze and float off into the bushes. I had to walk farther up the walk when the paper was light.

Thursday and Friday editions were heavy. I couldn't carry many at a time, but they went where I wanted them to go and hit the step with a satisfying thud. A Friday paper hitting against a cheap storm door was amazingly loud, but it ended up where I wanted it.

In an apartment building for old people, the hallways had seasonal decorations—Valentine hearts taped to doors, plastic Easter eggs hanging from light fixtures—and, year-round, crocheted crosses and little American flags. A television was always on behind one door, probably twenty-four hours a day, like my mother's was near the end of her life.

And everywhere in the building there were signs: Please put the paper under the door. Please put the paper in the bag, not on the floor. Please knock loudly. I do not have my hearing aids turned on. No smoking—oxygen in use. He is risen. God bless you. Think spring!

As far as I know, I'm the only person to have subscribed to, written for, and delivered the *Star Tribune*. I once delivered an edition with one of my book reviews, quite a sensation, as I recall.

Once a woman whose house I was cleaning recognized my name on a review in the Sunday paper while I was there. Another odd sensation. It was the first time I'd cleaned her house, and it was a mess. I told her I made more money cleaning her house than I did reviewing plays for the newspaper. She never called me back.

Felt

When a Cat Goes Out

He'd patrol the doorway waiting
To make his break
Or he'd scratch around the threshold
As if he could dig himself out
All he knew was out was where
He wanted to be
When the opportunity
Was right he'd bolt
When he went out that last time
Looking for whatever he craved
Then attempted to return
There was no there
There anymore
No familiar arms to welcome him back
Nor nimble fingers to massage his weary head
No food in his dish
No breast to fondle
No open door
No one knows where a wonderer
Goes when a prowler goes out
He sees what others can't
Because of askance perspectives
He makes patterns of disappearing
After having been on the scene too long
And they speculate about where he's gone
"He's got a woman cross town" Ray said
"Who won't come out with him or
Hang with the likes of us"
"He has an alternative personality that's
Shy and reclusive" Dana chimed in
"So he hides to sulk and write
He's often manic and won't
Come out in his depressed state"
But that last time he went out

Out swallowed him whole
So he stayed there in the belly of the beast
Too long to remember his way home
And when he arrived in a place he thought was home
Everything recognizable was gone
Out has black holes that eat light
Especially the kind in cat's eyes
That wide eyed bright enthusiasm that
Expects stuff is depowered
Blacked out
Like New York in a major storm
Scent of a woman and
Radar of voices bouncing off each other
Work like bat intelligence when
Sense of sight is rendered invalid
So he closed his eyes and blew his saxophone
Listening for echoes feeling around for
Osmosis believing in aural perceptions
What he heard confirmed he was still alive
Though he had lost his way
He was out in front of something
He didn't know about
Home was not an avenue or a building
Where he used to live
But somebody who knew him
And put up with his shenanigans
In was not the songs he already knew
But the ones he'd never heard
That insisted on entering through soles
Of his feet
Before exiting the bell of his horn
When a cat goes out
There are no guarantees
The locks will accept his old keys
So he crawls into a window
When the front door's on fire
He rewrites his story to accommodate
Strangers
To introduce himself again
In a world he thought he knew
In woodwork that's lost his scent

Heartsong for Our Father

9/18/1918 to 1/27/99

For My Brother, "Topper"

All these wounds have names
From your circumcision,
to your scarred knees,
to your bypass.
Although we say we love it,
    who says this road is not *rough* on a man?

Our father has given himself heart and semen,
Our father has witnessed with his hands and labor,
    we boys grew, flew through years like we were racers,
    and it took you Pa not a few beers with whisky chasers.
    You know, we moved beyond Dad's possibilities,
    Grandpa's dreams and great-grandpa's living nightmares
    and time passes, time passed and
    Pa you were there—heart and soul,
      body and soul you were there,
        you are here where it counts.

Our Father, our Father, our Father
    has clicked off the bathroom light,
    has tripped into twilight.
the newspaper is at the bedside,
the all night jazz station whispers in the dawn,
the majesty of the blues possesses the song,
and lingers on, lingers on,
it is the hue of this room
and there is silence hear . . . ?

I never really believed that I had a story until my father began to lose his memory. He'd always been forgetful. When we woke him up from a deep sleep, he didn't know where he was right away. Sometimes if he woke up with a start, he would call out the names of his sisters, "Emma!" and "Julia!", then my mother, "Jeanette!" and then me and my brother "Topper!" This was a startled litany that would bring him back to present time *if* he stayed awake.

My father seemed to always work at odd hours that put him out of sync with the rest of the family. He seemed to always have some part of the night watch and slept some part of the day. I remember for a while this seemed to work to my advantage during a time when he would be there at home and prepare some lunch for me. I can still remember a fried pork chop sandwich with mustard and black pepper on it. Although it disgusts me now and I haven't eaten pork in years, somehow this is still a pleasant memory for me.

Father! I call forth all the passion you never expressed,
All the words unspoken,
All the songs unsung,
All the injustices unchallenged.

Father! I call you forth from loss and failure perceived and real,
All the would-have-beens,
All the could-have-beens,
All the dreams deferred,
All the bad luck that stuck to your shoes.

Father! I call you forth from woundedness and rage suppressed,
All the betrayals, slammed doors and Jim Crow demons,
All the lies, lost friends, deceitful salesmen and second-hand cars.

Father! I call you forth to the truth of who you really are:
   "You are compassion,
   Mother loving,
   Skirt flirting,
   Rough red-brown earth hands full of beauty,
   Rose hearted, car fixing, little girl teasing, scat singing,
   Go-to-work-on-Monday,
   Too-tired-for-church-on-Sunday,
   Angel Daddy risen up from Arkansas' red clay soil,

Who ain't no 'farmer' or an 'old lady.'*
Sweet, sweet Daddy, your face is in the son,
      Is in the Sun.
You nurtured with the power of a Mother-man
And my Soul rises up in wonder
Of the Strength in a man like you.
Tenderness,
Endurance,
In spite of it alll, in the face of it allll,
You were there,
You are here,
Where it counts!"

*"Old lady" was a term used by my father's Depression-era childhood running buddies, Wade Watson and Bill Farrow, expressing their affection for one another.

OnScene

Stepping
Lightly
Over the roots of trees
Which will no longer be
Themselves
Planted in this community
But beneath the feat of it

Feet
Feeling a pressing need to leave
Crashing leaves wake people from their sleep

This morning
The sky was sheepishly silent
Painfully purple
Violent Orange
A humbling hurting
Natural

Disaster is an understatement

Says a student
Half dressed in depressed
Entirely uncertain
And gracefully gangsta
    Hey yo you good
                Your peoples good

He is reaching for a connection
Before cutting across shards of glass
To aid those who cut their eyes at him a day ago

Particularly
Mrs. Middle-Class Illusion
Who posed with her nose up each time he passed
Her prior to the present

Posturing now with her hand out
Poverty looks like his hand pulling her up from the ground
Him hearing the call she was too wounded to make
He is a gang
    Member of this community still
Tomorrow
Horses will heal these displaced men
And we will be condemned to weep for them from behind our doors
Half exposed
Home has holes in it
This is rescue
It takes weeks

Giving off an aroma of distance
New found proximity to self
Truth begins seeping in like sewage
On the first level
Filling lungs
Surging through a city blocked
And guarded
Movement soon to occur
Forced into a higher place of consciousness
And the people pulling you up from the stench you were drenched in
    will be draped in blues
They will not be cops
Shit
Smells different

A tornado hit North Minneapolis
Children ducked beneath decks to survive
Lives were shifted
Forever became a fable term
Time stop
Foreigner amongst friends who dwelled in its fantasy

So many weak after
This city has been redecorated
Sectioned off by vouchers

And an elder
On the porch
In a chair
Rocking
Whispers

> *That tornado let sooooooo much light in*
> *Uprooting all dem trees like dat*
> *Don't look so dark round here no mo now do it*

Love Across the Middle Passage

from *An Essay for June*

> *Love is profoundly political. Our deepest revolution will*
> *come when we understand this truth.*
> —bell hooks

> *"I think love comes first and then the reasons follow. When*
> *I am with him, I feel that I don't need anything else."*
> —The character of Olanna,
> speaking to her sister in
> Chimamanda Ngozi Adichie's
> *Half of a Yellow Sun*

I haven't wanted a man all my life, but during the parts that I did, I wanted a sweet man. Someone I could curl up around, someone who would cook me scrambled eggs or a BLT or french fries when I needed something to look forward to. Someone who would tell me stories in bed, and share in my rabid appreciation for all things nerdy.

Someone who was easy.

You might say that travelling all the way to Liberia, West Africa, was not the easy way to go about getting a man, and you would be right. Luckily, it wasn't the reason I went there at all. Four years ago, I was embarking on a journey of an altogether different kind—in search of a different flavor of love: that of story. I was gathering research for the novel I am still plodding away at, a tome-like odyssey of fiction about one family, half African American, the other Liberian, and their struggles to come to terms with the violence that has created them. Never, for even one second, did I imagine that I would meet my future husband during the course of this trip. Neither could I have even remotely entertained the possibility that in some way, the historical family drama I was plotting was actually the story of my own family, the family yet to come. Had you suggested either of these notions to me as I was packing, anxiously awaiting the arrival of my visa, or kissing my dog goodbye for a month, I would have laughed in your face. For a very long minute. And yet, here I am, four years later, married and mothering an energy-saturated toddler, after battling the U.S. government to allow said husband to set foot in this country, and all the while insisting that mine is not your run-of-the-mill American melting-pot/love-conquers-all narrative, but instead, that these love affairs—one with my husband, and the other with the written word—exist only within the constant negotiation, nuance, strife and commitment. And that it is this ever-shifting tension that gives them meaning.

When I saw Ballah standing there that day in June and took in his easy poise but open vulnerability, what caught my thirty-three-year-old eye was a strength about him—something intangible to my First World eyes—that was different from most of the American men I knew. Maybe it was living his childhood through fifteen years of civil war. Maybe it was his love for his mother, who kept them alive during this time by tending a garden on whatever land she could cultivate and selling water and other necessities at a kiosk, as well as additional creative enterprises she devised for survival. Maybe it was simply his sheer social intelligence—he seemed to be able to make anyone feel at ease, without artifice. But when I ran into a group of male students gathered in the brown dirt landscape of the University of Liberia campus in Monrovia who surrounded me, the light-skinned foreigner, eager to engage in a conversation about presidential candidate Barack Obama's chances of winning, I knew that this trip was going to be a lot more complicated than I had anticipated. *What will he do for Africa if he is elected?* The young students asked me excitedly, not used to having "white" Americans on their campus to pull into such discussions. *I don't know if he will do anything at all for Africa*, I told them honestly, trying to explain what I understood as the line Obama had drawn between his heritage and the Kenyan father he had never really known, and the pragmatism of his political ambitions—which wouldn't allow for what would be seen as the "frivolity" of "charity," in the case of aid to the continent. The students pulled back from me when I said this, clearly not pleased with the direction I was going. *You are saying he is less African and more like you*, they said. *White.*
    I shuddered.
    Having spent a year in West Africa in my early twenties on another research adventure, I was well aware of the racial politics here, and the regular substitution of race for nationality. In this world, whiteness was equated with a U.S. or European passport, and blackness was synonymous

with being African. It is a kind of shorthand that is an accurate descriptor in many instances... except if you are African American. Given the massive chasm of history and culture that collide every time a poor, West African person (who are, after all, the majority of West Africans) encounters an upper-middle-class African American (the majority of Africans Americans who travel to the continent fall into this category), it is perhaps inevitable that the shorthand in the West African mind would become "American = White." All shorthand serves the purpose of facilitating communication and interaction, but there comes a time when you need to start filling in the blanks. It was during this trip, my second to the continent, that I realized that I was now ready to begin this process of education with my new friends and colleagues.

I hoped that they would be as open to my perspective as I was determined to be about theirs on the history of African American domination of indigenous Liberians for the more than 130 years leading up to the bloody civil war. And they were. Even though they were struggling to learn in a university whose library had almost no books, whose science labs had no equipment, whose professors had no access to books in their field published in the last fifteen years, or even classes with fewer than 150 students, I was buoyed more than I can express by the fact that these students before me were determined to get an education, however or wherever they could find it. If it was in the middle of a cemetery of decimated tree stumps in the center of campus, talking to a mouthy American woman who insisted that she was Black, and that Obama winning the presidency wouldn't really change things for Africa, then that was where it would happen. This was what they were teaching me: *Make your own opportunities.*

But what I noticed through the course of all this back and forth—although I was trying hard not to—was that my attention kept on going back to a medium-built, young man with a wide smile and glittering eyes. *There's something about that guy that I really like,* I said to myself, and I wanted to keep talking to him. So, I did.

I had determined, during my first trip to the continent, that I would never date or marry an African man—a fact I shared with my future (African) husband-to-be minutes after I met him. Ballah had just told me that I was beautiful, and then inquired about what my thoughts were about African men. So I told him some things I had observed during my year in Ghana: That most African men felt not only compelled, but actually empowered, to have at least one woman on the side, and that there seemed to be very little that the women could do to object to this. And of course, it went without saying that a woman attempting to have extra-marital lovers was seen as heretical. That fact alone was enough to make me want to tear my hair out, I told him, but it pointed to a much deeper problem: A fundamentally different understanding of the gender roles in Western and African cultures. Women were expected to exercise their power primarily within the confines of the family and home, while men were entitled to rule the rest of the world. According to most of the African men I met, I told Ballah, a woman who is powerful and making waves in her career, who is outspoken and does not always "obey" the wishes of her family, and who sometimes defies traditional cultural expectations, is "trying to be white, and Western." These women were described by these African men as "rejecting their cultures and identities. They are colonizers, trying to accelerate our cultural annihilation even further." Of course, as a twenty-three-year-old Black feminist, I found these arguments less than convincing, especially when confronted with the fact that most of the West African women I encountered on that trip worked from before the sun was up until long after it went down: waking, feeding, and caring for the children; working in the gardens, the fields, the kiosks selling water and goods; cleaning the house and preparing the food for the family; and generally seeing to their own needs last. Most of the men just seemed to sit around for most of the day, telling each other tall tales and playing drats. Some of them did go to work, but the work had a starting and an ending point. For the women, the work was endless, and unacknowledged. From my "colonized" eyes, all I could see was women's labor making the whole continent go round.

Ten years later, remembering these facts while eating rice and cassava leaf with a young Liberian student whose round face and curiously amber-flecked eyes were clearly African, clearly male, I wondered how it could be that something deep inside me, something I had almost forgotten was there, kept opening to him in spite of this knowledge, over and over again.

> *The vision of an African continental family or a sable race standing shoulder to shoulder was born by captives, exiles, and orphans and in the aftermath of the Atlantic slave trade. Racial solidarity was expressed in the language of kinship because it both evidenced the wound and attempted to heal it. The slave and the ex-slave wanted what had been severed: kin. Those in the diaspora translated the story of race into one of love and betrayal.*
> —Saidiya Hartman

"Why?" Ballah asks me while we are driving around our neighborhood in South Minneapolis one afternoon. He is pointing at several Black youths, hooded, and with sagging pants and an exaggerated gait, smoking on the corner. "Look at your people. Look at who Boisey will be."

We have developed our own language within ordinary language, as many couples do, after living together for almost a year now. Ballah is not asking why these Black boys have gathered, he is asking why they are allowing themselves to be stereotyped as "gangstas" by passerby, especially by area police. He is provoking me by offering his own response to my oft-uttered statements about how much Black Americans have been through in this country, how much we are still going through, and how strong we have had to be in order to endure it all. And he is expressing his fear, only recently admitted, that our son, who is both Liberian and Black American—but who will be raised primarily here, and who will, therefore, be primarily Black American—will see the only expression of Black manhood as the one that these boys have clearly chosen, which could have very negative consequences. We go back and forth on this matter frequently—Ballah saying that Boisey will end up with the wrong friends and on the wrong lifepath, and me responding that there are many different ways to be Black American, that this particular version of Black manhood is the only one that gets transmitted to Africa is intentional, and that it is up to us, Boisey's parents, to make sure that he is exposed to the full multiplicity of what it means to be a Black man in America today. Half the time, I know that Ballah is just teasing me, trying to stir the pot, and that the other half of the time, he is confronting his profound worry and sadness around the treatment of Black males in this country—and the unfortunate fact that the person he may love most somehow falls into this category in the eyes of the world. How does one save a Black child, in a culture that wants no Black children? I get this, I get that he's working through this big, festering cesspool of identity and disappointment and powerlessness, but it still pisses me off.

"Boisey is fine," I say, gesturing to our eighteen-month-old, who is firmly strapped into his car seat behind us, munching on a pear. "Your son is not interested in hoods and designer pants. Just how much fruit he can fit in his mouth at one time." I grin back at our solid, thirty-pound chunk of child, and he points back at me in acknowledgement, babbling something that only he understands.

"For now," Ballah says, frowning. "Soon he will be taller than me, swaggering, and not listening to either of us."

I peer at him sideways, trying to gauge if he is kidding. I decide that he isn't. "What? You think he'll be raised by wolves? He's got two parents here—two *actively involved* parents who will be heavily present in his development throughout his life. And he's got a community that will also make sure he keeps on the straight and narrow."

Ballah waves his hands. "With Americans, the kids can do anything. Nothing is a problem. They don't have to listen to anyone." He is half-smiling now, probably remembering some obnoxious kid that has come our way recently, misbehaving in any number of ways that would be completely unacceptable in an African context. Hell, it would also be unacceptable in a Black American context, for that matter. "You love your children too much here," he says, sighing.

I decide to side-step this particular discussion right now and instead refocus on the cause of his malaise: our son, and how he wants him to grow up to be a happy and productive member of at least one, if not both, of our societies. "These boys may not have had parents who are as involved as we are," I tell him. "They may not have other people and men in their lives making sure that they don't get into things they shouldn't. That's a big difference between them and Boisey." As I'm speaking, however, I can hear the damning statistics ringing in my ears: half of all Black boys eighteen and under living in our county will have some kind of contact with law enforcement, even though they make up a tiny percentage of the population here. Black boys in Minnesota are six times more likely than white boys to be suspended from school, mostly because 95 percent of teachers here are white and not culturally competent. It's almost like I'm trying to convince myself that our son will be okay growing up in this environment, where the very presence of a Black male body is seen as menacing. I am well aware that although everyone thinks he's "such a cutie" now, as soon as he turns the corner on twelve or thirteen, and begins to grow into the adult male body that is his birthright, another, far more sinister reaction will greet him when he moves through public spaces. That these particular Black adolescents have decided to embrace an image that grants them the most powerful (if often negative) response available to them only confirms how relatively little *real* power they feel they have in their lives. How will Boisey confront this maddening contradiction at the heart of our daily and moral lives: Although we state that all human beings deserve to be treated fairly and humanely and not be prejudged, we in America do not extend these laudatory goals to our view and treatment of many groups of people here—but perhaps most shockingly and disturbingly to those whose bodies he shares through no fault of his own: Black males.

"And we can always send him to Liberia to stay with your family if it looks like he's really getting out of control," I say, more to myself than to Ballah.

He nods.

Of course, it would be wonderful for Boisey to spend any amount of time with Ballah's family, and for him to have the opportunity to really deeply explore the Liberian side of his identity. But the irony of this situation—one that is shared by hundreds of Somali and Liberian mothers in the Twin Cities—is not lost on us. That you would send your own flesh and blood to one of the poorest countries in the world, a place where 85 percent of the population is still without work, where wide swaths of the populace are illiterate, where the daily security of its citizens is threatened by the lingering effects of the fifteen-year civil war that decimated it, and by the ongoing devastating fight against Ebola that has taken thousands of lives in the West African region; that you would do this as a parent, as someone who loves your son so much that you would do anything to protect him; and that you are nevertheless certain that America is still the richest, the most powerful country in the world, home to what is still, despite its deficiencies, a world-class education system, unparalleled research and innovation, a solid, if embattled, middle class, which the majority of the Global South sees (for better or for worse) as a leader in humanitarianism and good governance, a society with arts and social justice movements of paramount importance; that you would take your only child out of this vast sea of opportunity—this effectively damns the very country whose ideals of liberty and freedom you toil and labor so hard to express. It is exactly as James Baldwin described it almost fifty years ago, in his formidable essay, "My Dungeon Shook: Letter to My Nephew on the One Hundredth Anniversary of the Emancipation":

I know what the world has done to my brother and how narrowly he has survived it. And I know, which is much worse, and this is the crime of which I accuse my country and my countrymen, and for which neither I nor time nor history will ever forgive them, that they have destroyed and are destroying hundreds of thousands of lives and do not know it and do not want to know it . . . But it is not permissible that the authors of devastation should also be innocent. It is the innocence which constitutes the crime. (Baldwin, 1965)

. . .

As it turns out, things are not so different for Black boys and men growing up in Minnesota in 2011 as they were for Black boys and men growing up here in 1965 . . . or even 1865. These may be facts, but they are also a set of stones piled and piling up between the three members of our family: me, a light-skinned, hyper-educated mixed Black woman; my husband, a new immigrant from Liberia; and whoever our son is and will be: a curious and extremely physical *African* American child of this new century.

"I never knew how fortunate we are, to have a real home," Ballah says, slightly smiling, slightly grimacing. "In Liberia it is hard but . . ." He watches the young boys on the corner disperse, waving goodbye to each other. Then he turns back to me. "Our country doesn't hate us. Even though you Black Americans have more access to education and jobs, you really are stuck. I see that now." He sighs. "This is your home, but not your homeland."

Now it is my time to sigh. For the two years we made our relationship work over the phone, and over Skype, I vividly remember my frustration when trying to explain American racism to him. After all, how do you explain something that makes no sense at all? "Why do you hate the white people so much?" he would often ask me. "People are just people. Who cares if they're white?"

I would wonder if he could hear the sound of my teeth gritting, thousands of miles away. Then, I would try to explain some basic aspects of Black history in America, structural versus interpersonal racism, and racial profiling to him, before realizing the futility of my words and the exhaustion they were bringing on. "You just have to be here," is what I always ended up saying. "Then you'll understand. I can't describe it."

Now that he is actually experiencing American racism—understands intimately its simultaneously wide-sweeping, and individualized effects, its ruinous consequences—I want to go back to the time before his hope was busted. I want to hear the lightness in his voice again.

Instead, I say, "Just don't forget. You may be African, but you're also Black American now."

"I know," he says. His shoulders are sagging, his eyes faraway. "I know."

It's Like a Miracle

from *I Would Know You by Your Feet*

In 2006, through a lucky DNA match, David Grant found and reunited with one line of his long-missing kin from the transatlantic slave trade. The day after his arrival in Accra, Ghana, he was escorted by new-found cousin Gideon to the family's ancestral village of Tegbi.

The highway east from Accra to the river crossing at Sogakope had been the best stretch of main road that Gideon and I had traveled since I'd arrived in Ghana. Only about two hours after escaping the insane traffic of the capital, we were crossing the Volta River into the family's ancestral home country of Anlo.

Not many years ago, there was a ferry at the place where the bridge now stands, and that was the only way across for many miles. This was true even back in the days when Keta, a few miles to the east near the border with Togo, was a major port. During the dark era of the slave trade, when this stretch of river was deeper, slave ships used to lie at anchor just south of here in the delta. On this particular afternoon, a few fishermen in dugout canoes were the only river traffic, but during the dark days of "the trade," slaving ships in the delta would be lying in wait for dugouts like these and larger war canoes to come downriver bearing cargoes of slaves from the interior. The Volta wasn't the first African river to serve as a water highway for the transport of slaves, but it does have the dubious distinction of being the last. The very last ship known to have carried a cargo of slaves from Africa to the Americas, possibly within sight of this bridge, weighed anchor for Brazil from here in 1866.

From Sogakope to the Togolese border, the road narrows and its quality isn't quite as high, but compared to the roads on our trip west during the week before, it was still easy going—much like traveling a typical two-lane blacktop "blue highway" in the U.S. We veered south to connect with the road that carries travelers east along the coast through Srogboe, and

Anloga, the regional capital, then through Woe and Keta and finally, Denu and Aflao, the last two towns before the border. The big "First Ghana Building Society" logo on Gideon's truck had the desired effect, and we were waved through every police check point with a nod or sometimes a salute and a smile, without even having to slow down. We were getting close now. The butterflies that had earlier come and gone soon morphed into a whole swarm. I'd never experienced exactly this kind of nerves before. This must be, I thought, like the case of nerves the groom in an arranged marriage might feel before meeting his prospective bride and her family for the first time. There's so much riding on that first impression ... for all concerned. Will we feel like we fit hand in glove, or will we somehow feel just all *wrong* together? When we first look into one another's eyes, will we see a glimmer of mutual recognition there—enough to recognize one another as family in any real way—or will we see ... nothing? Or worse yet, will we feel repelled, or simply disappointed, sorry that we'd gone through all the trouble to arrange this meeting in the first place?

I knew Gideon was nervous, too. There'd been a generally warm and positive reception to the news of my coming. But still, as Gideon had said on our journey here, even though he'd been back and forth between Accra and the village a few times, it had been twenty years since he had actually spent a night there. The process of fence-mending after a long time away is always awkward and complicated at best. Figuring out where and how my own agenda might comfortably fit into the mix could be like tip-toeing through a minefield, given the complexity of Ewe social etiquette—especially when my first introduction to the culture would come at the very same moment as my first introduction to the people who would be my hosts. But neither Gideon nor I felt like talking about any of it now. In fact, this was the longest stretch of silence that there had been between us during the entire trip.

The silence lasted until we arrived in Woe, the last town before Tegbi, a stop where we had to take care of a piece of business which turned out to be an important preliminary part of the social etiquette I needed to learn. Half-way through town, Gideon slowed to look carefully down every side road until he spied what he was searching for: a little liquor store at a dusty crossroads. Gideon explained that I should give him some cash now so that he could buy, on my behalf, two bottles of schnapps as gifts for the elders: one for the clan elders at the old family compound, one for Uncle Wakachie. We'd meet with the clan elders today, Friday, and pay our respects to Wakachie on Sunday. In the old days before colonialism, libations to the ancestors would have been made with home-brewed palm wine, but during the time when this area had been part of German Togoland, it had become fashionable to use store-bought schnapps for this purpose instead, and the tradition had stuck.

The liquor store was shabby and dark and felt a little dangerous. My natural impulse, when a partner walks into a place like that, is to follow close behind and, literally, have his back. But when I slid over to get out and wade through the crowd to join him, Gideon turned back toward me and said, "Lock the door. I'll be back in a minute."

I did as I was asked and watched him disappear inside. A few more neighbors shuffled down the street and joined the people crowded around the truck. It's hard to be the object of that much attention, especially when you are truly not looking for any. If people stare at you when you walk by on the street, no matter how uncomfortable certain stares may make you feel, that's a different thing, because you know it's soon over. All I could do was relax, make eye contact with a few folks and nod. A few people nodded back and waved. There was nothing malevolent in their stares, just curiosity. I understood. It was a slow afternoon in a slow, hard-bitten little town, and the two strangers in the official looking government car were, quite simply, the only show in town just now.

Soon enough, Gideon emerged with the two bottles, wrapped in the ubiquitous black plastic bags which comprise half the litter in Ghana. (Many of these baggies—seemingly produced in the tens of millions—get reused, but eventually, they wind up on the ground or in landfills, and because they are one of the few items the equally ubiquitous goats won't eat, there's no getting rid of them completely. When the wind blows hard in Ghana, because the flora is tropical, very few leaves, other than a few fronds of palm, will come flying at your face along with all that red dust. What you *will* get is shredded bits of black plastic bag on your clothes, in your face, in your mouth and in your eye if you're not careful.) I slipped the bottles into my backpack, and we were off. Every once in a while, there'd be just enough of an opening through the trees and the underbrush to allow us a glimpse of the vast Keta Lagoon, which is the great, defining natural feature of Anlo-Ewe country. Many of Anlo's most important towns are sandwiched in between the lagoon and the sea, spread across a long spit of land that grows narrower and narrower as you travel east until, near Keta, both the lagoon on the one side and the sea on the other are each only a stone's throw away. Its shallow, brackish water was too hard for heavy war canoes to navigate, so it became a safe haven to which people fled during the slave trade. Its many small islands became densely packed homes for many thousands. We could see dozens of their descendants fishing its waters from small boats or working their nets as they waded the sandy shallows.

Residents know the pathways from island to island through the shallows very well. At low tide, you can see them trudging home with the day's catch or with sundries from the market balanced on their heads, giving the impression, from a distance, that this is a place where the people have mastered the secret of walking on water.

Just outside the gate of the old family compound in the heart of the village of Tegbi, there's a small, family-owned liquor store/snack bar called The Groovy Spot. As soon as Gideon pulled the car up next to it, several clan members suddenly appeared and crossed the road to greet us. We alighted from the vehicle and Gideon swung into high gear, working the group like a politician, managing the introductions in both English and Ewe as we walked together to the compound gate. There to greet us were the chief's secretary, Agibota, in his black leather cowboy hat, and a small delegation of respected elders, led by Mr. Dzisam. Youngsters Kofi and Kwaku opened the gate for us and we were ushered through it into the compound. "We have heard of you, Cousin, and we are very glad to meet you," said Mr. Dzisam. "We welcome you home." Madame Desawu, a distant cousin who has been caretaker of the place for many years, rose from her cooking in the big outdoor kitchen and approached so that we could be introduced to her as well. Following shyly in her wake came her daughter, Agnes, and Agnes's young children.

Our escorts spoke with one another in Ewe for a moment, and then excused themselves, saying they'd be back in a few minutes. They informed us that Old Kponyi, whom Lawrence and Gideon had hoped might be able to shed some vital light on the possible identity of my ancestor and how he might have been taken as a slave, was no longer with us, but a couple of elders who *were* available on this particular day would be joining us soon.

Agnes's children peered at me from behind their mother's long skirt and giggled. Madame Desawu spoke animatedly with Gideon in Ewe while I had a look around. I'd been warned that the old family palace built by Gideon and Lawrence's Grandfather George (Haxormene I) was in a complete state of ruin, but I wasn't prepared for what I saw. It looked almost as if it had barely survived wartime damage from bombs or shelling. But it was only time and neglect which had done the damage—time as measured by the relentless pace of ruin in the tropics. After George's son, family patriarch John Kofi Agbemabiese, moved his large family away to Kumasi and Accra in order to be close to his growing business interests, there were no more direct descendants of that line left in Tegbi to occupy either the palace compound or the stool of chieftancy.

A building made of unadorned stone might last here, but there was little native stone to be had. A building made after the European style—with materials and a design originally meant for a temperate climate—simply won't survive a tropical seacoast locale for long without constant upkeep. The cycle of dry and wet seasons, each of them hot, conspires every hour of every day, year in and year out, to rot everything beneath the sun away, most especially anything built by human hands. The salt air makes it hard to keep even a coat of paint looking fresh for more than a year or two. Still, the old palace's advanced state of decay made it hard to believe it was built only a little more than a hundred years ago.

It took a lot of imagining, but I began to see, as I poked around the place, how truly grand it once had been. It had eight bedrooms and two indoor baths at a time when these were rare anywhere on the continent. When it was built in about 1902, it was one of the first "story" buildings—simply meaning a building more than one story in height—built in this area *by a Black man for himself*. During the entire first half of the twentieth century, most other buildings of this size anywhere in West Africa would have been built as colonial administrative offices of some sort, or as the headquarters for some European-owned business. They say that for years after it was built, the sheer audaciousness of the project drew people from a hundred miles around just to see it.

While I explored and took photos, Kwaku, Agnes and a couple of others helped get white plastic chairs set up in the center of the compound courtyard for everyone who was expected. Madame Desawu chatted excitedly with Gideon as they traded family news and passed along greetings from people spread far and wide who communicated their regrets that they couldn't be with us this day, but wanted to say they were with us in spirit. Many times, she paused in the middle of her rapid-fire conversation with Gideon in Ewe, looked over at me and smiled. Every time she did, I heard the same refrain. "She keeps saying, 'It's like a miracle,'" said Gideon. "She says she took one look at you, and she was sure it's true you are one of us. 'Oh, it's like a miracle,' she says."

Her words moved me deeply. When she saw that my eyes had welled up as full of tears as her own, she walked over and pressed my face between her hands. They were rough, calloused, country woman's hands, but somehow, as soft and comforting as a warm blanket on a cold night. Then she abruptly wheeled about and returned to her cooking. Gideon, Kwaku and I sat nearby under the courtyard's nearly two-hundred-year-old mango trees to await the arrival of the full delegation from the Tovie clan.

While we waited, Kwaku peppered me with questions about my life and family in the States. The smell of Madame Desawu's food on the fire, redolent with just enough vaguely recognizable notes to summon memories of long ago summers in the country with my southern relatives, the squeals of the children at play, the casual wandering of the odd farm animal across the courtyard here or there, and the warm conversation, all worked to make this entire scene very comfortable and familiar. My earlier apprehensions about the day melted away. In fact, I found myself feeling more relaxed and content than I had in many months—maybe years. I had expected my first meeting with these long-missing relatives to be complicated, with at least a few jarring notes of culture shock. But so far, this had felt like the afternoons I used to spend on summer vacation in North Carolina, out "pop calling" with my father or my grandmother, visiting far-flung relatives we hadn't seen for a while. We'd turn up some long driveway and one of them would say, "Well, this is Althea and Robert's place, David. You remember Althea and her children, don't you?" There'd be a pretty good chance that I might not remember any of them at all. But they were family—or very close friends who, over the years, had *become* family—and that was all that mattered. And as a bonus, there was always sure to be some good eating too.

Narratives of Longing

As these long-lost kinsmen and I sat with each other in the compound courtyard that day, I began to realize that some of them had found a similar way in which to think about their relationship with me, too. It felt as if most of them found it hard to wrap their minds around the idea that one of their ancestors had been taken long ago as a slave to America, and that one of his descendants had found them through a DNA match, and had now come to seek them out. It was far easier to think of me this way: as the son of some long-lost branch of the family who'd been away in America his whole life, but who had miraculously returned to them. In West Africa, extended families are large, and with relatives often spread out over substantial distances these days, it's practically impossible to keep close tabs on everybody. People emigrate to neighboring countries for work, and seldom get back home as often as they'd planned. People emigrate to Europe, Canada or the U.S., and many of them get back home only rarely. Some never come home again at all. So the narrative of an almost entirely unknown but long-missing relative suddenly come home seemed to be a familiar and comfortable fit in this situation. It's a narrative that's simple and benign. A long-lost kinsman has returned. All that this situation would require of them is their hospitality, and then our mutual commitment to a happy family reunion.

As the men who had greeted us at the gate returned with their wives and the other clan members who'd been asked to come, it was pretty easy to guess who among them were thinking of our relationship on the basis of this narrative, and who among them might be steeling themselves to deal with me from another, less comfortable one. Unlike the people who were beaming at me, or simply trying to get a good look at me without seeming to stare, the clan members preparing themselves to deal with me from this other narrative looked sober and grim, because they knew this second narrative requires confronting slavery—always a difficult subject for Africans and African Americans. The lives of their ancestors and mine were viciously savaged by the same prolonged, almost incomprehensively brutal holocaust, but in the midst of that evil time, our stories diverged. My ancestors were among the twelve million souls who were its victims, carried away as slaves or killed in the process. *Their* ancestors were among the millions who found a way to ride out the storm and survive. One of the strategies the Ewes used to survive that time was to become major players in the slave trade themselves. Like the Yoruba-speaking Oyo Empire to the east of them and the Ashantis to the west, they raided other communities in order to capture slaves whom they could trade for guns and powder, which were then put to use to capture more slaves, as well as to prevent their own people from being captured by others. The ancestors of the people gathered around me had been successfully protected by this Ewe community from capture. Mine hadn't. Why?

The subtle tension rising between us around that circle in the courtyard was due to the fact that both I and these clan elders knew that I would have some questions about this that they couldn't answer . . . or would rather not. The bitter truth is that the slave trade lured many Africans into victimizing their own. The most familiar image of "the trade" is of slavery on the *wholesale* level, where kings and generals and strongmen devastated whole communities, afterwards selling the farmers and soldiers of the losing side along with their wives and children to the Europeans, perhaps keeping some slaves for themselves. Much less familiar is the gut-wrenching reality of slavery on the *retail* level—the cold-blooded and tragic choices made by ordinary commoners to sell away their own kith and kin. Poor families who became desperate enough might sell off a child or two so that they could better manage to feed the ones who remained. A man might lose a son or daughter, seized to settle a debt he couldn't pay. Chiefs sentenced some criminals to captivity as punishment. And so it went, decade after decade for hundreds of years. If the reason for my Ewe ancestor's captivity had a story like this behind it, it was easy to understand how this was the kind that might survive as a dirty little family secret for a couple of generations, eventually to be lost completely. These aren't the kinds of stories that people tend to cherish and commit to passing down for posterity.

But I also knew there was another over-arching reason the elders might not be able to answer many questions about my ancestor. Since the beginning of their exile in the New World as slaves, Africa's scatterlings have nurtured a longing for "home" and a sense of reconnection with African kith and kin. But for generations, the transatlantic slave trade and the people who went missing because of it *simply haven't been very much on African minds.* This is because the African narrative about slavery is so different from the African American narrative. Their narrative is about survival, resistance and triumph, first over slavery and then over colonialism. It's also a celebration of deep cultural roots and continuity. The narrative *I* inherited about slavery celebrates survival too—and the courage and faith required to achieve it. But mine is also a narrative about the loss of deep cultural roots and continuity, about feeling "like a motherless child, a long way from home." These Ewes have a heritage of songs and stories that celebrate the history of their resistance and its heroes that are widely known and frequently sung. I was told that there are also songs that tell of and mourn some of those who went missing during slavery, but no one gathered that day knew any of these, nor could they think, at that moment, of anyone who did. Elders in far-flung villages who might be able to sing us these songs or tell us these stories are being lost to us, one by one and two by two with every passing year. I was promised that they will ask around until they find someone. Essentially, they were saying, "We'll get back to you on that."

In the meantime, the elders who gathered to meet me made it clear they would do their best to tell me as much as they knew. And so everyone took their seats, Mr. Dzisam made introductions all around, and the formal part of our meeting began. There were twenty-four of us in the courtyard now, including the children. Kwaku was sent out to The Groovy Spot to buy soft drinks. These would be refreshment for the women and children. By tradition, only the men would be passing around the schnapps after the opening libations.

As soon as Kwaku returned, Kwadzo, aided by Eric, used the alcohol we'd brought to perform a libation ceremony, asking the ancestors to enjoy this auspicious moment with us and to bless it. Eric scooped a little dirt from the courtyard into a bowl and swirled some water into it. Kwadzo poured in some of the schnapps and swirled the mixture again. Whether they had planned it beforehand as a group, or it was a spontaneous expression from Kwadzo's heart—or perhaps a whispered inspiration from the ancestors themselves—an attempt to begin to bring our differing narratives together began now with this libation. As Kwadzo chanted prayers, pausing periodically to pour some of the mixture upon the ground, he offered thanks that one who had been lost to them had returned, and asked the ancestors to bear joyful witness to this. But he also invited my ancestors to come and be with us, to bless and to be blessed on this occasion. In the distant past, my ancestors and the ancestors of the people gathered here were one and the same, but tradition holds that the ancestors' presence is strongest in the places where their lives were lived on earth. So mine, who were among the many ancestors torn from their midst long ago and made to live out their lives on foreign soil, were asked to come join us, too.

As Eric and Kwadzo closed the ceremony and returned to the circle, the women and some of the other men spontaneously offered up additional prayers of thanksgiving. Then, while Kwaku handed out soft drinks to the women and children, the men passed the bottle of schnapps, each reverentially pouring a little onto the ground for the ancestors, then taking a sip before passing it on. Everyone gave me strong eye contact when my turn came. Everyone except Agibota. He didn't seem hostile, just cool and reserved, still perhaps a little unsure about me, unsure about this whole enterprise. Who could blame him? My sudden appearance among them, and the way in which it had occurred, was a big thing for people here to make peace with and fully comprehend. So far, it had been hard for me to discern, anywhere in popular African culture, a cultural space where it's possible to feel much of a genuine sense of an African longing for *us*, at least one that is anything like the longing that many of us have felt for a close and authentic sense of connection with *them*.

But it's crystal clear that the Ghanaian government, at least, was bound and determined to help create just such a popular cultural space during this auspicious time. The spring of 2007, just months away, would mark the fiftieth anniversary of Ghana's independence, which, in a powerful bit of synchronicity, just happened to coincide with the two hundredth anniversary of the British abolition of the African slave trade. A variety of big public events had been planned, most of them designed to "inspire the diasporans to come home": people of African descent from the U.S. and Canada, from Central America and the Caribbean, and from Europe. One of the biggest of these initiatives, aimed specifically at the descendants of African slaves, was The Joseph Project. The project's two major goals were: 1) to publicly apologize for the role of Africans in the African slave trade; 2) to invite people of African descent, after they'd heard and absorbed this apology, to "come home" either literally or figuratively, in order to help build

Africa's capacity to successfully lift itself up and out of poverty, and then soon after, to launch itself into a new age of prosperity and leadership on the world stage.

Whoever it was at the Ghanaian Ministry of Tourism that thought up "The Joseph Project" really knew what they were doing. The biblical story of Joseph and his brothers has a powerful and evocative resonance for Africans and people of African descent, offering a shared narrative which both can use as a way to confront the slave trade and its legacy together—side by side. The story of Joseph and his brothers shows how reconciliation is possible even after the most grievous of wrongs. Jealous of the special favor shown him by God, and by the special place he had always held in their parents' hearts, Joseph's brothers plotted against him. They stripped him of his fine clothes, beat him and sold him into slavery. Soon afterward, the family suffered financial ruin and became desperately poor. But Joseph, after years in bondage, gained his freedom and eventually became a prosperous man. Word of his remarkable reversal of fortune reached his suffering people back home, and they sent a delegation to beg his forgiveness and ask for his help. When his brothers found him, they were genuinely glad to see him again, relieved to know that the stories of his survival and rise to prosperity were true. They marveled that, in spite of everything, he was glad to see them again, as well. He accepted their apology for what they had done to him, and they were reconciled. Joseph returned to his people and helped restore their house to its former glory.

That's the best of all possible happy endings for a story that seemed destined to end very badly. There had been much written about The Joseph Project in the daily press and much said about it on television and radio too, so everywhere I went in Ghana, people had heard of it. In this country of pious Christians and Muslims who share the same prophets and the same treasury of Old Testament stories, people seemed to understand and relate to the story and its meaning on a visceral level. But did this mean that everyday Ghanaians were actually taking this spin on the Joseph story to heart, giving birth to a new narrative in which Africans feel a spiritual need, a longing, to reconcile with their long-missing kin and welcome them home? I don't know the answer, but I do know it isn't a simple "yes" or "no." The old Pan-Africanist dream has taken a serious beating, but it still has its true believers. For them, and for a few diverse allies on both the political left and right, I'm convinced the answer is "yes." But I'm also convinced that for most, it will take some time for that new narrative to grow and take root, because there's a lot of ambivalence, indifference and downright hostility to overcome. There is too little mutual knowledge of our histories and cultures. There are too many years of cynical talk about why we diasporans spend so much money to come all that way just to stand in the slave forts and cry. There are too many years of boasting by vendors and shopkeepers and unlicensed "tourist guides" about how simple it is to take advantage of us. We come to them so needy for a little recognition and acceptance that we make ourselves easier marks.

But the man whom the Tovie clan had welcomed into their circle and into their family through this ceremony at the compound in Tegbi wasn't invited in because he was "one of the Josephs from the diaspora" that the radio and papers kept talking about. He was invited in because he's *their* Joseph. Today's ceremony was a specific embrace offered to a specific person they had decided to recognize as their own. Perhaps the problem with The Joseph Project narrative is that when you attempt to make the story apply in a broad and general way to millions of people, it's just too abstract. But there was nothing abstract about the depth of the welcome I had been offered this day in Tegbi, nor about the strong eye contact we were sharing with one another around that circle. Nor about the presence of the ancestors. I could feel them.

The schnapps burned as I choked it down. I had taken a bigger gulp than I intended. It scudded into my mostly empty stomach like a malevolent wave. As I passed the communal cup to Gideon, I swore I could feel the alcohol already going straight to my head. Someone in the circle offered water, and I gulped it down to the last drop. Now that the cup had made it completely around, Mr. Dzisam announced to the group both in Ewe and English that they knew I had come with many questions about family history. They regretted that they could not tell me the thing I most wanted to know. They had no idea exactly who my ancestor was or where he fit on the family tree—but they would share their knowledge of that family tree with me to the fullest extent that they could.

Then, Mr. Dzisam ceremoniously pulled a battered old notebook out of his briefcase, and for nearly an hour, he read from it the entire known genealogy of the Tovie clan. As he intoned the names, it felt like being in church on some high, holy day. Elder clan members who had heard the entire family history read before and the younger ones who had not listened with rapt attention and drank it all in, swaying slightly with the rhythm of his voice.

When Mr. Dzisam had finished, I thanked him and asked if I could please look the book over to see how the names in it were arranged. As I received the notebook, Gideon leaned into me and said that if I had any cash I could spare for the clan's communal coffers, now would be a good time to make a contribution. I didn't have much, but I'd been told the weekly dues the clan has traditionally asked from each family has been set at three cents a week for quite some time now. Quickly doing the math, I figured the sixty dollars in my pocket would cover my own family's back dues to 1966. I promised I'd pay up all the way back to the probable time of my ancestor's departure the next time I saw them. That got a good laugh out of everybody, even Agibota.

Gideon and I looked at how the names were arranged in the book and sighed. It's an interesting arrangement, full of intriguing information, but it's hard to read for someone used to using the kind of genealogy chart that's become standard in the west. The familiar western model is linear, designed to enable tracing a direct path back to an ancestor whose place in the family tree proffers upon descendants the rights to property or a family name. This less linear African model seemed to be all about establishing the broad blood ties and shared history of the inter-connected families of the clan. The chart they presented to me looks like it probably gets us back to the late eighteenth century, but that may be too late to identify an ancestor who might have been snatched from them considerably earlier. And in any event, no one was aware of anyone in that list of names having been taken as a slave. But Gideon and Lawrence have drummed up support for searching the oral record of diverse clan elders, not only in Anlo, but farther upcountry where members also live, for clues about known historical events that can help us date some of these "begats" on the chart—also, of course, to see if we can find that ancestor of mine buried in the middle of some barely remembered story or a fragment of one of the old songs. I asked if I could make a photocopy of the chart. They told us that would be fine, and that there was a copy center just down the road in Keta. I thanked them profusely.

Agibota smiled broadly. He seemed to have warmed up to me a great deal. "Come back and see us at Easter," he said, "and we'll slaughter you a ram." Everyone smiled and laughed. The meeting was over.

Science

Gideon and I sat there for a while and talked about the next steps we would have to take from here in order to parse out the tale of my ancestor. Would I be able to find a record dating his arrival in Virginia or North Carolina, a date that could then be tied to a specific story about an ancestor who went missing from the African side of the Atlantic during that time frame? A scenario like that would be the most likely path to the "Kunta Kinte moment" we'd craved.

From the very beginning of this journey, I'd been mindful of the need to pay due respect to the science involved in this kind of search. Before you can make any real sense of a Y-DNA match or near-match, you've got to be able to construct a reliable record of "begats" to positively identify a missing male ancestor and see where he fits into the family tree you're attempting to flesh out. A near-match on eleven out of twelve "markers" like ours could mean our common ancestor lived as recently as seven generations ago. It also *could* place him as far back as twenty-two generations distant. But because of Ewe culture's oral record regarding the traumatic years of slavery, and because the family from which this ancestor of mine appears to have sprung is prominent now and was prominent *then*, we knew there was a reasonable chance that there might indeed be some specific stories somewhere out there about him. We knew that the written genealogy chart we were now holding in our hands might prove to hold a critically important piece of the puzzle. Gideon said he'd be ready to head into Keta for our copying mission in just a few minutes.

Even though we'd been sitting in the compound yard for hours now, my heart was full and I was feeling very relaxed and content—in no hurry to go anywhere. The children were off running around and playing. The men had scattered across the courtyard, talking quietly in small groups. But the women were still seated, all eyes still on me. It was as if another, less formal meeting had now been convened. I took a very tentative part in a couple of different conversations going on between the men, but I was really only paying cursory attention. My focus was on the women, as Mrs. Dzisam, Madame Desawu, and the others talked with quiet intensity among themselves. Even in a profoundly patriarchal culture like this one, the wise understand that every minute of every day, it's important to try to intuit what *mother* wants too. There are many spheres of daily life, large and small, in which she is the quiet power behind the throne. Men's voices had held sway in the formal part of the meeting, but now, the floor belonged to the women. I could hear them trading notes about me, mostly in Ewe, so I was able to understand very little. But the tone and sound of their voices, like honey, and the warm little glances periodically thrown my way told me everything I needed to know.

In every culture on earth, it's women who are the ultimate keepers of the family tree, since they are the ones who bring each new generation into the world. They are the faithful keepers of all "the begats," recorded in the pages of the family bible, or perhaps not recorded at all except in memory. In the rural South I remember, if a young man was alleged to have gotten a young woman pregnant, at some point, the women in his family needed to see this baby and pass judgment. Only five percent of the examination was about easily observable physical things. "Well, he's got our nose . . . and hands like Big John's . . . and our color." There have got to be a thousand subtle things that go into that determination, most of which the women who pass that baby around the parlor couldn't really explain to you if their lives depended on it. But somehow, they just *know*. If great-grandma snorts and says, with certitude, "Now, you know this child ain't none of ours," that's probably the end of the matter. But if indeed that turns out to be the final word, it could never represent a callous or casual rejection. Every little baby who comes into this world needs and deserves love. It's just that if somebody who can't even hold up his own head yet is about to be given: 1) all your unconditional love, 2) the keys to the family treasure, 3) a whole lifetime of everyone's blood, sweat and tears, 4) a license to break everyone's heart as only a family member can, they'd better damned well be right about this fateful judgment they are about to make.

That's another kind of science. And by the end of a long afternoon beneath the shelter of these towering mango trees, having now been scrutinized in a somewhat similar way, I knew that by the time the women rose, certain their work was done, they had unequivocally decided to recognize me as one of their own. Case closed.

Now that, as far as they were concerned, my place among them had been affirmed, Madame Desawu came over to me with a piece of personal business. As she pressed her body close and put her hand on mine, Agnes stepped over to interpret. "My son Richard went away to America fifteen years ago," she said. "For the first ten years, he called and wrote, and sometimes, he'd send money. But for five years now, I've heard nothing from him. No calls, no letters. No one seems to know where he is. When you go back to the States, will you please search for him for me?" Agnes placed a well-worn piece of paper into my hand. Richard's last known telephone number and address were on it. "I'll look for him," I said, "And I'll tell him he needs to call his mother." Now I had two missing people to track down, my ancestor and Richard, and I left solemnly committed to searching for them both.

At the End of Myself

For Angela

There used to be a chasm, yawning darkness
from one horizon to the other edge of space
at the end of my being. My muscling heart
used to shudder in perplexed wonder,
my mind racing with fear that itty-bitty me
would be so much fine dust in vast eternity.

But at the end of myself—after I've rolled the rock
to the mountaintop and cried my lips sore,
after I've borne this weight in the crook of my shoulders,
shifting my back out, straining hips some more,
after I've cricked my creases and bruised my palms raw—
there is you, with scripture and salve and Gilead's balm,

humming healing at the end of that hanging rope,
over the edge of that dangling cliff, beyond
the bounds of that thrown ball—beyond it all
there is a blessed sound enfolding me,
a brilliant breathing with a sweet hold of me.

At the limit of myself, there was brooding night,
an abyss of cool agnostic doubt;
it was hunger and thirst, this void in want of light—
now there's word made flesh, and a need to shout

thank you for catching this fallen striver
on his broken-down, sour-frowned face,
for plucking me out of the maws of darkness—
thank you for your snatching grace—

for bringing me back with renewed strength,
for showing that at the end of teeny-weeny me
there is a great and endless blessing—thank you
for every divine word to which I belong,
for every honey drip of your sweet, sweet song.

Lilac Week

It's lilac week.
Everywhere you
look/lilacs.

Heard these punks
Running down the
alley
Laughing their fool
heads off,
Old Lady Duncan
yelling at them about
stealing her lilacs.
It's lilac week.

Hey, man!
Some good shit!
Meet me back
in the alley
Smell those lilacs.

Purple
Blue
Red
Pink
White
and every shade
between,
accented
by
the
Green.

It's lilac week.
Lilac week.
The world
surrenders to lilacs.

The Bank Robbery

On November 10, 2002, my eldest son was sentenced to ten years in the federal penitentiary. Ten years hard time in maximum security. This wasn't the first time Steven was given a number to replace his name. He has spent most of his life behind bars; a short sentence here, a longer one there. But this time it was serious. This time my #1 son robbed a bank in a lily-white suburb of St. Paul, Minnesota, a blue collar burb with a shamrock as its logo, a 36-mile area fifteen miles south of the Twin Cities whose census data in the year 2000 reported a population of 14,619 white people with a smattering of Asians and Latinos and one or two black folks for diversity; a community with a median income of $65,916 derived primarily from heavy industry—refineries, industrial waste plants and the like.

A few years earlier, Steve was feeling frustrated. "Mom," he complained, "nobody wants to give an ex-offender a decent job or rent him a decent apartment, especially if he's a felon." But my #1 son had held on tight and, to his surprise and my great pride, some good things started to happen for him, a series of firsts; he worked his way off parole for the first time since he was a teenager, he landed a job driving a semi—the job he had dreamed of since I bought him his first set of *Hot Wheels* when he was barely old enough to walk—the kind of job that allowed him to feel powerful as he guided a mighty rig across the highways of the U.S. of A. praising God for the beauty of the plains, the hills and mountains, the rivers and the oceans that he witnessed along the way. For the first time in his life, my #1 son had the means to buy a brand new car and, for the first time, he was blessed with a child of his own.

But one morning when Steve showed up for work, ready to hit the road, he was faced with the shocking news that the company had closed its doors, leaving all of its workers jobless and leaving him vulnerable, in danger of reverting back to his old patterns. Ex-offender/convicted felon seeks employment. Baby's mama screaming on him cuz the rent's late and baby needs shoes. Powerless. Ashamed to tell the shrink he didn't have the money for the meds that kept his bi-polar disorder in check. Powerless. Ashamed to call his Narcotics Anonymous sponsor or anyone else, for that matter, including The Almighty, to ask for help.

Shame has amazing power. It can cause a person to turn something around so that it begins to look like what happened was your fault, like Steve was to blame for the company's problems.

Shame.

Shame buried just beneath the epidermis, the top layer of his skin, ready to jump out and bite him in the ass at a moment's notice. Shame stored in his genetic memory, imbedded in his DNA. Shame that started when his great-great-great-grandparents were shackled and forced to walk through the Door of No Return, locked up on ships that carried them through the middle passage shitting and puking all over themselves and their relatives, friends and neighbors chained close together like they were in a can of sardines, then stripped of their history, their identity, their language, their religion. Shame passed down to him through three or four generations of family members who suffered the pain and humiliation that started with slavery and mutated into deep anger and self hatred, one of the far-reaching effects of the phenomenon known as post traumatic slave syndrome. It's the kind of shame that has no place to go except to be visited upon those less powerful, like spouses and children. My mama praised me for having put an end to the child abuse that's been in our family for all of those generations, but by the time I learned how to show my children that I love them, it was too late for Stevie. Shame. Shame. Shame on you.

It only took a few weeks for the positive energy Steve had built up over a few short years of living productively to dissipate. He began to spiral out of control, sinking into that familiar black hole of drugs and alcohol. And on November 20, 2001, two months and nine days after the attacks on the World Trade Center, a year and ten days before he was sentenced to the federal penitentiary, my #1 son imploded.

Dear Mom,

Donna threw me out and I was living in my truck so I decided head out to Denver. I liked it when I lived there before but it wasn't the same this time. I got with this beautiful hooker named Celeste and got stranded when she stole my SUV. I tracked down the guy who hooked me up with her and pressed him to tell me where she was. He took me to her place and I met her grandfather. I told him she stole my truck and he got upset, frustrated with his granddaughter, saying, "I don't know why she keeps doing this to me." The old man, Calvin, let me stay there for about a week, until the police found my truck in the impound lot. I didn't even recognize the signs that said I was once again reaching the bottom of my life . . . which is always the stop before prison.

I had no money at all, so I called my little bro and he sent me enough to get my car out and get back home. I promised to give him the money as soon as I got back to Minnesota. In fact, I asked him to pick up my unemployment check and hold it until I got back, which he did.

I called him when I was about six hours away and told him that I would be there around 3 or 4 in the morning. He stashed my check on his front porch so I could pick it up without disturbing his family.

I blazed into town around 4 AM. Stopped off at my brother's and picked up my check from the hiding place on his porch, hit the freeway and headed to the check cashing place on Lake Street and First Avenue. It should have taken me about a half hour to get from his place in the burbs, but at that time in the morning, when there isn't much traffic, it only took half the time.

My plan was to cash the check and run back out to Julian's crib to give him the money I owed him. But I ended up at the crack house instead. My custom has always been to get my dope and then look for a woman. Not necessarily for the sex, it was more about the company. I found this pretty, petite little Chicana and for the next day and a half, we went bar hopping, went back and forth to the crack house and holed up in a motel in south Minneapolis.

I don't know what it was about this girl that made me want to keep her. With street women, time's up when the money runs out, so I was trying to use whatever brain cells I hadn't smoked up to figure out how to keep her from leaving. When we couldn't stay at the motel any longer, I pulled into a liquor store and stole a bottle of vodka.

We polished off the vodka in a matter of minutes, and right about this time the edge was coming off of the dope. I asked her if she had ever robbed a bank. She said no, but she knew of a way to rob banks by computer. I really wasn't trying to hear that because I was one of those here and now type niggaz. I didn't have the patience for all of that long term hustlin'.

It was Tuesday, right around noon, and we were getting hungry. I pulled into a Burger King knowing that all I had were some bad checks from my account that had been closed, so I went inside where I could write a check instead of tryin' to order something at the drive-up window.

When I came back out, the girl was gone. I guess all that talk about robbing banks scared her off. But by now I had been talking so much about robbing a bank that I convinced myself to do it. So I pulled into a convenience store and stole a pair of those dark, mirrored sunglasses so no one could tell what I was looking at, and then it was off to the bank.

The first bank I went to was crowded so I left. Jumped back into my truck and just sat in the parking lot for about 20 minutes. As I sat there, I saw where I was heading—back to prison. I thought about all that I had lost in just a matter of thirty days; a good job that I loved, my woman and my little baby girl. I began *to feel tears well up but, Mom, I can't cry—not one tear fell from my eye. It was almost like those bitter tears were backing up into my soul.*

I was in Apple Valley, not far from Hastings where there's a detox center so I thought, "I'd better get to detox, that's the only thing I can do at this point." I pulled myself together, started up the Bravada and headed off with full intentions of getting off the freeway in Hastings and droppin' at the detox center. But as I was rolling through Rosemount I caught a glimpse of a sign that said "TCF Bank Grand Opening."

Very impulsively, I pulled into the parking lot, a Cub Foods supermarket with a TCF bank attached to it. I circled the building and found a place to park, then I wrote a note demanding money. I put on my shades and my baseball cap which read Female Body Inspector (F.B.I.—how ironic), and went into the bank and scoped it out. One of the tellers stood out, she was so beautiful. So I walked in, half mesmerized by the beauty of her caramel-colored skin, her long, thick black hair, and her honey-colored eyes; and half desperate for the money. I talked with her briefly and she told me that she was Persian. Then I slid her the note. I should have slid her my phone number instead and asked her for a date.

She looked at the note and then looked at me like she was confused, like she couldn't believe what was happening and then she nodded her head in agreement. When she opened the money drawer and began pulling out the cash, I noticed a slot in the drawer that was stacked with $100 bills. Little did I know that slot had the device that would change the next ten years of my life.

The Rosemount newspaper reported that Steve "used a threatening note and the suggestion of a gun to walk out with an undisclosed amount of money." Witnesses helped identify him. "As he ran out of the bank he had shoved the money down his pants and a dye pack exploded, which attracted the attention of a number of people. One wrote down his license number."

I imagine Steve dropping the bag of loot down the front of his pants and trying to run to the Oldsmobile Bravada, the SUV he had purchased brand new just a few months before, when he was employed. I see him looking over his shoulder cuz he knows that a black man stepping into a new car in small town Minnesota will raise some eyebrows. I hear the dye pack explode. Pow! And I see this red substance cover the front of his pants as he climbs into the truck.

Listen. Can you hear the crowd? Can you see people spilling out of the building? Do you hear them yelling "Catch him!" "Don't let him get away!" "Give me a piece of paper. Gotta get his license number."

And I see my #1 son peel out of the parking lot, out of his mind from the pain in his groin and the crack cocaine that gave him the guts to stop off in white town and rob the bank, his dark eyes shining with a mixture of sadness, wonder and surprise, glazed and sparkling like stars in a clear sky on a summer night.

I imagine him taking his right hand off the steering wheel and reaching down to unfasten the holster where his cell phone is locked, lifting the phone and dialing somebody's number, then parting the mustached lips that hide his perfect teeth. But before he can get the first word out, the dye pack starts to burn in his crotch, making the insides of his bones scream. He muffles the screams, recalling instead the confusion on the bank teller's face when she realized that the glassy-eyed black man who stood on the other side of the bulletproof glass, the ginger-skinned desperado dressed in dark glasses, a baseball cap, tight jeans and a brown leather jacket, stinking to high heaven cuz he'd been up smoking crack and drinking whiskey for three days and three nights, had slipped her a note commanding her to fork over the cash. But he can't hold the screams back for long. He has to keep moving before the cops catch up with him but where will he go? He has to get that bag of hot money out of his pants before the substance ruins his ability to father another child. He's trying to keep control of his ride while his crotch is burning so hard that he wonders if he has finally made it to that place where it's rumored that Satan makes his home. I imagine him digging his sweaty hand down where the Sun doesn't shine and coaxing the offending bag of cash away from his parched skin, a long, guttural moan barely making it past the Adam's apple on his thick, brown neck. And I imagine Julian, my younger son, who has built a happy, prosperous life with his wife and three sons feeling hurt, bewildered and disappointed; wondering why his big brother ripped him off.

I put the bundle of money on the passenger seat and when I picked it up again it was still smoldering, traces of the red dye had burned through the tan leather seats. I attempted to see what I could salvage from the bundle. Now picture this, Mom. Here I am blazing down a dirt road with my pants and underwear down around my ankles, kicking up a thick cloud of dust behind me and tossing all of the destroyed, banded bundles of money that I couldn't salvage out the window. Then it was off to Rochester where I had a delicious steak dinner and left the waitress a $20 tip.

I hooked up with my dope man when I got back into town. It was the Tuesday before Thanksgiving and I had promised him a month before that I would take him home to Detroit to see his mom for Thanksgiving. You know me, Mom. How could I refuse a request like that? He was just a 20-year-old kid. He called me "Unc" and I called him "Nephew." I spent $400 with him, then holed up in a hotel room close to his house smoking crack and tweaking so we could hit the road on Wednesday.

I was still on fire from the burn I got from the dye pack so I showed it to the kid on the way to Detroit. He asked me what had happened. He grimaced and then told me that I needed to put some peroxide and ointment on it so we stopped and got some. Sure started feeling better.

Soon as the youngster and I hit Wisconsin, my cell phone rang. I knew it was Donna. She asked where I was and I told her I was on my way to Detroit for Thanksgiving. She asked me to come back and spend it with her and the kids but all I could think was, "You got some nerve. You threw me out of the house, I've been sleeping in my truck, and you didn't care when I was stranded in Denver for five days, and now you want me to have Thanksgiving with you?"

I talked with her again while I was in Detroit, told her I'd be back at 6:00 on Saturday morning. I remember telling her that I was on my way to greatness (whatever that meant) and she started crying. It didn't dawn on me until later what her tears were about.

Anyway, we started back to Minneapolis on Friday night. The youngster was tired from all the rippin' and runnin' we'd been doing so I took the first leg of the trip. Mom, I know you're familiar with Divine Intervention. Well, I believe that's what happened for the rest of the trip. God was not willing to let me go through with my plans for the next 24 hours.

I drove for about 4 hours and right around 6 AM as we were pressing through Gary, Indiana about to head into Illinois, I got so groggy that I had no fight left in me. I turned the wheel over to the youngster and was about to nod off to sleep when Donna called again and asked where I was. I fell asleep just as we were about to cross the Illinois/Wisconsin border.

About four hours later, the youngster woke me up in a panic. "Unc! Unc!" he cried out. "We're getting pulled over!" Being a trucker, I knew how the troopers were in Wisconsin, so I said, "Boy, I told you not to speed in Wisconsin." He assured me that he had set the cruise control at 60 m.p.h. so I told him to pull over and we'd straighten the whole thing out. But he said, "I don't think you understand. We are getting pulled over!!!!"

I flipped down the visor and opened the mirror and when I looked out the windshield, what I saw was like something you only see in movies. I swear, Mom, Wisconsin state troopers and federal marshals were everywhere. They had completely shut the highway down! You would have thought I was Osama Bin Laden, the way they came at me.

A few days later, as the marshals were transporting me to the Federal jail in Madison, Wisconsin, I naively asked, "What is a marshal? Is he like a deputy or something?" The marshal arrogantly replied, "Let me put it to you this way.

I can go anywhere at any time and arrest anyone, including the President of the United States."

I thought, "Man, what have I gotten myself into?" Then I asked how they knew where I was. He said, "You guys all make the same stupid mistake. We know that if we really want you, all we have to do is hook up with your girl and she will lead us right to you." I learned very quickly what Donna's tears were about when I told her that I was on my way to greatness. She knew otherwise. She knew I was on my way to jail. And not only that, she knew that all the while she was working with the feds to catch me.

Something else I found out (speaking of God's intervention) was that, if the police would have caught up with me 10 miles later, I would have ended up going to jail in a county of Wisconsin that is run by the Ku Klux Klan. So here I am, Mom. 10 years for a bank robbery that I only salvaged $1,000 out of. That's $100 a year, less than 37¢ a day. Now that's crazy!

All my love,
Your #1 Son

Mama

from *The Days of Rondo*

Evelyn Fairbanks wrote about her childhood, her adoptive family, and St. Paul's Rondo community of the 1930s and 1940s, before the neighborhood was destroyed by the construction of a freeway.

Throughout her adulthood, Willie Mae Brimberry Edwards weighed at least three hundred pounds and stood a firm five feet ten inches tall. She was a warm breathing mountain of power and womanhood. To this day, womanhood and bigness are synonymous to me. Mama worked hard to fatten me up, but I've rarely weighed more than a hundred pounds, except when I was pregnant, and I stand only five feet, one and three-quarters inches.

The resonance of her voice filled the room and all its corners, whether she was speaking normally or whispering quietly to me.

Everyone was afraid of Mama except for Daddy and me, and with good reason, because Mama intended to have her way 100 percent of the time. Since Daddy and I had accepted this, our lives, while governed by Mama's wrath, were not filled with fear, for her wrath was tempered by genuine love for us.

Like most people her size, she spent a great deal of time with food, producing it, canning it, cooking it, serving it, and eating it. But the part that fascinated me the most was what she did with the food from the time she put it on her plate until she ate it. With deep concentration she mixed, seasoned, arranged, and rearranged her food. The right amount of vinegar on the greens, to the drop. The raw onions and tomato cut up with half of the greens, meat cut up with the other half. The hot-water bread torn in pieces to be used to pick up the food with her fingers. Although Mama taught me precise table manners at an early age, she rarely used silverware to eat. The food on Mama's plate looked better than any other food. Sometimes I would ask her to fix my plate like hers and she would, but it still didn't taste the same. Many times I would beg for her food. She'd always say, "Ba', it's the same food you've got on your plate." I'd always answer, "But it's not fixed the same." Then she'd shake her head and smile and I could hear that soft rolling laugh deep inside her chest as she extended her fingers and thumb and picked up food from her plate and put it on mine. Whether it was biscuits and syrup or crackling bread or navy beans, the food from Mama's plate was the best food in the world.

Mama was a strict disciplinarian and believed that if you spared the rod, you spoiled the child. She had no intention of spoiling this "grave responsibility that God has given me." My behind and legs knew the sting of the freshly cut switches Mama used for her rod all summer. I can't recall what she used in the wintertime, but since I also can't recall going without spankings for half of the year, I suppose she laid in a supply in the fall.

Mama's discipline, however, was balanced by the sense of security she placed around me. I may not have been afraid of Mama, but I had acquired the usual number of childhood fears about other things. Mama made it very clear that she intended for me to walk through the world as fearlessly as she did. (The only person I ever heard of who walked through the world as fearlessly as Mama was Harriet Tubman.) She taught me that all fear could be overcome. For example, after Daddy died, she made me responsible for looking after the furnace at night.

Banking the furnace for the night was the easy part. The light at the top of the stairs lit the bottom of the stairs, but I had to walk through the dark to turn on the light by the furnace, which left the storage space behind it and the other half of the basement, containing the furnace for the up-stairs tenants, in deep shadows that stimulated the imagination more than total darkness. To bank the fire, I shook the ashes down from the grate into the bottom, put any clinkers in a bucket by the furnace, and opened the damper and the furnace door. Then I went back to the coal bin, unlocked the door, and carried the coal shovelful by shovelful from the bin to the furnace, carefully picking up any I dropped on the way. Then I covered the coal with ashes, closed the furnace door and the damper, relocked the coal bin, turned off the lights, and the job was done.

Some nights this was all there was to it. Mama went down in the morning and brought the fire back to life. But sometimes I didn't do it right, and in the middle of the night Mama would wake me up and say, "Ba', I think the fire's going out. It's getting cold in here." That meant that I had to get up out of my warm, safe bed, put on my one-piece red snowsuit, go down to the basement, and fix the fire.

I was always scared to go down to the basement in the middle of the night, but I knew that nothing I said would save me from the trip. The sooner I got up, the sooner I'd be back in bed.

I usually found that I had left the damper open, which had caused the fire to burn too fast. I had to repeat all of the steps that I had done earlier. It was worse when we were almost out of coal because then the coal was way in the back of the bin, where the light didn't reach. Not a glow went into the darkness. I would stand there looking into the blackness, feeling with my shovel for the pile of coal. When my shovel didn't find it, I had to go into the darkness, step by step, pushing the shovel ahead of me on the floor, until finally it struck the small pile in one of the corners. But each time I went into the darkness, I did so with a bit more bravery, until I had all of the coal I needed.

It wasn't just the near-empty coal bin that held terror, for even when there was plenty of coal, the big empty space behind the furnace and on the other side of the basement seemed to be full of things that made tiny noises when the rest of the house was so quiet. I kept dropping coal on the floor that I had to pick up, all the while being watched by those things in the shadows. I wanted to cry, but that would have made too much noise, and I wouldn't hear the things; and besides, Mama would get mad if I cried.

And then, one night, the worst thing that could have happened, happened. I was almost through putting the coal in the furnace, just two more shovelfuls and the ashes, when the light by the bottom of the stairs went out. I was standing by the furnace under the light, and all around me was dark—the space in back of the furnace, the other side of the basement, and the space by the stairs where the coal bin was—and I still had to get more coal. That night I did cry. I didn't care if I couldn't hear anything, I cried *loud*. I screamed and cried until I heard that wonderful angry voice.

"Ba', what's the matter with you?"

By that time she was at the top of the stairs and saw what was the matter with me. She came down the stairs, slow and heavy.

"Girl, I thought something had happened to you. And here you are crying just 'cause the light went out. Hurry on and get through. I'll stand here and wait for you."

Mama was fussin' at me, of course, but I didn't care as long as she stayed in the basement with me.

Naturally, from then on I was afraid that the light would go out again, but it never did. Mama didn't stop me from being afraid, but she had trained me to overcome that fear. I would remember the nights in the basement the first night I stayed alone in the woods.

Mama loved to fish and didn't miss an opportunity to go. We went several times in the fall and spring, always with Brother and Sister Tiffin because they were the only people we knew who liked to fish and had a car. Most of the time we went to Buffalo, a small town west of the Twin Cities, but sometimes we fished on the Mississippi River near South St. Paul where the packinghouses were. I didn't ever see the packinghouses, but that's what they said was smelling so bad when the wind shifted.

I don't remember much more about the fishing trips, but I do remember clearly my sense of shame on the day after one, when I took the note to school. The note simply explained that I had not been present the day before because my mother had taken me fishing. If these trips had been planned, with the school's permission given before we went, I would not have been embarrassed. This was not the case. Mama went fishing any time the spirit moved her to go, and the spirit moved her every time Brother Tiffin offered to take her.

The teachers never objected, perhaps because early in my educational career they had seen my mother's wrath. When I started kindergarten at McKinley elementary school, Miss Tobias sent a note home to my mother saying that I showed exceptional natural talent for the dance and that I should be given lessons. Mama didn't say anything when she read the note, but the next morning she walked me to school.

All the other kids remained at a respectful distance as we walked a half block down the alley, turned, and walked another half block to the corner of Mackubin and Rondo. The kids had to stop there to wait for the police boys to hold up their flags. You didn't have to stop when you were with a parent (and after all, there were no cars coming in 1933). So we walked across Rondo with kids on all four corners looking at us. Mama had taught me *never* to walk with my head down, so I had to look at them. There was every expression imaginable on those faces, but now and then I would see a look of sympathy.

As we entered the playground, the children stepped aside to make a path for us. Adults never changed their pace or direction when they walked through a group of children, and you could always tell the bad boys in the group because they would dart out boldly in front of the adult. Boldly, but with a clear escape route.

"Where's your room?" The voice held the anger, but I was so relieved that it wasn't for me that I ran ahead of her to lead the way through the side door and down the basement stairs to Kindergarten B room.

Here the memory fades, except for Mama with her hands on her hips and the words like "Devil," "Christian," and "dance." I don't remember Miss Tobias saying anything at all, but I do remember sitting and watching from then on while the other kids danced.

Mama's ability to stand toe to toe with anyone and everything in this world was based on her absolute knowledge that God was all-wise and all-powerful and that He would use that wisdom and power to guide and protect her and her loved ones. I heard her speak these words hundreds of times. She was always saying, "God can do anything."

To prove her point, she told me about the miracles recorded in the Bible: the parting of the Red Sea, Jonah's experience in the belly of the whale, King David's triumph over Goliath, the Flood and His mercy toward Noah and his family, and on into the New Testament and the miracles that He performed through Jesus Christ. She told me about the miracles that had happened to people we knew, people who had been born in destitution and had been lifted to lofty positions as doctors and preachers, people who had been given up to die by physicians, but who had recovered after the Saints in Mama's church had stormed Heaven with prayers on their behalf. When she talked about God's miracles, she always included my coming to her and Mr. Edwards as one. It was important to Mama that I share in her belief in prayer.

One day when she was sitting in her rocking chair and I was hovering around—even though she half-heartedly kept telling me to go someplace and play—I got my foot under one of the back rockers. I must have made a terrible noise, because Mama jumped up, looked at the blood on my foot, picked me up, and carried me to the bathroom. Mama usually didn't move that fast. She sat on the toilet seat with me in her lap and cleaned up my foot, all the time fussing about how she had told me to get away from her in the first place.

My big toenail was crushed and soon it was gone. The pain was minor in comparison to the fact that my toenail was gone. I don't know why that toenail was so important to me, but it was. I mourned about it for days. Mama kept saying it would grow back, but I didn't believe her. How can a toenail grow back? "You have to pray, Ba'. God can do anything."

"I don't know how to pray for a toenail."

"I'll pray with you."

Every day, Mama and I knelt down beside her bed and prayed. I had heard Mama pray in church and at the table before we ate a meal, but I had never heard her pray so hard. She begged God to replace my toenail, not only because I wanted my toenail, but because it would create in me a belief in prayer. Little by little I began to understand that God had to be listening to Mama, 'cause she was praying so hard. I began to pray hard too, even though I still wasn't quite convinced. And, sure enough, one day when Mama was changing the white rag that she tied around my foot, there was a little bit of toenail starting to grow. Mama and I immediately got down on our knees and thanked God for this miracle. The real miracle was that I prayed harder than Mama, because now *I* believed in the power of prayer.

Mama was big and loud, demanding and controlling, unswervingly passionate in her love for God, Daddy and me, loyal to her friends, giving to sinners with hopes of saving their souls, and satisfied with life. Mama.

Faces

from Born to Be

Taylor Gordon grew up in White Sulphur Springs, Montana. At the age seven-teen, he moved to St. Paul, Minnesota, to take a job as a driver.

Tempering My Nerves

One glorious September morning, the eleventh, 1910, found me riding the eastbound Chicago, Milwaukee and St. Paul Railroad, my cheap suitcase packed with shirts, socks, underwear and overalls and an extra pair of pants that did not exactly match the suit I wore. In my pocket was forty dollars. In my mind was 286 Nelson Avenue, St. Paul.

While looking out of the window of the day coach, watching the blue peaks of the Rockies disappear behind me, my mind turned to the last instructions Mother and friends had given me. Many of them I neglected, but one thing Mother told me I heeded, that I didn't need my forty-five in the city, so I had left it behind. Why? The thought came to me as the train rambled farther and farther from home, and I began to feel alone. I always felt safe anywhere with Blue Steel Betty by my side: she gave me courage and protection at home when I was alone. They had pictured nothing but trouble in the city, still they convinced me that my forty-five would mean the worst. My nerves grew shaky.

Had I been on a saddle-horse at that moment, I might have turned back. But instead, I had to look at the fast moving ground and bid farewell. I mumbled to myself, Good-bye, sharp tops and deep canyons. I may never see you again, nor the heavy foliage that covers you, painted different hues by the rising and setting sun. No more shall I see the speckled trout hit at a fly-hook from behind a twig in rushing waters, or taste their delicious flesh, when it comes curling fried from a hot rock. I shall miss the bark of the pistol and the thud of a bullet when it brings down a blue grouse. I wondered if they rolled blue grouse in mud, feathers and all, then baked them in hot ashes in the city.

My melancholy musing might have lasted indefinitely had it not been for a noisy news-butcher selling his wares. He had a game to show me where I could get rich quick. It was only fate that I didn't pay him forty dollars for the idea. The train stopped at a town where a half-breed Indian got on: he sat down in a vacant seat across from me. When the train started again the news-butcher was coming through the car, with the intention to show me the fine points of the game. But it seems he had shown the same game to the half-breed sometime before for seventy-five dollars. It had proved unsuccessful, and the Indian wanted his money back. Because of that, I nearly witnessed my first murder! It was the conductor who straightened them out. The act proved to me that my old friend of the Hills—C. H.—was right: "Never play another man's game."

After another uneasy night, it was eleven o'clock in the morning when the train stopped in St. Paul. Mr. Scott's chief engineer of the Metropolitan Theatre was there to meet me. He took me to Mr. Scott's residence on Nelson Avenue, where Mrs. Scott greeted me. She showed me my room, then the engineer gave me instructions about the Locomobile I was to drive. Scott, who was in Minneapolis at the time, had a large private garage in his back yard.

After I found myself in the big city, I wasn't sure that I would like my job in it. Things seemed to be done so queer. A time was set for everything, and not the best hours, according to my judgment. Breakfast at 7:30, feeding the dogs at 8:00, take Mr. Scott to the office at 9:00, lunch at 1:00, to Minneapolis at 2:00 and 8:00 PM. Everything timed. They even did it to time. Had it not been that Mr. and Mrs. Scott were such nice people, I would have left the first morning, because Pernhagen told me so many things I would have to do on time.

My first trip with the car was taking Mr. Scott to the office the following morning. To me, it seems as though St. Paul was laid out by a cross-eyed Frenchman, following a milk cow's tail, so you can judge how the streets run. After inquiring from a couple of cops, I managed to get back to 286 Nelson Avenue. That afternoon Mrs. Scott had me take her shopping, and to a few other places I should know the roads to. I was used to mountain trails, so I learned St. Paul and Minneapolis streets quickly.

One afternoon I took Mrs. L. N. to a beauty parlor—I should say hairdresser, for at that time she was one of the most naturally beautiful women in St. Paul, for the newspapers had quoted her as being so. While waiting for her, I had a little pain in my stomach. I decided to step in a restaurant and get a bite to eat. I sat at the counter while the waiters ran up and down by me like white mice in a cage. It was in this restaurant I learned that the magic power of Uncle Sam's money didn't respond to me. Never before had I had plenty of the attractive paper and weights in my pockets, taken them out and laid them down for anything reasonable, that what I had desired to exchange them for didn't come a-hopping.

I saw the bill-o'-fare hanging up on the wall with many things listed. At the bottom was "Fresh Home-made Apple Pie and Milk—25 c." in large letters. I laid two bits down on the counter and as one of the waiters passed me, I said, "Give me apple pie and milk, please." He began getting red around his collar, then the redness quickly mounted to the top of his bald head, catching the ends of his ears. Then he grew deathly pale except for the lobes of his ears. Finally, he spoke. "We don't serve colored people in here." That was the first time I had ever heard that phrase, and I really didn't quite understand him, so I answered, "Just pie and milk."

Then he lost control of himself, picked up my money, throwing it at me with this remark: "Get to hell out of here. Don't you understand? Niggers can't eat in here."

Even at that I couldn't get it through my head why he should be mad at me. I hadn't done anything, but I knew he was hot. My right hand automatically fell to my left hip where old Betty always hung when I was alone. She wasn't there! I can't describe the lonely feeling that came over me. I have never felt like it since. It seemed as though everyone whom I knew had died at once.

Something told me that if I didn't move, I would have a fight. With boys at home, battles were head and head, but with a man, I felt I'd have little chance barehanded, so out I walked, cranked up the big Loco and drove to the Metropolitan Opera House to see Tom Owens the footman and porter. He had told me before that there were a lot of things that he must tell me in order that I might get along in the East. Tom had been a prize fighter and had travelled lots. I found him polishing the long brass railing which led to the balcony.

At the sight of me he said, "What's up? You seem to be all upset." In some way he could tell that I wasn't myself. I told him what had happened. He laughed, "Hee Hee"—an act that was done through his nose in high tones—then said, "Man, don't you know you's a niggah and can't do things heah like you did out home in Montana?"

I asked him to tell me all the inside stuff on this thing, nigger and niggah. I found myself to be pronouncing it again and again. I was sure the waiter had called me and all like me niggers and Tom had said niggah. Then I showed him the quarter I had laid on the counter. His answer to it all was that white people who wanted to be nasty called anyone like me with curly hair, thick lips and black skin, "niggers," but most any colored person would call you "Niggah," a word taken from an exalted ruler of Abyssinia, and not have any evil thought in mind at the time he said it. As for the lady on the quarter I showed him, he said that in a white man's hands she was a goddess, but in my hand she was a bogus bitch.

My time was up so I returned for the Madam. Tom's last words were for me to come to the flat any night, and that he'd tell me anything I would need to know to get along in the East; not to pay any attention to that waiter. I thanked him, as I was glad to learn.

The Madam was waiting for me in front of the hair-parlor, and as the car stopped she inquired whether or not I had been to another fire. I told her yes, but this time the fire was in my mind, at the same time nodding toward the restaurant. She asked my complaint. When I related to her the incident, a beautiful red tint came over her prized face as she answered, "Oh yes, I should have told you before of the different opinions of people in the U.S.A. If you drive slowly up Summerset Avenue, I'll tell you the things most essential for you to know." In two hours' time I got an emancipated Eastern woman's ideas and advice, in order that I might be enlightened. Many things that Mother might have told me but didn't, and that Sis read but couldn't understand, were told to me ...

Gratuitous Surprises

In St. Paul, I got my experience as doorman and porter at the Orpheum Theatre. The work was not hard but continuous, every day and night. By being a chauffeur I earned good tips, handling people's cars. I was satisfied with life for some time. Things went unusually smooth for me.

Somehow or nother a church-going girl came into my life. Mother had pulled us kids to church so much when we were little, I hadn't attended any church since I had left home. I thought it would be a nice thing to take this girl to the Thanksgiven dinner they were going to serve in the basement of the Methodist church, at sixty cents a plate. That Thanksgiven morning caught me broke not a soo in my pocket.

I remembered that, during the time I was railroading, I had loaned Guest, a tailor, thirty dollars to pay his house rent with. Two dollars of it I had gotten back. That was a coupla weeks after he had borrowed it. Guest owin' me came to my mind. I thought if I could get a few more bucks out of him, I'd be all set for the day. I cleaned up my work in a hurry, and walked down to the station where Guest had his tailor shop. He was pressing a pair of pants. I sang him my hard luck tale.

"I only got two dollars myself, an' I need that to take my gal to the same thing," he said.

We talked a little while longer, and I started to leave, hoping to get the money some place else, when a porter came running to the door. He hollered out, "Heah, Guest! Take this two dollars an' gimme my coat. I gota chance to make extra." He threw the two-dollar bill down on the table, grabbed his coat and ran out of the shop. I felt good.

"Well, Guest, we're in luck. You got two bucks an' I got two," I said.

"I can't give you this two dollars; I need six to make the day with my gal," he declared, and grabbed up the money. We got into an argument. He told me lie after lie, saying he had to rent a room—when he hada house; must take a cab—when the street car ran right by the church door. It got hotter and hotter. He tried to hit me with a big clothes-pressing brush, fourteen inches long an' four inches wide. Somehow I got the brush an' cracked him over the head with it. He hollered murder. A big cop came into the shop. Guest knew more about pleading to a city cop than I did, so I got locked up.

I had to stay in jail all day Thanksgiven: the next day was Sunday—no court until Monday. Then the judge told me I couldn't take a debt out of a man's hide in St. Paul, and he gave me the choice of fifteen days or fifteen dollars.

I couldn't get in touch with any of my friends, so, with ten other prisoners, they loaded me in the Black Maria, hawled by two black horses, and carted us up to the work-house between St. Paul and Minneapolis. We were measured and weighed in. My cell mate was a Mexican, up for stabbing a man.

Before we were in the cell ten minutes, two men came along with old pie-tins (like mother used to feed baby chickens out of) loaded down with hunks of beef, boiled potatoes with their skins on, stewed tomatoes and half-stewed prunes, all on the same tin. We each got one. Following them was a fellow with a big bucket full of tin cups. Then came a man with a large garden sprinkler (no spray) full of sunburnt-black-asphelt coffee. He poked the pipe through the bars and filled our cups. I ate some of the garbage, but I couldn't go the coffee.

They were just getting ready to take me out on the rock pile, when Johnny Davis came and bailed me out.

The girl's parents stopped her from speaking to me.

Never try to compensate for gratuitous surprises.

. . .

I quit the theatre for a while, and got a busman's job at Uptown Charlie's restaurant, on Fifth Street, just across from the St. Paul Hotel. At that time, they had all colored waiters. Jim Hunt, a big six-foot yellow fellow, was the assistant headwaiter, and a young German was the headwaiter. I stayed there about a month. That was a job that meant long hours for a stomach full of food. They only paid ten dollars a week to the bus-boys. I never did get a chance to wait there—even on the help, so I quit and went to the roof of the St. Paul Hotel as busman and waiter. I graduated there into getting a chance to feed the help, clerks and headwaiters. I couldn't keep room-rent off me at that job, so I quit again. The doorman at the Orpheum Theatre got sick and I found myself back at the old job again, as foot-man. I was much better off at that. I couldn't break anything, and if I did, I didn't have to pay for it, like I did in the restaurants. I held this job for about a month and a half, during which time I got the feeling that St. Paul was too small. I must move on.

Kwame J. C. McDonald

He faced death with courage

Hotep. Kwame McDonald was a much-loved icon in the community. He was well traveled and well known across the country. My relationship with him—a relationship of associating and working together—lasted over thirty years, right up until the time he died. This is also a story about the manner in which he died, his whole attitude about life and death, and the acceptance of his fate. Never in my whole life have I seen, in the face of death, such a demonstration of courage, determination, and thoughtfulness—which not only affected him, but affected all of the people he knew and loved. He was careful to minimize any and all gestures of pity, sorrow, and grief; yet at the same time he did want people to know he was dying.

Mary K. Boyd—a well-known and much-loved educator—Kwame, and I made up a team that taught leadership training, cultural wellness, and life skills at Johnson High School on St. Paul's East Side. I joined the team in 2009. I will miss the mornings when he and I would ride together in his car to the school, listening to "Lean On Me," which he always had playing on his stereo. He loved that song and was fond of the principal in the movie, Joe Clark. We would discuss what we were going to teach the students that day, and how we would encourage the young men in our class to be critical thinkers, to know who they are, and to love themselves.

Kwame was an avid sports fan who could be seen at many high school and college games. He was recognized and much loved by coaches and athletes across the state. At Johnson High School games, he always encouraged me to sit with him—most of the players were members of the class we taught. Kwame was easily recognized by students because of his regular attendance and his symbolic African dress. You could see the admiration in the eyes of the students, who would come up to him or wave at him. They all seemed to say, "We need you here in our school. You make us feel the importance of education."

When he turned eighty, we had a party at the school during classtime. He asked all of us, especially the students, "What do you think it will take to get to eighty years old?" Before anyone could answer, he talked about all he had done throughout his life, and most importantly, how he had never smoked or drank liquor. He didn't talk about it like anyone else shouldn't do it—just that he didn't, and that those were some of the choices that contributed to his long and productive life. I was a smoker and he knew it, but out of respect, I never smoked around him. Yet knowing how he felt about it, together with other positive influences in my life, I stopped cold turkey on the first of September 2011 and have not smoked since. I never told him that I had quit, and he never asked.

There are many, many things that I could write about in terms of my relationship with Kwame, but I can't help remembering the time I directed him in a play called *Somewhere Before* in the late '70s or early '80s. One day during rehearsal, he stopped in just to see what we were doing. He was so impressed with the play and the people in it that he said, "Man, I want to be a part of this." Right then we started talking about it and wrote him into the script as a character called "BB Boldacious." He was an instant hit in his role. We performed it in different places around the Twin Cities, including the Penumbra and Guthrie theaters.

Kwame was a man whose swagger complemented his tall and handsome figure, and he was a good dancer. It was during the three school years we worked together at Johnson High School that his illness became apparent. I began to notice how difficult it was becoming for him to walk, and the pain he was suffering, but he never complained; he would just say, "My legs ain't working too good today." Still, he seldom used the walking stick that he brought home from Africa.

In early October 2011 I called Kwame to see when we would meet with the new principal at Johnson High School and talk about our next classes. He said to me, "Yes, we'd better do this soon, because within two weeks or so, I will be leaving."

"Leaving?" I said. "Where are you going?"

And he replied, "I'm about to die."

I rushed over to the Golden Thyme coffee shop, where I knew he would be, and sure enough Kwame was in his regular chair by the door, talking to the people who usually gathered there when they knew he was in the house. They all had looks of disbelief and wonderment on their faces. I glanced over at Kwame, and there was this expression on his face that suggested his satisfaction at having informed the community of his demise.

After Kwame left, the crowd looked at me and asked, "Elder Bobby, what should we do?" It was quickly determined that Kwame should "smell of his roses" while he was still alive. On October 7 we hosted a gathering at St. Paul Central High School. More than four hundred people came from all over Minnesota and beyond to show their appreciation and love to Kwame. There were proclamations from the governor's office, county board, state legislature, city council, school district, and more. I arranged for SPNN to tape his last statement to the community. At the end of the celebration, right after his son Mitchell told some humorous and wonderful stories about life with his mother and father, the tape was played. Kwame admonished everyone to look out for one another, love themselves, and be watchful for opportunities to be of service. He spoke of his appreciation to everyone in the St. Paul community for adopting him and his family and making them feel at home.

In late October 2011 Kwame was in the Sholom Hospice, where many people came to bid him farewell. So clearly was his courage, his fearlessness, his self-determination, and his understanding and acceptance of his fate revealed. It was rather tickling when people would tell him to eat so that he could get some nourishment, and he would look at them as if to say, "I'm dying, I don't need nourishment!"

The last time I was with him, he asked, "I wonder what's taking so long?"

"What do you mean, 'What's taking so long?'" I asked.

"Death," he replied. "Why are you taking so long? I am ready." Kwame passed away early the next morning.

In conclusion, I'm reminded of something my godfather used to tell me when I was very young. He always reminded me of what a gentleman is and should be. He would say, "Son, a gentleman is one who is gentle and refined in manner. He is courteous in deportment, magnificent in disposition, and temperate in habit. He doesn't give in to strife or evil speaking, but maintains proper dignity and self-respect. He is mindful of the rights of others, and he's truthful, honest, patient, benevolent, and humane." He then would go on to say, "I like to meet a man who's glad that he is Black, who is conscious of his color and realizes that fact. I like to meet a man who's glad that he is White, for color makes no difference—any color's all right. But I like to be with friends who distinctly understand that character makes a person, no color makes a man."

In addition to all of the other good things about him, Kwame McDonald was a gentleman with much character. Farewell, beloved friend, teacher, and brother—you are missed. *Hotep.*

My Rites of Passage

Da' Kwamsta' was my Rites of Passage. From the moment we first met.

I was raised by my Aunt/Mother Willie Mae Johnson at 718 West Central and St. Albans. Willa Mae was very Old Skool, born in 1918: Faith and Trust in GOD. Sincere Prayer was number one at 718 West Central. I thought the world was coming to an end when I was in the first grade.

In 1992 I was hired by the Inner City Youth League to create effective programs for this new generation the elders had a difficult time communicating with. It was a challenging time; we went through four EDs (Executive Directors) in less than six months. Meanwhile . . .

About to turn twenty-one in less than three months: two children, round three stacks in debt with Child Support Enforcement Agency. Where are my Rites of Passage?

I'm on a speed of sound . . . Japanese train to financial devastation, not only for myself. Not knowing, I would force my children to eat and digest the unfortunate meal of poverty and want. I was so confused; I couldn't explain what I was feeling inside of me, this formless matter affecting me daily.

The next day at work, I received a memo stating that Kwame McDonald was hired and would be starting the following Monday. I smiled and said, "The Creator always answers every one of my prayers!" Immediately, Elder Kwame started talking to me about harnessing my anger, channeling it into positive actions, ways I can give back to where I came from: my village.

Da' Kwamsta' taught me that I must work on changing my thoughts to learn how to do what pleases the Creator: love myself, love my village, love my community.

Da' Kwamsta' taught me how to make money with the gifts the Creator blessed me with. Every day Kwamsta' would express to me, "It's all about the children, and if that is not your agenda, then you're just wasting your time here!"

Da' Kwamsta' always told me, "Kemet, you don't have the type of atmosphere to work for anyone but yourself!" He would explain to me over and over about the loopholes, the codes, to survive as a young Black man. He would express to me in parables that this road that I chose was a very,

very lonely road. Self-love was critical to further my faith and trust in the Creator, and to my personal growth and development.

The Wonderful, Tiny, Short Moments Before

It started on a very cold morning. I always hit my favorite spot in St. Paul, the Golden Thyme Coffee Café, early in the AM to run over my daily schedule: projects that need to be completed, guarded from procrastination. The owner of the café informed me that Kwame was looking for me. At the time my mind and heart were so heavy. It was one of those moments . . . missing my mother so much—just to talk to her . . . for a few ticks . . .

A couple weeks went by. I was in my regular spot at the window listening to the wind howl against the glass pane like an opera soprano. Seconds later in comes Da' Kwamsta'. He enters, sits in his chair, looks at me.

I say, "The Kwamsta.'"

He replies, "Everythang is Everythang. Kemet! I been looking for you. You change your number again? I mean . . . What's up with that, man?"

I said, "I know, Kwamsta' . . . just been going through it . . . like Whoop-Tee-Whoop . . ." My head's down as I'm writing on my blank sheet of paper.

"Are you working?" Kwame asks.

"No, sir, just got fired yesterday."

We both look at each other . . . [Pause] . . . then a hard laughter that I really needed. This is how this small moment in time begins.

Almost every day after that, Da' Kwamsta' created some work for me to do, knowing that I needed something. He could see the pain, hurt, heaviness, and darkness, the "I'm about to cock the hammer" look.

Da' Kwamsta' would take me to lunch and begin to teach me like I never heard him teach. I would always say, "Kwamsta', do you mind if I write this down?"

He would reply, "Please do. That's why I'm buying your lunch, because you listen."

I laughed—holding back tears at the same time. He would glance through the window with that thousand-yard stare all Black men have when you choose to be on the Front Line. And then he'd begin to teach again. He answered so many questions that plagued me for years—questions only the Creator knew about.

I was asking the Kwamsta' . . . "Am I really off or crazy like people saying I am? I still don't fit in anywhere."

He chuckled and replied, "Kemet, don't you ever change, the Creator gave you who you are."

Da' Kwamsta' started having me do li'l errands here and there for him, and wow, the teaching was getting more intense. All I would do was record what he was expressing to me.

A couple of weeks after that, the Kwamsta' started not feeling so well. The weeks before he was called Home, he left me a message that he really needed to speak to me. Understanding the timeline, I called Steve Winfield to see if he could run me to where Da' Kwamsta' was at.

I get to his room, saying, "Da' Kwamsta.'"

He says, "You got it, Kemet."

I sat down with my blank sheet of paper waiting for his knowledge to hit me like an unexpected uppercut while looking the opposite way. Steve handed Da' Kwamsta' the newspaper, and he goes right to the sports page, and says, "Let's go get something to eat and see what the Gophers . . ."

I'm sitting like . . . um . . . what? In my mind, I was like what is this all about, what am I to get out of this? Am I being selfish, this is not about me? I wish he would just tell me something important. But it never happened. I had to go to Drill Team practice.

On my birthday, 10-26-2011, I got a call from Steve. I hang up and was like . . .

On my birthday.

Complete silence.

Kwame really loved me.

He really loved me.

Now who will tell me it's okay that I got fired? "Just create your own," when at this very moment, most don't really care for me. He was the one to work with a very confused, lost child from his village.

Love you, Kwamsta.'

He gave me my upcoming book title: *The Many Mistakes I Made on My Way to Heaven.*

Da' Kwamsta' was/is My Rites of Passage. From the moment we first met.

» TAIYON COLEMAN

Decay

For Momma

your right front
tooth is brown
and you are going
to get it bleached
making early morning
Saturday appointments
because you can't miss
work

a Dun and Bradstreet
supervisor
down town behind
a glass window
with a yellow phone book
on your metal desk
you sit drinking coffee
taking calls
and watching for workers
slipping over the edge

your dentist's office is near
the place you put
my c flute
in lay-a-way

fifteen hundred
over three years
forty-one sixty-six a month
plus interest

and I stop playing at 18
over eight years
fifteen hundred
fifteen sixty-three a month
with no interest

your babies carry bone
from your body
and your husband
leaves you alone
with five kids and only one
damaged tooth at the root
and you are lucky

in your knowing smile
that even with insurance
and many morning
Saturday appointments
the darkness in your mouth
will never turn

I Hear Myself Say (MMA)

After the woman in stilettos and neon bikini
jiggles her way 'round the cage—a primary number
hoisted high above her bosom, where a man,
unthinking, could form a loop and just rock—

an insistent bell chimes. Two mixed-martial arts fighters
pop out like wild seeds to its urgent ring. They
fly out like bats from a church attic, like dogs
from Pavlov's grave, like crows to a carcass.

Heads a-bob now, like courting pigeons, they circle
each other, jabbing. Quick-quick, they fold into each other,
grabbing hold, grappling hard, gripping. Feral hunger shoots
beads off their foreheads, their hands lunge and punch and . . .

I favor one, in blood orange trunks, perhaps
because he is pinned now and eating a volley of fists.
My body starts to writhe to show him how to twist
out of the trap, to slide out and reverse just so.

My guy suddenly jerks the jerk off and they're up
again, circling. They tangle, and my hands and elbows cup
a long, invisible watermelon. Here, against a sofa pillow,
my body jerks and twists and turns

some more. I bring down the hammering fist
on the cushion beside me. *Kill him,* I hear
myself say. *Hammer the head so.*
Do I really want to see him dead?

Do him in, yes, make his eyes swell
enough to not see well but he should be able to

walk again. He should rise, though spindly
like a newborn fawn.

Somehow, through the blue light and
flickering screen,
through the roaring, baying crowd, my thoughts
conduct into blood trunks, and my fighter

lands a good one that fills the screen
with cherry squirt. I quicken. *Kill him.*
I hear my tongue give voice. My throat
tightens on my breath, that shallow thing,
as I pan for medal. I sit up, hankering, for blood.

The Night Before

It was the night before the service. Most of the details had been set. When everything would take place, who would speak, and for how long. The seating charts.

Frank sat at the kitchen table with Harriet, his mother. Frank had taken care of all of the arrangements. He negotiated with the church, the funeral home, family and everyone else who wanted to get involved. It was complicated, and at times, petty. The previous week felt like a month.

Karl—Frank's father, Harriet's husband—died in his sleep the previous Saturday night. He would be buried Saturday morning.

For most of his life, Karl was active in some type of sports. Basketball, softball, bowling. He tried running, but got bored. Even in his sixties, he kept active, if only making sure he walked for a least a half hour a day. A couple of years ago, his body began to break down. First, the right knee. Then, the left. Then, a hip replacement. In between surgeries, he got around well enough, but he wasn't the same. The lack of mobility began to wear him down.

During the recovery from hip surgery, Karl was withdrawn, irritable, less interested in exercising, and he slept a lot. For a few weeks, Harriet lobbied Karl's doctor to prescribe something for Karl's mood. Convinced and worn down, the doctor agreed. A short while later, Karl began to come back to life. He was walking more, cooking, helping around the house, taking Harriet on long drives, and talking dirty to Harriet the way he did when they first started dating. Harriet had Karl back. Last Sunday, when Harriet went to get Karl up for church, he didn't wake up.

The official report said that Karl died of natural causes. He just drifted off to sleep. Harriet wondered if the new medication contributed, but Karl's doctor assured her the meds were safe. However, the doctor said, "There is no way to know for sure." It was neither comforting nor reassuring. Harriet wondered if the drugs she asked the doctor to prescribe to bring back the old Karl also took the old Karl away. Frank wondered the same thing, but never said anything about it, nor would he.

The house was now a restaurant and control center. There was food everywhere. Store bought, homemade, fried, baked, slow-cooked, raw. Cold or hot dessert. The food would last for the next two weeks, even with the constant dispatch of plates to relatives and friends dropping by or stuck at home.

Although almost everyone at the house had their own cell phone, folks would call the house to check on Harriet and find out what the schedule was. Frank offered to set up a quick Web site, but Harriet said the phone was enough. "Don't need to go through any of that technical stuff," Harriet said.

"It's really not that complicated," Frank said. "I could set it up in half an hour."

She wouldn't go for it. Frank did convince Harriet to get call waiting on the home phone, but that was as high tech as she would go.

The dependence on the home phone number also meant that the home cordless phone was always in Frank's hand, since he knew the schedule and details better than anyone. And, he was a buffer for Harriet, so that she didn't have to take every call. It also meant Frank had a good read on who was coming, who to watch out for, and who not to sit by whom. Frank hated the phone, but the intel he gathered from answering could not be beat.

As expected, there was a lot of traffic in the house. People stopped ringing the front door bell and just walked in. Normally, Harriet and Karl unlocked the screen door to let anyone in. That routine was put on hold during the day, but back in play in the evening once everybody was gone. So it was a surprise when the doorbell rang that night.

The last folks had left a half an hour before, and it was already 10:00 PM. Harriet started to get up, but Frank waved her down. Harriet sipped on the cup of cold tea in front of her. It had been a long week, but the constant movement was a way to forget the loss of the man she had been with for the last fifty years.

Frank came back into the kitchen with Edith, a cousin of Karl's. One of the earlier seating discussions focused on how close Edith would sit to Harriet. The final agreement was that Edith would sit a row behind Harriet, three seats in. Edith would be close, but no so close that Harriet might lose her mind and rip Edith's hat off her head.

"It's dark outside the house," Edith said. "I didn't know if anyone was home."

"We're up," Harriet said.

"It's a heavy day, girl," Edith said. "But I think we're all going to be okay."

In an effort to keep busy, Frank asked Edith, "Can I get you something to eat? Did you get a plate?"

"It's a little late to start eating, but no, I didn't get a plate," Edith said. "Is there anything left?"

"You know we have plenty of food," Harriet said.

Without another word, Frank began putting a plate together.

"As long as it's no trouble," Edith said.

"No trouble," Frank said.

Edith made her way to the table and sat down where Frank sat before. "So how are you holding up, girl?" Edith asked.

Harriet looked at Edith for a moment, and sighed. "Minute by minute."

"I know," Edith said. "Me, too." Without missing a beat, to Frank, "Could you get me a glass of water?"

Frank brought over the water, anticipating the request.

Harriet took another sip of tea. "Did you need something, Edith?"

"I came to check up on you," Edith said.

A few years ago, there was a situation over a piece of jewelry that belonged to Karl's mother. It was an antique ring, white gold with two cut diamonds. Everyone knew the ring was supposed to go to Harriet when Karl's mother—Priscilla—passed away. Priscilla had put the ring in her house for safekeeping, but for some reason, Edith was the only one who knew where it was. When the time came for Edith to give up the ring, Edith claimed she could not find it. No one believed her, but no one could prove she was lying. A year later, on one of her yearly visits, Edith showed up with a ring just like the missing one. She claimed she bought it online. No one believed her. As she sat in Harriet's kitchen, she wore the ring.

"Thank you," Harriet said.

"You know it's no problem," Edith said. "I just wanted to say 'Hey' when everyone else was gone. People have a heavy heart. Just wanted to let you know, I'm looking out for you."

Frank continued working on a plate, hoping his mother would let that one go. She didn't.

"What do you mean?"

"Girl, I'm just talking," Edith said. "Don't mean nothing." Harriet took another sip, lest she said what she was about to say.

Frank listened for his cue to jump in.

"You know Cletus Johnson, family used to live down on Livingston?" Edith asked. Harriet didn't answer, just sat looking at Edith wondering where Edith was headed. "His boy, C. J., he's an investment broker . . . banker . . . something . . . He told me if you wanted some help with Karl's affairs or anything like that, he'd be right there for you. No charge."

"You talked to somebody about my finances?" Harriet asked.

"About Karl's finances," Edith said.

"What's the difference?" Harriet asked.

"Karl's stuff," Edith said. "His estate."

"You're not serious."

Avoiding the point, Edith said, "About estate planning . . . planning . . ." Edith looked to Frank for some help. "Is that what it's called? Stuff that might need to get settled?" No help.

Done with the plate, Frank positioned himself between Harriet and Edith. "All done," Frank said.

"Why would you talk to someone about that without me being there?" Harriet asked. "What's wrong with you?"

"Excuse me?"

"What . . . is . . . wrong . . . with . . . you?"

"I was at the store, and I saw Cletus with C. J.," Edith said. "They came up to me. The boy gave me his card."

Trying again, Frank said. "Do you want some dessert?"

"And so the night before the funeral, you just drop by to tell me this?" Harriet asked. "Why didn't you talk to me about this earlier today? Did you run into Cletus and C. J. tonight when you stopped at McDonald's on your way home?"

"Mom," Frank said, hoping to ease the tension.

"I'm just trying to help you," Edith said.

"This isn't helping," Harriet said.

"I don't understand why you're so upset," Edith said.

"Have you lost your mind?" Harriet said.

"Aunt Edith," Frank said, "we can go over this later. I'll call C. J. myself." Edith did not back down. "Look, I didn't go up to Cletus."

"You should have told him it was not your place to talk about it," Harriet said. "If that didn't work, you should have walked away."

"I don't have to stop talking to people just because of what you're going through," Edith said. "I was trying to help."

"This isn't about you," Harriet said. "Can you not see that? Talk to people about your business, not mine."

"You don't need to talk to me with that tone," Edith said.

"When things settle down, we can figure it out," Frank said.

"No, we won't," Harriet said. "There's nothing to figure out. This is not something we're going to go over by committee. There's no family meeting. There's no vote."

"Mom—"

Waving the conversation to an end, Harriet said, "Stop. It's not happening."

"I am here trying to lend my support," Edith said.

"Every time you come back, it's about you," Harriet said. "You got no kids, nobody at home, and you come back here like you know what I'm going through."

"Why would you say something like that?" Edith said. "You owe me more than that."

"I lost my husband," Harriet said. "I owe you nothing. Not before, not now, not ever."

Frank picked up the plate and told Edith he would walk her to her car. Edith got the hint. Edith gave Harriet a hug, promised to see her in the morning, and left.

As Frank walked Edith out, she told him that she would be there if they needed anything. Frank asked if she was planning to move back home. He knew the answer. "Oh, child, no," Edith said. "I got too much going on. I'm not moving back. But if your mother needs me, you know I'll be there. This is family."

Edith hugged Frank, got into her car, drove away. Frank waved and watched her go, wondering if tomorrow would be as strange as the last hour. He knew the answer.

When Frank returned, Harriet was in the bathroom, in her nightgown, washing her face.

"Is there something I should know?" Frank asked.

Without looking at Frank, Harriet said, "About what?"

"The drama is usually left for an audience of four or more."

Harriet stopped cleaning and put her hand on Frank's cheek. It was a gesture she used to make when Frank was younger. Before he got taller than her, Harriet would cradle his cheek, and look into his eyes. It was her way of telling him she was happy to have him as her son. She struggled to remember the last time she had done it.

"Your father and Edith spent a lot of time together when they were younger, right up through their first year of high school," Harriet said. "Karl would help around Edith's house because Edith's father left and her mother was raising five kids on her own. One day, your father went over to the house to cut the grass, or something, and he heard some sounds coming from the house. But no one was supposed to be home. He went inside and found Edith having a private prayer meeting with the pastor's son. Buck naked on her mother's couch."

"Oh, snap," Frank said.

"The pain was Edith moaning, I guess," Harriet said.

"That image is going to stick."

"She said they were taking a study break," Harriet said.

"Who was on top?"

"You need to quit."

"My bad."

"Your father kept it to himself, but word got out," Harriet said. "Edith's mother found out, put Edith on lockdown for a month. Edith said your father told. But he didn't gain anything by telling what happened."

"So, Aunt Edith is worried about that coming out?" Frank asked.

"I have no idea what that woman is worried about," Harriet said. "I just don't trust her. She moved away thirty years ago and only comes back on her birthday and when someone dies. Like some weird pigeon-buzzard. Whatever she's thinking, I want nothing to do with it. I don't need her mess."

Frank just nodded, remembering how often his father would look down and smile whenever he was around Edith.

Harriet went into her bedroom. A little slower than usual, she got into bed. She still wasn't used to having the whole bed to herself. Frank walked in just as she was about to turn out the light.

"Do you need anything?" Frank asked.

"No, I'm fine."

Frank walked over to the bed, sat on the edge, the way Harriet had done many times in Frank's room.

Frank placed his hand on Harriet's cheek. "What is it?" Harriet asked.

"It's not your fault."

Harriet kissed his hand, trying not to cry. The next day would have more weeping than she could handle. She would be a mess at the service. She didn't want to start now.

"This feels like a bad dream I can't wake up from," she said.

"I know."

"And Edith's an asshole."

"I'll tell her tomorrow," Frank said.

"I think she knows."

"I'll put it in the program."

Harriet smiled. "We need to get some rest."

"Good night."

Frank returned to his room and sat on his bed, looking at a picture of himself with Karl at Frank's high school graduation. He thought about how that was the first time his father had hugged him. He thought about the conversations he never had with his father. Love, sex, finances, race, family. He thought about all the time he spent in the house. He thought about the homework done, all the TV watched. He thought of the times he looked out his bedroom window wishing he were somewhere else. He thought of the times he felt like an outsider in his own home, in his family. He also knew that these regrets would have to stay with him, at least for now.

He had to get some rest. Tomorrow he would see his father for the last time.

The Brawl in St. Paul

During the Civil Rights movement, most youth felt that the leadership of their community was inadequate and didn't speak to their concerns, and therefore they would "take matters into their own hands." Little did they realize that their methods and tactics were causing more problems than they were solving, that they had the effect of polarizing the community; as a result, there were constant disputes and conflicts, stemming from those who thought they knew the most about what to do, how to do it, and who would do what about the problems that were plaguing the community.

These disputes would sometimes turn into ugly fights between opposing families, groups of friends, girls against girls, boys against boys, blacks against whites, etc. Every day there would be reports of clashes that were mostly instigated by people who held personal grudges that often bordered on petty jealousies, mistrust, fear, hatred, and uncertainty. This brought negative attention to the African American community, which gave rise to a lot of police presence. Much of that presence resulted in police brutality, arrest, and injuries that further caused parents who were formerly good friends to turn against each other in defense of their children.

In St. Paul in 1967, we formed an organization called The Inner City Youth League, and immediately set about to change this behavior and persuade the combatants that there is a better way to deal with their frustrations. All across the nation, there were youth organizations cropping up to teach the young people about the Civil Rights movement, and, more importantly, how their help was needed, and how violent actions were detrimental to the cause.

The youth responded to our call to have meetings and tell us "older folks" what their concerns were. Could they justify their behavior? Their arguments were as follows: "We don't have any decent places to go, no activities for us, and there are no jobs available, we have to go out of our neighborhood to school. The police are brutal and disrespectful to our whole community. We have no black businesses. We're crammed into houses that are not decent to live in, our so-called leaders are someplace else and don't listen to our concerns. Who is here to teach us what we need to know?"

No one could deny or dispute the stories they told or the arguments they made. In fact, we agreed with most of the things they were saying, but we couldn't agree with the way they were dealing with the problems. There was a void in leadership in the community; in many cases, adult members of the community were frightened by the youth.

We attempted to convey to the youth that we understood and in most cases agreed with their arguments, but there was still a need to embark upon different approaches to solve these problems. They could get involved with the movement, go to meetings where these things were discussed, engage in peaceful protest, learn some trade skills. They could show more love and concern for family and community. But the problems were so well entrenched that no amount of words were going to get them to fully understand and change their attitudes and behavior. That meant that a new approach was necessary, but what? How could we persuade our youth to try our way of doing things?

One answer came in the most unexpected way. A rumor was circulating around the community that a long-simmering feud was about to boil over into some serious violence involving two families and their friends. These families contained two well-known and influential "street guys," known as Billy P. and Chum, whose reputations were all about unrest and keeping tensions up in the community. Due to our credibility with most of the youth, we were expected to help squash this problem.

Part of the program at ICYL was to go out and break up fights and skirmishes in the streets. We often took the fighters to our gym where we had a boxing ring, and we would fit them with boxing gloves and make them fight it out under the supervision of Rock White, a professional boxer. No one was admitted who might be there to instigate in a negative way. In this case, we confronted the two men who were threatening each other. We asked them if they would be willing to fight it out in a boxing ring, at a recreation center with the community in attendance. We would charge three dollars admission and they would split the proceeds between them.

When they agreed, they were told that they would be required to train for the event every day at The Inner City Youth League under the watchful eye of our trainers. We embarked on a serious advertising campaign with pictures, flyers, and posters. This would be a takeoff from the Muhammad Ali vs. Joe Frazier "Thrilla in Manila." We called it the "Brawl in St. Paul," and we promoted it just like the professionals do. We had a doctor at ringside, three judges, and a "trainer" in each corner, in the personages of Dennis Presley and David McCall, who were up-and-coming boxers at Inner City. Lansing Thompson, a.k.a. Kokayi Ampah, was the announcer. There was a timekeeper to ring the bell, and some sisters sold tickets at the door. Robert McLain took pictures. Inner City's video class was on hand to record the fight.

On the night of the fight, a large crowd of almost two thousand people showed up to the gym at Oxford playground. It seemed as if the whole neighborhood had turned out, and there were people of all descriptions. We couldn't be sure of what might happen, but we kept our fingers crossed, and I remember thinking of how beautiful a gathering it was of our community. The lights were lowered, and the fighters entered the ring. The crowd went wild, and they were given instructions by the referee. The bell rang and after forty-five seconds of wildly swinging, ducking, and dodging they were so tired that they could not continue. In fact, they looked more like lovers than fighters the way they were leaning on each other at the bell. (A strong indication that street fighting is quite a bit different than organized boxing.) After the fight, we all went back to The Inner City League, where a celebration was held. The money was split up as we had promised. Billy P. and Chum became good friends and are still good friends to this day.

A few days later, a large group of youth came to The Inner City Youth League and wanted to know if they could start some programs there and get involved in learning more and being active in the Civil Rights struggle. Through this process, the youth learned that there are more viable solutions to problems than they had heretofore experienced. This creative approach was valuable instruction to both the youth and the community as a whole.

What mode of persuasion will we use to deal with the problems of today's youth? How will we reach conflict resolution? My conclusion is simply this: Conflict can't always be resolved by talking alone. Persuasion often calls for creative action.

Akhenaten's Dream: SunRise!

Beyond your flesh
Beyond your room
your house
your piece of ground,
your town.
Beyond your state, region or country,
Beyond your continent or island,
Beyond the 3rd Stone from the Sun—our sweet Mother Earth,
Beyond your mother, father, family, nation, race, class and gender
Beyond all that . . .

Yeah, beyond capitalism, socialism, racism, class-ism, nationalism,
and the FASCISM that loves all our ISMS of whatever flavor,
Yeah, beyond Jesus, Jonah, Buddha, Mohamed, Musa, Joseph Smith,
and all the Devine Mothers cradling us,
cradling us all, all,
Beyond our hunger for oil, gas, coal, uranium and wood
burning, burning, burning,
daily choking
the life from the precious air we breathe
and all that breathes us,
Beyond roach dust,
mercury and lead choking the life from the lungs, brains and nervous
    tissue of our babies,
Beyond our tears of joy or rage
Beyond all our graves!
Beyond
Politics,
Sociology,
Spirituality,
Our humanity or the latest theory—
Which we now think explains it all,
Beyond all we believe is either grief or joy

Who really knows distances in this vastness called Universe?
Who really knows the cost of our comfort?
Of all the petty energy-consuming stuff we think we have a right to:
"Central heating
Air conditioning,
Cars,
Airplanes
Electric lights
Inexpensive clothing,
Recorded music, movies, hip replacement surgery and
Your national defense!"
If you love your Country more than the Earth that cradles her,
If you keep burning the fuel of fossils,
You are dumping in your living rooms
You are torching your rafters
Feeding your babies a formula full of arsenic, mercury and lead.

Wake up and live now
In Sunflower Splendor!
Open Morning Glory!
Wake up for the first time and LIVE!

What you have a right to is the Natural World.
What you have a right to is your movement through Seasons.
Embodied or not, as everything turns, turns, turns . . .
We are dancing inside Nearness
Dancing in the Sacred Web of Life made of
Mud and starlight
Semen and seasons
Novas and notions
Stardust and the chorus of all singing planets known and un.
(What? There's a new one now???)
Anthills' industrious grit and constellations spilling
'cross the unnamed expanses of sweet home AllWhere,

Ultimately, who we are is not the bag of skin we are in.
Our energy spreads throughout all that is Creation:
Tendrils woven and weaving through all Mother-matter, touching.
We are touching all things all the time in Unity,
whether we know it or not.

We are flying-spinning through Space,
All the time timelessly, endlessly, eternally, infinity!
What a trip! Feel it!

And now I press my palm against your heart-breast,
I speak softly to you, as you see it and feel it now too:
I see you now with the eyes of my heart,
No enemy, no other . . .
Transformed, revealed, awakened and naked,
Crying for a Vision now quaking,
Beyond this global war zone of our own making,
The stuff of conflict, greed, arrogance & fear,
Will this be the inheritance of our babies' babies' babies?
Will our babies have babies?
Will they survive?
Will they *want* to?

Touch me brother with kind hands,
Embrace me sister with hope-heart (we are safe in this wisdom).
Death has no dominion over Life,
Death is a twin to Life   a ying/yang unity of unending Life
In all its forms and possibility.
Touch beyond all boundaries and identities fearlessly,
Let us all Touch the Earth with our naked feet
And *be glad!*

For the Earth to live America must die . . .
Yeah I said it!
For the Earth to live America must die!
For the Earth to live ALL nations must die.
For the Earth to live Germany
Spain
England
Egypt
Azania
China and Guatemala and all their sisters,
All must die, must be transformed.

The Snow will make us friends.
The Rain will make us family.

The Sun will melt all hearts,
All Gods chillin gonna have rhythm now.
The Wind will teach us a New Song that everyone can sing,
ROBUSTLY! Rooted in a Deep Democracy beyond what we know now.

Listen!
My friends are committing suicide now . . .
To me it says something about how toxic our environment has become.
They don't want to be here anymore.
It's become physically, spiritually—toxic!
To me it begs the question of,
How do we recognize what is Sacred in our lives and be centered in that?
How do we recognize the green sprouts coming through the concrete and
    treasure that?
How do we recognize where the renewal is emerging and become one
    with that?
How do we "Walk the Way of the New World"?

Wherever we are going, we must all go together or not go at all!

There are spaces in the Heart as vast as the Universe,
And who knows distances in this vastness . . . ?
I see you now. I see you now. I see you now . . .
So touch me now with kind hands
In this mornings' glory!
Transformed, revealed, awakened, naked
With kind hands, hand in hand in hand . . .
Gripping! I got you now! I got you now!
Stepping gently on this Holy Earth
Now striding toward . . .
SunRise!

Take my hand
And together we can make it.
So when I am afraid
I know you are there for me
As I am for you.
I am because you are
I am because you are
We are lovely locked together

Oh blessed curse!
It is natural compassion
A green & verdant celebration
We are rescued from our egos
Our world is spinning & springing into renewal
... and yes it hurts like hell—that's the way it is, isn't it?
We feel there is no beginning and no end
There was never any more beginning than there is now
Nor any more youth or age than there is now
And will be never any more heaven or hell
                  than there is now
Man & woman, man & man, woman to woman, all!
Mating in mirth and magic
Manifesting a new world with our breathing and being
There is no sanctuary except in compassionate action
There is no sanctuary except in compassionate action
No nation, no race, no religion, no gender
Blossoming burst of energy on our Liberation Day
On the radiant Kundalini ground
We shudder in Holiness
   Earth is home, Earth is home, home, home, home, ooommmmmmm!

The Pork Chop Wars

A performance novel

(All the voices move on to space in tiny washes of light with open hands and single fingers pointing the way/ This is the road of shadows at the end of a long journey/ These are the old tellers with visions restored/ These ones remember their legs, turning from one another, leaning into songs, into streets/ Horns center the movement/ claves accent stomps of rhythm/ Melody holds hands with these refugees/ Walk/ Wail/ Tell it when you can/ Start before night)

THOUGHT I

Iona Pearl
Woman and dog hungry, howling/ Found cross town when Iona got the
    news/ Her name washed big in buckets of fried frogs legs specialized by
him/ A good recipe turned back round with the sauce so sticky, vinegar,
    peach meat mashed, long wait, all manner of pepper, and dried
Tamarind/ Doused cross his lap she went to hang her legs over where he
    could see what he wanted/ So he would have all of this long fall to look
    at and touch in any way he wanted to/ She smoothed herself open in his
    hands so deeply fragrant/ Lifting her wide and closer with his thumbs
    he washed his face/ Afternoons like this as his knuckles broke through
    her in the few weeks gone by eased her/

No longer would she dream of the silk coat with so many colors that the
    scoundrel would not buy/ He kept all the money and counted careful
    never to get her what she wanted/ To keep her from the beauty of the
    world seems to have been his life work/ The most beautiful coat and
    he would not let her have it/ He laid on top of her and give her the
    damn babies/ At his age still full of juice/ Stingy dirty scoundrel!/ Two
    children both of them for him to look at and sing to on their birthdays
    cause they were his/

If she wanted some part of him he would measure the time to be sure she was left dry/ Too much noise for a decent woman to make with a man/ There were woman who he loved to listen to when the deal was good/ When he had bargained hard with whiskey and cash/ Women who would hum, burn, or bark just for him as requested, as bargained for/ This wife of his didn't listen to his requirements/ She leaked her unskilled sonatas unrestrained and this was not expected from her when they married

Twenty four Iona was when her father introduced them in the parlor of their palatial home/ On this street in Memphis slipped the best colored folks in and out of their gracious dwellings, tidy, respectable and gently used/ Everything from back yonder time crawled and sat under the nails/ Way back imperatives of roughness were waived away with lace, with gentility/ They scrubbed and washed with purpose all the time daily/ Nothing from the street absorbed the rugs nothing, no dust, or muddy satin shoes/ Under the glass cut lights even in French no hair on fire made entrance here/
The best pomades cooled and dressed these diverse torrents of ribboned controversy/ Everyone had their own comb and brushed their secrets to be burned in the plate so the birds would not get them/
Just sweet music/
Only the sweetest music was ever played on her piano/ No Rag Time/
None of that in here ruled Mabah/ Not in this house she whispered/ No Rag Time in here, no, no, no, no Le Jazz Hot, no/ The ongoing interrogation of Boleros continued at every gathering of invited guests/

Only the best people ever associated with this family here in the new south of colored entrepreneurs/ The family that had come up from Mississippi wood laid a foundation solidly into the future/ First there were the general stores owned by her uncle, her father and later by her twin brothers and first cousin/ The very best funeral parlors to serve any clientele in Memphis Tennessee enjoined their sterling reputation/ All details were executed with distinction by a skilled and well trained staff/ Nothing got past em/ Taking notice of hair pins/ emerald broaches/ leather braid belts/ stockings/
Watches/ Hats important at all times no matter where you are on the ladder of life/ Hats were gonna tell it all/
Despite her behavior they would advance to run the state and the nation with their intergenerational finesse/

Where the hell had she taken her wayward black ass now? Leaving the children alone in the house with just his nurse/ It was not her responsibility
to feed them after all/ Children were not the reason why she had been
retained/ The patient needed his dressing changed every three hours/
Poultices of turpentine and oil of sage placed beneath the open wounds
in his scrotum/ Prostate cancer had eaten him away even though he had
been worked on by the very best doctors money would buy/ Under a
small tent on linen changed twice a day he lay open to the air/
Now as the afternoon slipped into dusk Peter heard the firecrackers marking
the days celebrations/ Into the end of his life his children moved toward
his face to kiss more and some more again/ Tiny lips trying to sing a song
for him/ Juanita and Milagros clapping softly for their father going now,
today/ Fourth of July every one today told them fourth of July today is
the fourth/ They had lemon custard as well as plum candy wrapped in
paper at their Mabah's house/ It's the way they called her name unable
to say grandmother/ Juanita started to call her this way cause she loved
it when ever her grandmother held her close to her own heart/
Milagros had arrived too soon/ Juanita wanted the world for herself a little
longer/ A beautiful child so dark in his arms, a jewel, holding her, child
of his old age/ Juanita returned his hope that some kind of sweetness
was possible in his life/
His young wife tried too hard at all the wrong things/ Yes indeed she is a
great cook/ A great cook and she knew how to keep house/ She kept
a cleaner than clean house and she could sew anything/ She sewed
clothes for the children, made beautiful crocheted doilies, precise faggot
stitches/ The girls were very well kept, very well behaved, well man-
nered, so sweet/ Milagros just three years old kept up with her sister,
got into everything, sang/
Clap hands clap hands
Till daddy gets home/
Daddy has money
And mommy has none/

THOUGHT 2

Look at that Gal dance/
They no longer desired to chew on sticks, crumble bones, mash leaves under
tongues, fill cheeks with plum pits, and grind the rinds between to
soften/ Sucking back salted spit little Imah crowned the air in billowing
smoke/

Tiny words/

Skin off lips/

People can think what ever they like/ You know that/ They think what they want to think/ Whatever that is/ What they think really cant bother you/ You cant let people get to you with what they say/ Everything they say is not always true/ they can lie/ Lie about you/ Lie behind your back/ Lie and they don't even know you/ Don't know any thing about you at all/ Never met you/ Start lies like they know/ Go around telling people lies about you when they know they are just lying/ Do it for no good reason/ Do it to make themselves seem important/ Lie on you so people think they know something about you and what you do/ They don't know any thing/ They think they know so much/ Think they can say what ever they want about you and your family and your life/ As if the world cares about any thing they have to say, cares what they think or say or do/ Who cares about them/ You don't have to think about what other people think/ I have lived my whole life just like I wanted to/ I aint asked nobody for a damn thing/ I done ate dirt when I've had to and damn sure aint dead

Yet/ Though some of em always talking bout what they know done gone way from here long time ago/ Gone and never coming back and some of em aint missed worth a damn/ People always talking/ My whole life washed floors and cleaned spittle from off crazy people/ I am knowing for myself that life is sweet/ Not always tender and sometime just bald head/ These things I know/

When you love some one who don't love you that's a mess/ Mess is the worse thing in this world/ Life was not meant for every thing to be all up in the air all the time/

People can see you/ See you with your hair on fire and what are they gonna do?/

what?/ Cept look, talk, spread lies, smile in your damn face/

THOUGHT 3

Look at that gal dance/

Milagros that girl dancing a music in her/

The girl stepped over to one side/ Broke/ Crossed those legs while she swung close down to the floor holding the left leg above her head/ Milagros takes a toss with her smile a blaze out front of the world/ No back crossed dreams where those lean legs tap/ When winter froze the

rivers her heart light took out sweet morsels of sun that warmed days
to night/

Any one can crush apples/

I'll have no reasons to cry anymore/ The boy who loves me speaks when
he can through the stutters to say how much I mean to him/ The boy
who loves me fights for each word so hard to give me his message/ The
swiss dot dress is still over to Anne's and I have got to borrow it again
for Thursday/ When people tried to tell him to get away from our kisses
Smitty coughs up curses in their faces/ A man of music he is/ If I take
back Margo's shoes she will let me keep Nedra's for a few days/ My
Smitty who is so good looking girls want to fight me over him/ None of
them can dance like I can so none of them can win/ Smitty is mine and
when he says his iiiiiiiiiiiIiii lllllllllLLLooove yyyyyyyyYyyyyou in my ear
I just wait till he can get all of it out then we kiss some more/ We have
this life to make just for us/ just for how we want it to be/ Stuttering is
talking not dancing or playing music/ It's just talking/

Off to the Big City

from *Nellie Stone Johnson: The Life of an Activist*

Nellie Stone Johnson, union organizer and civil rights activist, treasured her agricultural background. Her family farmed in Dakota County, where she was born in 1905; they moved to a larger farm in Pine County in 1919.

Tenth grade was as far as school went up in Clover Township. If I wanted to go on for two more years of high school, Hinckley was fourteen miles away, and I did just not want to drive that Ford car to get there.*

I really didn't like driving the car because in the spring the road was muddy, and I didn't like the ice and snow either. I'd carry a five-gallon milk can of alcohol to keep the radiator from freezing. I remember once when I was in my twenties, I was up at the farm for a while when my mother was ill, and I was going to some political meeting, I think it was a Unitarian meeting in Askov, Minnesota, which is nearby. Well, when I got there, I reeked of alcohol.

I had a vivid opinion about leaving home. I was going to finish up my high school education at the University of Minnesota; that was more common then, through their extension side. Nobody wanted me to go to Minneapolis—my father and mother didn't want me to go. But there was no argument; I just wanted to continue school. My parents made the argument many times that I should stay at home and go to Hinckley High School, but they knew how hard it was for me to get there. The ride was so bad that lots of girls from my area left Sunday night and stayed in Hinckley until Friday. There was a Mrs. Fry in Hinckley; she boarded most all of the farm girls for miles around. She had ten to twelve rooms in that big old house.

To be able to leave, I just kept talking—talking and yelling and carrying on. I bugged my parents half to death. I wanted to learn everything I could learn, and I couldn't do it there. I knew that was a soft spot for them,

*This narrative is by Nellie Stone Johnson, as told to David Brauer.

because of how much they believed in education, and that's why they never told me outright not to go. They didn't give me any arguments, but they said, we'll see, we'll see.

It was kind of a split thing in me, because I knew my mom was ill, and she needed me for heavy things around the house. At seventeen, I couldn't keep up with all that needed to be done. It was rough—Cortland, Clemmy, and Almeda were all in school, and the old man was busy, in the winter he was cutting ice off Crystal Lake and Orchard Lake. He survived because the older boys weren't around the house, so he didn't have to take care of them, and Cortland, Clem, and Almeda, they were getting to the point where they took care of themselves. There were some things no one else around the house could do as well as I—washing and cooking; I did that since I was ten years old.

They never said they needed me more here, but I could tell by the other arguments they gave me. They said all cities are dangerous places for young girls to go to, but I always felt I could fight my way out of everything. Of course, that wasn't true. I never realized then how bad it could be, sexual harassment.

I came to the city, Minneapolis, in September 1922, after helping all through the summer to put up barrels of sweet pickles. I had to work to get out of there! We used these great hardwood barrels for the pickles, and I remember doing fifty-five-gallon barrels of sauerkraut. There was no shortage of food when I left. I remember I sewed myself two dresses that summer—not what city people wore as far as style, but they'll do.

I didn't think it was that bad moving here at all. I had a job when I came down to the Cities. I was taking care of an apartment and three kids on Spruce Place, right by Loring Park in Minneapolis. One child was seven and the other was almost a teenager, plus there was another baby. They were white, and I lived with them. I slept on a roll-away in their apartment. There were too many people in that apartment! There was only one bedroom, and I slept in the back hallway. It was good only because the apartment had two entrances. I had to leave that family because the baby cried all night.

I had gotten the job through the church we went to, Bethesda Baptist. Mrs. Helm was one of the founders of the church, and she got me the job with this white family, and a second family, too.

The second job involved two older kids, teenage girls. We were close to the same age; we'd go out and walk, and go over to Loring Park. They liked to play tennis a little bit. I didn't know the game, but I was much stronger, so I did OK. Their mom gave us money to go over to the Orpheum to see movies. These were thirteen- and fourteen-year-old girls, and I remember thinking, I was taking care of a whole family at that age! This place wasn't far from the first place I lived at on Spruce Place.

One day, after a big dinner of roast turkey on a Sunday with my uncle Clarence and aunt Delia in North Minneapolis, I just stayed all night, and then I just decided to stay for good. I told that second family I had been living with that I didn't want to stay, and the woman didn't have a fit about it. I wasn't a natural nanny or babysitter. It was not my natural calling to cook and make breakfast for them. Even so, it wasn't as hard as farmwork. Here, we had power machines, like an engine to run the washing machine.

My uncle's apartment was a flat, a five-room apartment—three bedrooms, a living room/dining room, and a fairly large kitchen. All with good hardwood. There was a piano in the living room, good furniture, and rugs. It wasn't really a big change from home—except we had linoleum back home and six or eight kids running around!

The great piece in my aunt's living room was their Victrola. We really cranked it up when we put records on. I remember our neighbors back in Lakeville got one before there were flat records—they had a cylinder that made the sounds. The thing I'll never forget about that Victrola was the little dog they used to sell it—listening in to hear his master's voice. The thing that interested me was that this little needle brought a voice out!

There were a lot of mom-and-pop businesses on both sides of the block on Sixth Avenue North, a lot of Jewish business owners. You know the old saying about when you get three Jews together, you've got an argument. Well, the same is true when you get two blacks together. So that was a lively place. It's right where Olson Memorial Highway is now.

My uncle's apartment was right over the People's Bakery. The bakery was two units, with a billiard room right on the corner of Jewitt and Olson Highway.

You remember the smells. I could smell bread when they first started making it at five AM, the Jewish bread, with the braided top—what do you call that? Challah? The Viennese bread, those loaves were all the same, heavy European doughs. When the loaves were coming out of the oven, I was there to pick up my loaf.

The billiard room was a rough place—a lot of young Jewish males arguing with each other. They were playing cards, though we were not supposed to know that. My uncle said they were coming to fight because they were playing cards, and that was a natural result. Their format was like black billiard rooms and club rooms on Bryant all the way to Lyndale. Between young Jews and blacks, there was plenty of activity. People today don't think that the two groups are very similar, but they were both on the low end of the totem pole, and there was plenty of discrimination toward each group, so there was a lot of anger and a lot of scrapping and criminality.

Every other place on our block was a business of some kind, usually Jewish owned. On Colfax there was a black grocery story, and on Bryant, another black-owned grocery. I didn't know too much about those groceries, because I shopped mostly at the Jewish grocery stores nearby. There was quite a large barbershop on the block, and a delicatessen, with a couple more across the street.

I took to the area right away because it was a convenient thing for me. I was still wearing pretty rough clothes and shoes, but I could buy new stuff right there. After a fashion, I had the money. I had skirts and stuff and sweaters; I had made my shirts.

The rest of the population in town thought it was bad. The consensus of every white European who lived outside of there was that it was all niggers and Jews. I remember in Pine County, there was a neighbor of ours named Mrs. Irvine, who told my grandmother Allen that nobody lives on Olson Memorial Highway except niggers and Jews! She was just saying it familiar because Grandma Allen was a white woman, but can you imagine some old fool saying that to her? I think Grandma wanted to hit her with her cane!

You'd see a blond-headed little kid in town here, going along talking about niggers and kikes! The blond kids who were not Jewish talk like that all the time—*nigger* would just roll out of their mouth. I didn't hear it every day, but more than I wanted to. It was kind of like today. You don't hear it, but you know it's just below the surface.

It took me until I was twenty to understand the meaning of all that—*shine, bootblack,* all the bad names, I learned them up here. I had just learned the idea early on at home that any discrimination was a lack of being human. There were people in the country who were racist, as I told you, and used the word *nigger* all the time, but they never had all the names they called us in the city.

I think if I'd grown up being called nigger, I'd have been in a fight every day. I think I would have been a little more hateful, but I would have eventually learned the right way. My father wouldn't like to mix up personal grudges with a political or economic thing—what you were working for was so much more important than the names they would call you. I was bad enough, fighting, so I'd hate to think what I would have developed into if I'd heard the word *nigger* all the time.

I remember walking with my aunt back from the flophouse joint she was a maid at. I was talking about getting a sandwich and a Coke at the downtown Woolworth and she said, "You don't have any idea, do you? I don't know if you can get anything in there." I wanted a cold drink—I was never one for a Coke, but it was hot, so I was just going to step into Woolworth's and get it. This will tell you what it was like growing up for me in the countryside—I was so used to getting what I wanted and just going about my business.

We had stores in our little towns from one end to the other, and I could just step into a store and buy cream soda, ice cream, whatever. In the big city, you could walk in, but not get served; in the city, there were many more people that I guess grew up not knowing you. In our small towns, it was hard to be exclusionary to one family.

Many years later, when those children who sat in the lunch counters in Woolworth's, Kresge's for civil rights in the early sixties, they did it with our strong moral support, because of things like what happened when I first came to Minneapolis in 1923.

The first summer I was here, I would see a lot of black kids out on the street along Olson Highway, standing in diapers with their bellies hanging out. They were malnourished. I was so busy thinking about school that I couldn't think about that a lot, but it affected me.*

And the people there who weren't working full-time, like their white neighbors were, I wondered about that. It was a rude awakening when I delved into the employment field myself. I'll never forget the feeling you get when you don't have a prayer of getting some job. You don't really feel so hurt you want to sit down and cry. What you want to do is double up your fist and start going after somebody. Pound some intelligence into their heads. That's how my reaction to it went, anyway.

But as I said, living with my aunt and uncle in north Minneapolis was not too bad a change—I was definitely used to working. I cleaned the house. I wasn't the best cook, but I made the bread. Aunt Delia had a job at the old Maryland Hotel on LaSalle. I went to help her do maid work one day a week. It was an apartment hotel, with small apartments, kitchenettes. I would wash dishes, especially kitchen areas, for my aunt.

My social life wasn't much. I was quite a skiier and skater yet, and at Sumner Field, they had a court to play tennis. I was never a good tennis player, but got my exercise. And at Sumner Field, we also sledded.

I went to dances once in a blue moon, at one old place I remember, the Kissler Building, named after a Jewish doctor who owned the place, on

*This paragraph and the next one are quoted from Steve Perry, "The Good Fight," in *City Pages*, May 29, 1991.

Sixth and Lyndale Avenue North. I was always chaperoned—I made my youngest uncle, Roscoe, take me. The black Elks would put on a dance every Monday. I met a few boys there, and I knew most of the folks were sons of women friends of my aunt, mostly railroad people that my uncle worked with. At that time, I was getting my—what do I want to say?—my initiation to jazz music, but I like the old-fashioned one-step and two-step waltzes more. Later, I came around a little bit on jazz, but still don't care much for it. That's why I'm not a bebop and rock fan. They incorporate jazz into these new-fangled styles. I guess that's how old I am; jazz sounded too modern for me.

I remember one time, I went to a dance and stayed out late, past nine. The next morning I could hardly get myself out of bed. That wasn't like me. I was home at nine the next time, I was so tired from that one little episode. Even with barn dances back home, I would come home early to get some sleep. I always did like to sleep, to the point that my body felt rested.

Anyway, the atmosphere at these dances was very good, there were mostly church people, mostly going on to higher education.

I had my first boyfriend around eighteen. He happened to be a friend of my aunt's. He was part of the Jackson family. He was nice enough, but didn't have too much sense from where I stood. He was fairly nice looking, but he didn't know politics or organizing, which was kind of hard on me. People like that, who were just climbing the ladder, didn't make much sense to me. I was able to keep him at arm's length. I never got too hung up on a good-looking man.

My aunt Delia was kind of like that, too, looking to climb. My aunt had to go to the established social church in south Minneapolis. She kept asking me if I wanted to go to St. Peter's. I said no, those girls there are only looking for boyfriends. At that time, I wasn't into boyfriends. But I loved to talk politics with boys or girls.

As for the schooling I came down here for, I was taking extension courses, the equivalent of GED work, at the University of Minnesota. I didn't have any trouble getting into extension school because my grades were good. They didn't discriminate against me because of being from the country—lots of people were in those days. And it was obvious how much I knew about politics at my age.

The extension classes weren't very much—they were night classes, and that was a little better. It fit what I wanted to do better, and fit the families I worked for when I first came down here. I wanted to go to North High, but they had a tuition fee then, and it was pretty steep. My aunt didn't want to pay that.

I started at the agriculture school, and I just couldn't stand the students over there! They believed every cliché about what people believed about students of color, which would boil down to racism. I was too big and hard-looking, so they didn't say it to my face, but their body language said it all.

For example, on certain questions, teachers would ask for comments and when I raised my hand, I got looks from some students like, What the hell do you know? These were students who had never missed a meal in their lives, who didn't know what a student of color was like. Some of the teachers were shook up, too.

I don't think I encountered such racism in Lakeville or Pine City because people just didn't think of being racist in their own city—but they could be racist in the *big* city.

Look, the people I grew up around in Lakeville and Pine City were fairly intellectual people. They had a flair for very intellectual relations—they were all church people who believed just do unto others as others would do unto you. In those communities, if families were hungry, we saw to it that they were fed, no matter what race they were. If there was a new baby, everyone would flutter and do things for the baby and the mother, no matter what race they were. The only conclusion I could come to is that a little religion—of the right sort—is a good thing.

It was better then because I think there was more good Christian mentality as a way of life than there is now. Those families all talked the same, the mothers all swapped the same recipes, everyone put their feet under the same table. They certainly didn't think about it as being political. The basic thought was that it was Christian, the right thing to do.

So I went to the Minneapolis campus to do social science and political science. The whole U, it seemed like I was going off to another place when I went there. I learned in one of those old red brick buildings, over by Northrop Auditorium.

The situation was better because the students were there to study the same thing as you were. That wasn't the same for me on the ag campus. There was a lot of farm studies over there, but I had been there to study chemistry to become a pharmacist. That was my original plan. I wanted to be a pharmacist, because I had been introduced by my parents on how you test milk for sanitation. But when I went on to political science, I said what are ag people without political science?

My father thought farmers were very shortsighted in their education, because the politics of food, the price you were paid, the economic forces, were so important. So it was easy for me to give up my first dream, because I saw where I could go real easily—I could go far in politics. I thought the ag department would help me work for the quality of food and medicine, but politics would, too. I guess I was headed that way, but those ag campus people gave me a push.

I don't think a lot of minority students realize how interrelated they are—if they don't have a really complete equal opportunity, then maybe they should get involved with politics.

I always did well in class, and studying social science worked out fine. I knew more at eighteen about politics than most people ever will. I was still a teenager and I had two of the most renowned teachers in the state, Mills and Ziebarth. Everybody called him Easy Ziebarth—his initials were E. Z. They were two top-notch professors, and they did extension classes. They were played up as two of the greatest in the field of politics.

The campus life then felt kind of in between quiet and rambunctious to me. There were all these political parties there: the Young Communist League, the Young Republicans, the Young Democrats. There might have even been a Young Farmer-Labor Party, but I don't remember it. Anyway, it wasn't wild in the physical sense, but in the mental sense.

The young parties, they had assembly halls. We knew where these gatherings would be. There was some noise, and a little bit of yelling between groups, especially when we got to the time of Farmer-Laborites and Democrats, when they started trying to get the two together. There was not too much back-and-forth between Republicans and Communists because the Republicans were afraid some of that radicalism might rub off.

There were a couple of other black people on the campus that I used to sit around with. I was on the campus when they still were building Coffman Union. The minute they got the bowling alley finished there, me and another gal would bowl there at least once a week, maybe sometimes twice.

Whatever musical event they put on at Northrop Auditorium that I could afford, I'd go. I heard the Minneapolis Orchestra there for the first time. Paul Robeson, they'd hardly let him come to town without me hearing him sing. When I got to be part of the labor movement, I'd often go to cookies and coffee after his performance at some faculty member's house. It was because I was black and into labor, and so was he.

I remember hearing him talk about the great things happening in the Soviet Union—about people eating and having places to sleep, and entering the hallowed halls of medicine. I believed him because I read the press, and even though the press was anti-Soviet, once in a while they'd make a slip and write about the great advances. I don't think it was the Luce publications—*Time, Life,* and *Fortune*—[publisher Henry] Luce was very anti-Communist. I suppose it was more like if *Vogue* had decided to do a special issue on women, or there was a story in the *Ladies' Home Journal.*

I talked to Robeson quite a bit, every time I was invited to meetings, but usually some people would get him off in a corner. He was big as all outdoors, and I wasn't a withering violet either. When he sang, he'd rear back his head and poke out his chest, big as all outdoors. He was very gracious and very intellectual. He was associated with a lot of the scientists at the University of Minnesota. Within the arts and sciences it was hard to figure out who began where, but there seemed to be a lot of interplay between the faculty and labor.

One of the Oppenheimers went to school here, Frank, and I ran with him a bit. I rode with him in a wild roadster because we had to get to some DFL gathering quickly. It was convenient to get to St. Paul and burn up some gas. He was a pretty nice guy. I'd love to listen to his politics, which were DFL and radical. He talked of people having enough to eat.

Did you ever hear of a Dr. Near? He was in the rocket program and died a year or two ago. He was one of the people very involved in university political life. I know that one night, he had us over and put us all in a large living room and dining room. He put chairs out—this was a social event for Paul Robeson. I took my youngest sister, Almeda, who couldn't care less. That bothered me, because she had a very down-to-earth service job. I thought she'd be interested in it—and we had the same father—but I don't think she paid a whole lot of attention to him. For me, those meetings were interesting, those equity things for people, and how to get it.

Heard

Stones and Sticks

There are turning points in everyone's life, though we sometimes fail to recognize them at the time that they happen. One of those moments happened for me during a springtime video/poetry class in 1983 when the class met in a cemetery to record a student's poem about roller skating through a graveyard.

Everyone in the seven-member class was intrigued with the idea, and nervous titters made their way around the room, along with words like "spooky," "macabre," and "eerie," the night we discussed shots that might work well for Gretel's poem. At the end of the evening, we agreed to meet the following Sunday morning at the entrance of Lakewood Cemetery, where prominent Minnesota families, such as those who founded the Pillsbury and General Mills companies, and statesmen like Vice President Hubert H. Humphrey and Senator Paul Wellstone, are buried.

From the moment the decision was made, I felt disturbed, unable to come to grips with the thought that I might be complicit in the group's violation of the spirits of the deceased who lay peacefully in their graves. What right did we have to disturb them just because a callow young woman wanted to see herself on videotape skating through their resting place? And what about the mourners scattered throughout the cemetery? How would they feel when Gretel skated by with the rest of us walking closely behind her, gawking while they prayed for their lost loved ones or placed flowers on their graves?

Gretel had just finished lacing up her skates and was about to lead the poets into the enormous cemetery when I arrived. We followed her past curved, tree-lined paths and rows of granite plaques and headstones, large statues and imposing crypts as big as houses. The tall woman with shaggy white hair and a slight limp halted every few steps and looked around as though entranced with the scenery. And it was fascinating to see how the sun illuminated the golden highlights in the 30-something man's black and blonde striped mohawk. I was moved when I observed the young married couple weave their fingers together when they slowed down to read the names of the dead and their dates of birth and death. No doubt they were contemplating a time when death might separate the two of them.

Gretel mugged for the camera, impressing us with her knowledge, naming birds that flew by and trees that were as twisted and bent as the people who lay in the graves they protected. The class members, usually quite vocal, were somber as they examined elaborate monuments and pondered the messages written on both elegant tombstones and simple markers. Even without reading the dates, it was clear which graves had been there the longest: the older markers bore streaks of dark green, brown or black from having been exposed to the weather for many years.

Soon, Gretel took us down a narrow pathway that led to a thick cluster of trees bordered with pink, purple and white impatiens. She stopped and turned to face the group, then said something was in there that was really interesting. She spun around and began skating slowly down the path, glancing back to make sure we were following.

I was the first to see the weather-beaten statue of a woman who looked like she had been carved by a sculptor in the Greco-Roman era. Her figure was draped in a gown, belted at the waist, allowing her skirt to fall gently over the pedestal on which she stood. Her right hand rested serenely over her heart, and her left arm reached out in a gesture of peace. Her chiseled face was framed by long hair pulled back in a bun and she gazed down at me with a soft smile. Her eyes, though devoid of color, appeared kind. She looked so real that it was hard to believe she was made of stone.

The class stood in a semi-circle and watched Gretel's eyes take on a ghoulish sparkle. The instructor trained the camera on her and an impish grin spread slowly over her face. The group stood waiting until finally, the man with wavy blonde hair and gold rimmed glasses became impatient. "Well?" he asked. At that moment, Gretel's eyes grew wide. She spun around and skated up to the statue. She lifted her arm and stuck out her finger in a gesture that reminded me of Michelangelo's *Creation* painting, God's finger almost touching the finger of man. Then, as suddenly as she lifted her arm, she snatched it back and said: "It's a statue of a black woman. If you touch her you'll die." Then, as though propelled by a tornadic wind, she skated away, leaving peals of laughter ringing in the air along with echoes of her words.

I was paralyzed, unable to respond, as though a knife had been jabbed into my chest and slowly twisted into my heart. I took another look at the woman locked in that dark body made of granite and, in my mind's eye, her shoulders began to slump from carrying the weight of all that stone, and then to crumble under the burdens of overwork and underappreciation from cooking and cleaning for the families of Gretel's ancestors while desperately trying to care for her own family, the families of my ancestors. At that moment, I remembered every negative image I had ever heard of black women; *oversexed, breeder, wet nurse, mammy, hostile, nappy headed, ho.* Gretel's words named something I had felt vaguely all my life but could not describe with words of my own: The cautionary warnings my mother gave my sister and me: "You gotta work harder if you want to be seen as just as good as white girls." "Gotta go through a lot of pain to be beautiful (translation: hair straightened, butt girdled)"; the blue eyes that Toni Morrison's fictional character Pecola prayed for, believing that they would stop her from being seen as "dirt"; Sarah Baartman, known as the "Hottentot Venus"—the eighteenth-century orphaned south African woman whose large buttocks and extended labia caused her Dutch enslavers to turn her into a sideshow attraction; the degrading ways we black women are depicted in movies or shaking our asses in hip hop videos, the ways we are devalued in school and the workplace by our men who reject us and men of other races who look past us or leer at us with lust ... All of those images and more came crashing into my heart. The black woman has had to struggle with the perception that she is as venomous as a sting from the tongue of a poisonous asp or the bite of a black widow spider. Gretel's words made it clear that, in the eyes of the world, the black woman is poison. "If you touch her you'll die."

I have never been able to handle surprises very well, and that day was no exception. I couldn't gather my thoughts, so I bore my humiliation in silence. I looked at the class members, trying to gauge whether Gretel's words had affected them the way they had impacted me. None of them showed a reaction. I can't lay all of the blame on Gretel. Nor can I blame the group's nonreaction entirely on them. No doubt, Gretel was repeating what she'd heard all of her life. Her comment was likely unremarkable to the others in the group for the same reason.

I have three beautiful, intelligent daughters. I have had to help them maintain their self-images over and over again, even as I've attempted to heal my own self-image. The day after my middle daughter received a letter of acceptance to an Ivy League college, she left for school excited to show it to Chester McCoy, the African American male counselor who had encouraged her to apply. To my dismay, her shoulders were slumped when she came home. She tearfully explained that when McCoy proudly told his colleagues that she would be the first black girl from their school to attend Vassar, none of them showed any enthusiasm. Instead, one white female counselor started what turned into a chain reaction of discouragement, telling Tania that she was out of her league. When the news reached students, her black female peers, unable to imagine that they, too, might be as capable as she, insisted that Tania couldn't have gotten into a prestigious college because she deserved to be there. "They just let you in cuz you're black and they wanna look good," they asserted.

Lord knows I understand the horror of what is happening to our young men. I have a son who has served time in the federal penitentiary. But there seems to be a conspiracy of silence around our girls and women. Could this be that, in a large part, our incarceration is invisible? That we are locked up in our bodies?

Like countless black mothers, I have worked hard to train my daughters to be proud of who they are in a world that would have them be ashamed of their darkness. For black women, loving ourselves and passing self-love down to our daughters and our granddaughters is a difficult task. The constant negation makes us feel like we need to adopt a hard, protective shell, which is either praised as strength or dismissed as hostility. In short, we turn ourselves into stone.

I left the cemetery wondering what it would take to liberate us. And today, as I see my four granddaughters move through a world where some have tried to portray our first African American First Lady as a hostile black woman, even going so far as to call her trash for encouraging black children to do their best, I have to ask again. What is it that will set us free?

Who Would You Be?

Who would you be?

Who would you be . . .
If I tailored my attentions to know you?
If I were your guide to the beauty and worth of your subterraneous self?
If even your dark spaces were shared and accepted?

Who would you be . . .
If the warmth of my body melted your defenses?
If my light drew you to break ground
And you grew tall and opened?

Who would you be . . .
If I bore faithful witness to your deeds and disappointments?
If I wrought the rationale for your risks,
And abided your life in its wholeness with a swollen heart?

Who would you be . . .
If I made you laugh when you were taking yourself or life too seriously?
If I stayed unafraid when you raged or grieved,
Then held you when you were spent?

Who would you be . . .
If I opened my whole self to you?
If I said — Take what you need, I can make more,
And you did?

And who would you be . . .
If, when there was something that I couldn't give,
If I said — Well go on then, look for it . . .
May you know joy, may your dreams come true?

Who would you be?
Who would you be?
Who would you be . . .
If you were loved properly?

In the City, Homelessness

"Go away, you cannot stay. They'll be no niggers here today," said The Man. "Or any other day for that matter. No nigger children staining the carpets and crayoning the walls." And with that, this new landlord, who'd just bought our building, ceremoniously dismissed my three-year-old son and me from the duplex we'd lived in on Thomas Avenue in St. Paul for the past two years. Homelessness is about racism!

Broken lease, broken legality: The Man didn't even return my damage deposit, with interest, for only normal wear and tear. I was on welfare and couldn't afford a new apartment requiring one month's rent and security deposit in fifteen days. Normal operating procedure. Homelessness is not normal!

We were normal. And alone with each other, my son and I. I hadn't received a bipolar diagnosis yet, although my moods swung wildly and from time to time suicide seemed like a viable (re)action. I thought it was just a case of malingering post-partum depression counterbalanced by hits of speed. I was self-medicating while my son played with Legos and Luke Skywalker and Chewbacca action figures. He had no live-in father. Homelessness is about abandonment.

The year before I came to Minnesota and became an unwed mother, I packed to go away to college. I knew to bring four seasons' worth of clothes, my favorite books and LPs, especially Earth, Wind and Fire and Minnie Riperton—whose *Inside My Love* I'd planned to sing at the freshman talent show—my stereo, my portable black-and-white TV, my King James Bible, and a month's supply of Ritz crackers and Vienna sausage . . . just in case. Everything a college student needs. But what do you pack to become homeless? And it's winter. In Minnesota, where's it's nothing for the temperature to drop to 50 below zero. Homelessness is about cold weather fronts!

Someone once said no beautiful (read: skinny) woman would ever stay homeless for long. I, on the other hand, tried to fold my clothes as small as possible to shove inside a mountaineering backpack, no easy feat when you're a big girl and your clothes are made from yards of material and weigh a ton. My son's clothes were smaller and his sweaters were easier to fold. We were evicted during the winter. Homelessness is seasonal!

My parents offered to put us up in a hotel, motel, Holiday Inn, until we found a place to live. But I knew that if they did, the *four* of us would end up homeless: my son and I because of The Man, and my parents because they were middle class yet still living paycheck-to-paycheck, and the added expense would break their bank. Homelessness is about economics!

So I told them no hotel, motel, Holiday Inn, but was it fair to make my son a martyr, just so I could stand with those with nowhere to live? Jesus had said "Suffer the little children to come unto Me," and King had paraded children at the front of protest lines to which Malcolm strenuously protested. Was it fair to have my son sleep under a bridge? Homelessness is about lost childhoods!

I called every social service agency in St. Paul and finally got us beds at the Y on an all-men's floor. All men. How bad could that be? When I first went to Macalester College, I lived in a co-ed dorm, with men sleeping and making noisy love right next door. We'd shared the same showers. Would these guys be as cool as the stars of the basketball team? Or hapless as the nerds? Homelessness is about character!

Who would be among the homeless? Those with dreams and aspirations shot to hell? Or those with nightmares like daggers? Those who heard others speaking to them in parables and other metaphors, when no one was even there? The crazies who walked invisible dogs? Homelessness is about mixed messages!

My son and I were picked up by the driver of the homeless van and driven to the Y that housed the homeless. When I was a kid I used to take swimming lessons and modern jazz and African dance at the Y, but here was my kid ensconced on an all-men's homeless floor, living, eating, sleeping because there was no room for us niggers at our former inn. Wasn't my son precious, didn't he deserve frankincense and myrrh? At the Y men lined the floor like recruited soldiers, clung to the walls like cheap wallpaper. Men smoked cigarettes, one after another, incessantly . . . menthols or self-rolled ones with no filters. Or they smoked wacky-tabacky, Mary Jane, weed. Was my son getting a contact? I was! Homelessness is about inhaling noxious odors!

And then there were the penises. Penises, penises, everywhere, lined-up in front of stalls in the urine-saturated bathrooms. Penises, penises, everywhere hanging out in between unzipped pants. Penises, penises, everywhere standing up straight as swords, weapons used indiscriminately against homeless vaginas. I didn't trust homeless-at-the-Y penises around my three-year-old son, so I went to the bathroom with him, averting my eyes from penises streaming urine. I sat down to pee. Homelessness is about body functions!

I took my son to Head Start while I attended classes at the University of Minnesota, hoping my underarm Secret remained a secret. And in-between classes I called every newspaper editor and elected official I could get a hold of. I told them of my plight and my fear of penises versus fear of the under-bellies of bridges. Homelessness is about building bridges!

The newspapers were interested in my story. The local public broadcast-ing station was interested in my story and wanted to film a day in my life. They filmed me walking around the University of Minnesota. They filmed me with my son. The state legislature was interested in my story when I testified before them about race and child discrimination in housing. I gave utterance to the injustices of the rich and powerful, and those poseurs who wore their delegated power like sheep's clothing. Homelessness is about power or the facade thereof!

Not long after the documentary of my life aired, and the story of my plight had been published in a local newspaper, my son and I were given an apartment without the requirement of a security deposit and one month's rent upfront. It was full of donated furniture. Underneath a Christmas tree were gaily wrapped presents, including a coat and hat and gloves for me, and a snowsuit and hat and gloves for my son. He also got toys from Toys for Tots. Homelessness is about someone hearing your story and doing something about it!

Homelessness is about someone eventually caring!

Eventually . . . if you're lucky, or blessed, whichever comes first.

Smart Enough for Ford

At the St. Paul Ford testing facility, I sat next to a young, dark-skinned Black man with dreadlocks, who, I assume, heard the same thing about the tests that I had heard: they weren't hard. He said his job counselor told him to register for the assessments, that it was a good opportunity, the chance to have a job, at least until the end of the year, when the plant was scheduled to shut down after the last of its many reprieves.

Supposedly, there are no right or wrong answers. Of course, there are. There are ways in which we are supposed to behave at work—or ways in which we aren't supposed to behave. For example, it's not a good idea to hit someone or scream at him if you think he's doing a bad job. It seems like a no-brainer, but I know there are people who think acting in these ways is appropriate—or at least find themselves acting inappropriately, without pause.

I tried not to worry about taking the test, but I felt nervous. I had to do well, get through the questions efficiently. Although it wasn't rocket science, I didn't expect to do better than anyone else. I tried not to compare myself to the others, but I couldn't help it. While I was working on question 75, near the end of the first assessment, I glanced to my right to see the test booklet of the young man sitting next to me. He was on question 12.

We didn't know, at the onset, that we would be there for seven hours. Of course they knew, so they probably started us off with the easiest test that assessed workplace situational personality. So, how could it be that the young man was only on question 12?

Seeing this sent me spinning back to my grade school days in St. Cloud, visions of myself in versions of being on question 12, performing far behind all the white kids, who were supposed to do better, be better—and were, with few exceptions. They were well beyond question 12, while I performed at a grade level behind them in reading and still needed to be taught multiplication in the fourth grade. The teachers expected little of me.

They also expected little of my siblings, yet we now have four master's degrees among us. Both of my sisters had the same math teacher, who would never acknowledge their raised hands, requesting help or attempting to participate. Even one of my classmates suggested I take the easy science class, because there was no reason for me to take the hard one.

Although no degree was required for any Ford position, my master's degree really didn't give me any advantage in assembling cars, operating the machinery, no matter how complicated, or taking these standardized tests. I decided, however, do my best. To be a good student. I looked around the room at the other hundred or so hopefuls, who were corralled into this place to take the momentous first step toward glorious jobs in America's auto manufacturing industry. I worried that the young man sitting next to me was allowed to get to this point without learning to read and to decipher well enough to get beyond question 12 of an opinion survey in a half hour. His lack of preparation is a phenomenon that is too common in our society, and I live with unease when I consider why. I live with the grief that in too many ways, I'm still that young man.

I wondered if he had a child, as I did. Did he need the job as badly as I did? I felt anxious—for both of us and for many other Black people in the room. Despite the anonymity of the situation, I felt we experienced the same things, like the constant voice telling us that we weren't as qualified for these jobs or as worthy of having the opportunity even to apply.

In a not-so-distant past, it didn't matter if certain men had gone to high school, if they had done well in school, or if they had any training. It didn't matter because they were related to the men who had worked at Ford in previous generations. They didn't have to take a seven-hour test.

Today, people are no longer hired because a relative, church member, neighbor, or friend recommends them for employment. Now, folks are chosen at random from a pool of applicants who meet minimum requirements of reading and ciphering and have a non-dyslexic ability to fill in ovals on a test sheet. And the wages are far below what the UAW had secured for workers in the past. Now, instead of offering an opportunity to earn a great living, the company offers something just below a living wage for a family of two. You get ten-hour days, mandatory overtime, and wages that couldn't possibly pay for daycare, a house in one of the surrounding neighborhoods, a truck assembled by your own hands, and college tuition.

Today, the jobs are considered "good enough" for me. But am I "good enough" for the job? I have lived much of my life hearing explicitly and implicitly, through the persistent drone of negative propaganda, that I was not as good as my white counterparts. My adult life mirrored school, where it seemed predetermined that I wouldn't perform as well in reading or in math, or in anything else in which the white kids were proficient. The pattern repeated itself in the lives of my siblings. It also repeated itself in the lives of other Black kids in other places with predictability. Now it's imprinted on my mind.

Daily, I work to leave that pattern in old fabric bins of society. This was the work I needed to do before I sat down to take the Ford test. Someone told me that it would be easy, as if the only requirement was functional literacy, as if putting together cars still required little more than an eighth-grade education. But what if I fit the pattern of failure, after trying so hard all these years to not fit into it? In spite of my lingering anxiety, I got through the math test, while others did not. I did not complain or admit to them that one of the tests was really difficult. I filled in the ovals, pretending that I didn't care.

After waiting weeks for notification, a few months before the plant's shuttering, I received a letter, saying:

> You recently participated in a testing session as a requirement for consideration for hourly employment at the Twin Cities Assembly Plant of the Ford Motor Company. Thank you for your participation and interest in employment with Ford. Based on your test results, you have been accepted as a candidate for employment.
>
> Congratulations!

You can guess that my enthusiasm was quite high in learning that, according to their standards, I was smart enough to put together small trucks. To work in manufacturing, the company requires a greater mental capacity today than it did a generation ago. Still, I wasn't too impressed with myself.

After so many reprieves, the Ford plant's life is over. The last Ranger and Mazda pickup trucks have rolled off the assembly line. Whatever becomes of the space in Highland Park does not promise the magnificence of the great industrial age upon which much of America was built.

As for me, although I was considered smart enough for Ford, I didn't receive a call to that unlikely profession.

Zombies, by Andre Lord

Note & Disclaimer: Though this is addressed to a specific individual, it is for all thinking beings. And though Sarah is a real character, she represents a wide variety of colored folk. Additionally, this rant was written immediately after the incident it describes and thereby features profanity, as it serves to document my thoughts precisely as they occurred.

Dear Sarah,

What started out as a happy, glorious adventure to find the best books as a part of my graduation gift to you has turned into a quest for justice. Look how powerful you are, forcing hellful situations from afar. Allow me to expand upon my experience:

I enter Borders Bookstore, searching for two books: *The Great Gatsby*, by F. Scott Fitzgerald; and *Zami: A New Spelling of My Name—A Biomythography*, by Audre Lorde. At first, I'm having difficulty finding anything, because I can't understand the store's alphabetic system. Soon, though, I catch on to the logic. BAM! Found Mr. Gatsby and all his drunken American dreams turned nightmares. BAM! Found *Freedom*, by Jonathan Franzen, a book I did not intend to purchase but had heard such good things about that I wanted to read it for myself. Moving forward, I spot *To Kill a Mockingbird*, by Harper Lee. The cover, now in four different styles, has changed so drastically. They're all beautiful! I think of getting it for you, but decide against it because it is not the book I want you to have. I set out to carefully search, again. A. B. C. D. E. F. G. H. I. J. K. L. . . . ? She should be right here. Maybe I don't understand this system, after all. I travel back to the first bookcase, searching for *K* and *M* because *L* will be between them. I locate *K*, I spot *M* . . . ah, there's *L*! Still, she's not there. I start over: A. B. C. D. E. F. G. H. I. J. K. L. . . . ? What the fuck? Okay, this section is *Literature*. There's the *Poetry* section; maybe she's there. Here's a collection of European poets, there goes Shakespeare, Oscar Wilde, Pablo Naruda—I pick his collection up, sure that you'll enjoy it. I quickly put it down. Again, it's not what I came for.

At last, I spot a Black sales associate, or whatever they call their team at

Borders. Confident I have located an ally, I approach her kiosk. *"Excuse me,"* I say, *"can you please help me find Audre Lorde?"*

The pause makes me so uncomfortable I could slap myself or her, depending. She smiles, I feel saved. "Um . . . who?"

"Audre Lorde," I repeat more sternly.

"Like, who is she?"

I am attempting to keep my calm at this point. Not sure how to answer such a stupid question because I am, after all, in a fucking bookstore, I reply, *"She's a writer."*

"Oh," she says uninterested, "is that A-u-d-r-e-y?"

"No," I smile falsely, *"That's A-u-d-r-e."*

She moves her fingers in a way that looks like typing, but she was so withdrawn that I could no longer trust her, especially after she looked up at me, smiling as she was trained to, and replied, "We don't have her. Like, what type of writer is she?"

I knew what she wanted me to say; but I, so desperately, wanted to refrain from saying it. *I shouldn't have to,* I screamed inside my head! But I also, so desperately, wanted you to have this book, Sarah. I gave in, *"She's an African-American writer."*

Sure that she could help me then, she points her finger upward, "We have an African-American fiction section upstairs," she tells me so matter-of-factly.

I laugh. *"You don't have her at all, though?"*

She looks at me in that "What-did-I-just-say?" way, but puts on her best fake smile again and says, "No, ma'am."

I laugh hysterically, wanting to educate her, but knowing I had no place. *"Okay,"* I say sadly, walking away.

Maybe she's new, I reason with me. So, I locate another employee. *"Hey, can you help me find Audre Lorde?"*

He smiles, nervously. "I don't know. Who is that?"

I get to the point faster; I'm running late and really want to make it to your graduation party on time. *"She's an African-American writer,"* I exclaim bluntly.

"We have a section upstairs, on the back wall," he demonstrates with his hands. "Maybe you can find what you're looking for there." He laughs and starts to step backward, forcing me not to have any more questions.

Ah, what the hell. Sure, yeah, okay, I'll go upstairs. I tread the stairs. Locate the African-American section. *Hello, Sista Souljah; Hello, Eric Jerome Dickey; Zane, you're here, too, girl? What up, K'waan? No Lorde, good lord. Ah! Biographical! Of course,* Zami *will be there.* Zami *is not there. There is* a woman, though, helping a man, and she does seem more knowledgeable than the other two. I ask for her assistance, the same as I had done prior. She nods her head, making me confident she understands me. "Let's go look at the computer database." I'd already been through that but I was open to double-checking. "So," she says, "You're looking for *Zombies* by Andre Lord?"

I couldn't help myself, the blood boiled like water in old-fashioned heaters. "*What?! No! I'm looking for Zami by Audre Lorde!*"

She recovers from her embarrassment, gets the correct info from me, and does the search. "Looks like we're all out of that one." *Of that one*, I think, *Whew! That's a relief to know that, at least, they once had it.* She proceeds to do a search to see if it can be located elsewhere, "None of our other bookstores have it." *Ah, so they never had it.* "We can order it," she assures me, "It . . ."

"Hey, are you helping her?" a male voice chimes in. My mouth opens. Was *that* even a question? She was looking directly at me, in the middle of conversation! Yes, fool, she is helping my wide-hipped, big butt, nappy headed, chocolate-brown self. *We's read books, too!*

I did have a proud moment—when that bookseller simply looked at the man, said, "Er. Yes?" and quickly returned her attention to me. He did not catch himself, though, as he replied, "Oh, well, I need help." She ignores him. Thank you, ally. She goes on, "It would take three to eight business days." I smile sincerely, "I don't have that time, I'll go elsewhere. Thank you." I put down the other two books I had—if I could not purchase all at the same store, I would purchase none.

I got in my car, ready to cry, but determined to make it to you, Sarah, with *Zami* in hand. I started driving to Barnes & Noble, but figured I'd better call ahead. I did. I asked the woman to do a search. She asked me for the title. I replied, *Zami*—to which she said, "Oh! *A New Spelling of My Name*, or something like that, right?" I cried, *Yes!* She knew the author and did the search, "We don't have it, but you know who might?" She went on to tell me of a few bookstores that may carry the book and, even in my disappointment, I could appreciate that.

I do not have the book, Sarah. I am not done searching, either. I could give you my copy, but there is no justice in that. You will not see me until it is in my hands. When I do find it, I will be purchasing two copies: one for you and one for the Black bookseller at Borders Bookstore in St. Paul's Midway Shopping Center. I am sorry, Sarah, that our faces and histories cannot *simply* count as literature. I am sorry that we have to have our own section and books that "represent" us within those sections are scarce. I am sorry we are reduced to erotica and thug life. I am sorry that you don't yet have a new spelling of your name, or mine. I am sorry we cannot celebrate us, as mere *Americans*. I'm sorry that our literature doesn't count as such, especially if it's about blackness *and* gayness. And I'm sorry I'm not there to celebrate *you*, graduating from college. How badly, Sarah, I want to burn a copy of the *Catcher in the Rye* in front of Borders Bookstore and leave a note, requesting that they place its remains in the *Burnt Books* section.

Sabotage

When the boys were little, my family was the victim of a terrorist attack in North Minneapolis. Not many people know this—it was too painful at the time. After years of thought, I've decided to lay the blame at the feet of the Television Avenger, so the healing can begin.

One morning our four-year-old discovered to his horror that some miscreant had cut the plug off the power cord of our television. Having two freelance parents at home, he and his brother took it in stride and turned to my wife and me for entertainment.

My wife said, "Did you cut the cord to the television?"

"I'm shocked that you think me capable of such a thing," I said. "Children need exposure to as many marketing efforts as possible, and I'm suitably alarmed. Joe alone will miss upward of a jillion commercials a day. When he gets those multiple-choice questionnaires from people who would like nothing better than for him to mortgage the two of us in order to buy out their warehouse, he'll fall short. In the part about major appliances, his score will suffer. He will have no large purchases planned for the next three, six, or twelve months," I replied.

"You cut it! I knew it!"

"I think it's the Fifth Amendment. 'Take the Fifth,' is what I've heard. Or maybe 'stand on the Fifth.' So that's what I'm doing, taking or standing on the Fifth Amendment to the Constitution of this great nation."

"Did you?"

"Your efforts to force a confession from me will avail you nothing. This isn't some place where a person can go to jail without evidence of wrongdoing. Don't forget, I could drag this out for years in the courts; by then, that television will have pooped out anyway." This last was a telling point.

"This is very bad! Why would you just do that without discussing it?"

Because we'd still be discussing it. That's what I was thinking. What I said was, "As Bill Clinton said in some context or other, I'm sure you won't find any evidence against me. And as the alpha male here I feel keenly that I have failed you all. Our perimeter has been breached. My scent marking has meant nothing. Likewise leaving my stuff all over."

"Where is the plug?"

"What plug would that be, dear?"

"Never mind! I'll fix it myself!"

And she did.

When I got back after my meeting, the boys greeted me with great excitement, because the replacement plug had set off the smoke alarm. I gave up, but even as I trimmed off the burned insulation and prepared to swallow my principles whole, I felt in my bones that our television would never be safe again. We must be ceaselessly vigilant, lest we forget that the American Dream is mostly shopping.

On Performing "Berlitz"

(or Been Around the Mini-Apple, the Big Apple and the World)

> *This is not a language course. It is a simple way to learn these phrases . . .*

On "Berlitz"

"Berlitz" was commissioned by the Organization of Women Writers of Africa for their Yari Yari Pamberi: Black Women Dissecting Globalization conference in October 2004. It was my first solo performance art work in New York City; the first time I got flown in, paid, and put up in a hotel as an artist; the first time I got to do a workshop on performance art as part of an international conference; and, although the two remain very linked, the first time I really led with a performance artist identity, as opposed to a poet one.

"Berlitz" was also the only performance work of my early oeuvre to address hip hop head on, something that seemed required for a piece about Black women and globalization. No matter where I went in this whole wide world, moving images of half-naked, fake-haired, glazed-eyed Black women in hip hop videos had already preceded me. I remember hanging out with new friends in Europe while a muted video in the background showed a close up of a Black woman's ass shaking. I and the woman to whom that ass belonged were the only two Black women in the bar. (Been around the world, indeed.)

Debates about hip hop and feminism are quite old hat now. And it's clear that Black women's relationships to and in hip hop are quite complex. As are our relationships to sexuality, exhibitionism, and money. Even then, the intention of "Berlitz" was not to demonize women who listen to, love, or appear in hip hop videos. It was to embody and contrast different figures of Black women: the woman carrying the box on her head, the woman rummaging through the rag pile, the woman opening a huge birthday surprise full of festive balloons, the woman throwing down dancing by herself, the woman scantily clad, gyrating stiffly in a hip hop video. All of these figures raise questions about Black women's objectification through global capitalism. Archetypes, stereotypes, global realities. How does one person's burden become another's pleasure (and vice versa)? As Black women, what would be our new *lingua franca?*

Although "Berlitz" was chock full of images and ideas—I played language lesson tapes in Haitian Kreyòl and French, I recited a letter to my Haitian grandmother in Swedish, I offered an original poem name-checking powerful Black women writers and artists—the thing most people remember is the striptease. I wanted to contrast the way a Black woman's body could feel to herself, dancing joyfully without many clothes, to the way a Black woman could look objectified in the same attire in a different (global) context.

Interestingly, as I was working on the striptease part of the show, I had no shame or concern about my body at all. When did that happen? My colleague, psychologist Linda Siemanski, told me that American women have something like a 96 percent dissatisfaction rate with their bodies. Whether they're thin or fat, tall or short—their normal state is to believe that something is wrong with them. In fact, a mark of assimilation for immigrant women is their rising rate of body dissatisfaction. More than trying to fight body dissatisfaction, somehow I was overcoming it without thinking about it. Making and doing "Berlitz," I wasn't feeling bad about my body. Not for the first or last time, I took off my shirt and pants in front of the audience. This time, I put on high heels, pretended to be vacant, gyrated, and found myself trapped in a box. Literal, perhaps. But evocative. The materialization of my own brown flesh.

Berlitz

Sounds of Haitian Kreyòl enter the space from a Kreyòl language tape.

> *Leson 4* Lesson 4 Dialogue

A Black woman walks in the back door, wearing stretchy black pants and an old red t-shirt that says HAITI. She is carrying a very large brown cardboard box on her head.

Listen. The tape says in English.
Gaby and Tomas meet on the way to Port-au-Prince.

O Gaby. S'ak pase?

> *et ou-mem?*

The Black woman walks into the space from the left side of the audience, turns the corner to stand still before them, a large box on her head.

M'ap kenbe. Et ou-mem?

Et moun-yo ?

She kneels on one knee, sets the box down before her with care.

Now repeat the dialogue.

Gaby. Sak pase?
Gaby O Gaby
Gaby sak pase?
et ou mem ?
ou kenbe ?
m'ap m'ap kenbe
et moun-yo?

She runs away from the box. Smiles at the audience.
Picks up a striped mesh market bag, sets it down, rummages through it.
A few tiny balloons, not fully inflated, pop or float out of the bag like
  bubbles.
She grabs the bag from its bottom, holds it up, and pours
the entire contents over her head. A cascade of balloons falls over her head.
Some have never been inflated. Some look deflated.
Some seem to hold just a few breaths, tied off into small balls.
Her head and face are completely covered by multi-colored plastic.
She stands for a minute with the market bag over her head,
obscuring her face. Her arms are stretched up, her palms open.
She bends down, knocks the bag off her head and throws
balloons up in the air. It is either a celebration or chaos or both.
She gets down on her knees, begins searching through the rubbish pile.

The perky sound of a French accordion signals a change.
She pops up, begins to smile and dances with arms akimbo.
Runs to the big brown box that she has carried on her head.
Presses her arms to her heart, cocks her head, and smiles
with her mouth closed to the audience. For me? She seems to ask.
She saunters up to the box, eyes glittery with excitement.

This is not a language course. It is a simple way to learn
these phrases designed with simple effort and in a short time.
It is for those who have not the time or inclination to study the language.
This is Marjory Powell. I will speak each phrase in English.
The other voice you hear will give a French translation.

She opens the box and vibrant, fulsome, fully inflated balloons
pop out of the box. She burrows through the box, using handfuls
to pull out more and more of them.
Such celebration. Such joy. Such richesse.
Oh no—in her hurry to get to the bottom of the box, one of the balloons
    pops.
It's a shame. But there's always more.
She will speak each French phrase twice.
What is at the bottom of the box?
The Black woman finds a record with images of houses
from a different city. The title of the record: "Swedish for Travelers."

Now to begin. Here are some expressions you will use most often.

The Black woman walks with her present to stand between the dead
balloons and the now empty box with juicy balloons around her feet.

Can you speak English?
Parlez-vous anglais?

The Black woman starts to sing:
HAPPY BIRTHDAY TO ME /
HAPPY BIRTHDAY TO ME /
HAPPY BIRTHDAY DEAR GABBY /
HAPPY BIRTHDAY TO ME
Her singing drowns out the language tape.

She says: October 12 was my thirtieth birthday.
Yaaaaaay! she jumps and screams.
October 12 is Columbus Day.
Boooooooooooo. She pulls her arms down and shuffles herself backwards.

The first time I went to Haiti, my Uncle's friend
CURSED THE DAY COLUMBUS WAS BORN.

(She covers her face with her hands.)
Good Morning. Bon jour.

Well, I do like McDonald's cheeseburgers,
but I have concerns for the rainforest.
Jesus saves. (She presses her fist to her heart and raises it up over her
    head.)
In honor of this auspicious occasion, I decided to write my
grandmother a letter. Well, because my father never taught me
his mother's language, I decided to do something a little different.
You see, I've been to Paris, New York, San Francisco, LA, Barcelona,
Sienna, Geneva, Hamburg (on the way to Hanover), Pisa (for a half an
    hour),
to see the leaning tower. I've been to Santo Domingo, Port-au-Prince,
Port of Spain. Noooo, Nooo, (hands on hips) I've never been to Dakar.

I decided to write my grandmother's letter in Swedish.
Do any of you speak Swedish? Anybody?
Well, neither do I.

From the record sleeve which says "Swedish for Travelers,"
she pulls out a small 45. With one hand she holds it, and with the other,
she uses her finger as a needle to turn it around.
She begins to speak Swedish.
The test travel phrases in French still play in the background.
She pauses and says in English:
I had more to say, but I just didn't have the vocabulary.
She kisses the record sleeve that says "Swedish for Travelers"
and says, Ciao Mémé.

The record changes. We hear The Last Poets, chanting
"New York New York—The Big Apple!
New York New York—The Big Apple!"

She screams:
WE LOVE YOU STOCKHOLM!!!!!!
You feel me.
She snaps her fingers several times.
She becomes the blaxploitation diva.
I got a new one for you. I'm gonna take this one worldwide.

My exotic erotic Black body. (*intoned in the characteristic spoken word style.*)
At the Yari Yari Yari Yari. Yaaaaari.

Clichés.
Lost teeth kingdoms. Clichés.
She picks up a yellow balloon. Places it in her mouth.
Blows it up with air. Lets it fly away from her mouth.
She says: What's really at the bottom of the ocean floor?
All the languages of the world.
What's really at the bottom?
She picks up a yellow balloon. Places it in her mouth.
Blows it up with air. Says with it in her mouth.
~~of the ocean floor?~~ (sounds like *hrg hzm rugyh mrunn*)

What's really at the bottom of the ocean floor?
She blows up a pink balloon spits it out.
Fela's "Chop & Destroy" starts to play.
She begins to dance. Enjoys the tempo of the music.
She shimmies and struts, gives herself an embrace,
plays peek-a-boo with her top.

The striptease begins.
She pulls off her red Haiti t-shirt to reveal a black bra.
She rolls down her stretchy black pants to reveal black underpants.
She walks over to the brown box, discovers black kitten heels
bedecked with purplish blue metallic paillettes.
To the tempo of the music, she puts on each shoe.
At the end of the song, her arms are around herself in embrace.

A new song starts.
"Been Around the World" featuring The Notorious B.I.G. & Mase.
She goes over, pulls high-heeled shoes out the box,
puts them on. She steps into the box and pretends to be a video ho.
She dances with complete mechanical movements as if in a hip hop
    video.
She leans over the side of the box, presses her hands on the ground,
and begins to push her body up and down the side of the box.
She grinds. (The box rips).

She leans over, holding the edges of the box.
She dips her breasts low. She sashays her behind both ways.
She pulls the box close, lifts it up over her head
Slowly, surely she lowers it down over her body.
Until she is nothing left but a box gobbling up brown legs and high heels.

Been around the world and I I I
And we been playa hated [say what?]
I don't know and I don't know why
Why they want us faded [ahuh ahuh]
I don't know why they hate us [yeah]
Is it our ladies? [uh-huh]
Wanna drive Mercedes
Baby Baby Baby

The box engulfs her completely.

André Prévin & Kathleen Battle's "I Am Not Seaworthy" begins to play.
The Black woman pokes her head from the crack in the box.
She stands and says:

WHAT THE FUCK WAS THAT?!
Nigger you messed up my hair.
She picks up her clothes from the floor.
She grabs a couple balloons.

You know today, she says. Today is my birthday.
Dammit. And I was born in the Congo.
You know that shit. And Nefertiti was my first baby.
And Hannibal Lector was my son.
And he gave me an elephant.

She is picking up balloons one by one and throwing them
back in the box. She pops a few in her hands as she speaks.
And I blew my nose. And there was oil in the Arab world.

She takes hold of the box and drags it across the space.
She shakes her head and is speaking but not real words.
Just that ageless, timeless sound of a Black woman fussing.

She stops dragging the box, would be standing still if she weren't shaking.
Her head, body, mouth shaking. The clothes in her hands shaking.

Slowly she begins to relax.
Pulls her pants back on.
Pulls on her shirt.

As she delivers the next monologue—she passes to the audience
some of the small dead or partially inflated balloons.

they say we are dying. condoleeza rice.
will die soon. they say/ we are flourishing. the gap
between black men and black women / is the widest
it's ever been. newsweek. is this worldwide?
do black men still want us? essence.
if you have to ask you already know. my mother.
lick and blow. janine antoni. mouth. feathers.
sequins and horns. jayne cortez. ectoplasm
boogaloo. wanda coleman. if this were papyrus
what lacunae what fragments. abbey lincoln
picking up the tiny shards of glass. nothin but a man.
concrete poems in call numbers. a slave ship. a sugar cube.
all the scientists find. blues. a kente cap for sale.
a circling song. nawaal el saadawi.
a song I learned as a girl. *balloons balloons.*
come and buy my pretty balloons.
six women in a hot tub.
what do they say? rosamond s. king.
blood and salt. high stepping body.
all the languages.
all the languages
all the languages
in the world.

She takes a red balloon, puts it in her mouth, and blows,
holding its full body attached to her lips.

[*FIN.*]

On Audience

"Berlitz" premiered in New York, but was made in Minnesota. I built it in Patrick's Cabaret, the historic live art space in Minneapolis, which had no mirror (Deborah Hay would be proud), and I didn't use a video camera. Working on instinct, with key images and ideas in my mind, I tried to use my gut more than my looks. With "Berlitz," I was learning how to work on my own. How to go alone into a space, wake up the room (as Lois Weaver would say), and materialize something from thin air.

Because the turnaround time between my arrival in the Big Apple and my actual performance was short, I decided to stage a Minnesota run-through at Patrick's. Around twenty people showed up, friends and colleagues from my workplace. My dear friend and frequent artistic collaborator Miré Regulus was there (and perhaps another woman of color?), but the audience was pretty racially homogenous and overwhelmingly white. This was nothing new for me in Minnesota. Most of my work had been performed before majority white audiences, and I'd received diverse feedback from people who phenotypically seemed the same. Not all white folks are the same. And race is not the only, and in many cases not the most important, prism of identity.

Still, the cultural specificity of the particular white Minnesota audience that afternoon did not jibe with "Berlitz." My jokes were met with stony silence. My tongue-in-cheek spoof of nikki giovanni's "ego-tripping" received quizzical looks. When I talked about Abbey Lincoln or Wanda Coleman, the audience looked completely at a loss. And people seemed embarrassed for me during my striptease and hip hop transformation. At the end of the piece, after letting go of a newly inflated balloon, clenched between my teeth, I stood there looking at the audience looking at me. Dead silence.

Dear Sweet Lord Jesus, I needed to show this piece in just a day or two in New York City. Was it so terrible, so oblique, so inscrutable that it would flop?

All of my pride and excitement at having been invited to create and present new work turned into panic, a feeling I associate more with the development of a new work than with the actual reception of it. Should I rework the piece completely? But how? And with what time? I considered my elements. The babel of languages. Competing mother tongues. The box on the head. The dead balloons. Live inflated ones. Deconstructed afrocentricity. Hip hop. These were all things I wanted to explore in the piece. Maybe it sucked. But it was what I had.

In New York, the afternoon of the performance, I was jittery. But looking into the crowd at all of the bright, shiny, accomplished Black women, something in me felt hopeful. As I performed the work, I could see the glisten in their eyes, hear *Uh huh* and *Lord*, the chuckles at my jokes that turned into warm chortles. The hooting and hollering when I did my striptease. The Yari Yari audience died laughing when I became the "video ho." They hung on every word of my last poem/monologue. And many of them, including the writer Sapphire (who wrote *Push*, which inspired the film *Precious Inspired by the Novel Push by Sapphire*), gave me a standing ovation. Carrie Mae Weems winked at me when it was over. Another woman came up and asked if I had ever performed the piece for the community, and even asked if I was interested in doing it a Boys & Girls Club where she worked.

So often people say that performance art is insular and oblique, and here she was saying that my work was positive and educational. Such is the power of audience. Maybe the work was insular and oblique, but she felt empowered to understand. And so she embraced it.

Actors, dancers, performers of all kinds can all attest to the ways that audiences can change a work. Even if the steps, the lines, the actions are the same, the people in the room are different, which makes the way that you are understood among those people different. And particularly if you—your body in time and space—are the main material of the work, then this makes the work different. This raises an important point for performance art history, circulation and reception. To understand what happened, we have to think not just of who the performer is and what she did, but also who was in the audience, what was their context, and how the work resonated with their cultural references. For us as artists, we have to consider the audience relative to our intentions and our expectations about feedback and response. This doesn't mean that we should cater to the audience, per se. Or that we should dismiss audiences different from us in terms of their capacity to relate. It merely means that we should take into account the specificity of audiences in relation to the specific meaning generated by a work performed before them.

I don't believe that my performance in Minnesota was of substantially lower quality than the one I did in New York. But if I did manage to embody "Berlitz" more fully at Yari Yari, it was because of the rich, juicy, diverse, specific bodies of the Black women in the audience. Despite the non-linear, layered, abstract quality of the form, their understanding of my context and their familiarity with cultural representations of Black women's bodies allowed them access to my performance art work that my initial Minnesota audience lacked. This is not to say that all Minnesota audiences are the same or that multicultural Minnesota audiences don't exist. Rather, this experience simply highlighted to me, through stark contrast, the impact of audience: the need to find and claim people wherever we are—or elsewhere—to access the layers of our work. The affirmations of my work at Yari Yari spurred me on and let me know that the Black women in the audience were on my side. Wherever I am, I aim to be on theirs.

Liberia

1
Independent once
the waves breaking on shore were our voices

we were only a day's journey from ourselves
now our villages burn
    memories like scarred skin
    a nation waiting to be reborn

2
we lived here
before sunrise
among Kru
among Gio
Grebo, Gola
among Mano

we listened to the night
secrets gathered in circles
of women. meetings of Poro.

the market our journey
from kin to tribe
we returned home
with the sum of our dreams

before the Americos

3
we came running from
and running to Freedom
the best in ourselves

we came to bury haunted dreams
in the wide sea
plant hunted dreams
in our mother's soil
we came with prodigal returns
with whip-scarred needs
and empty promises
afraid of how the mirror might reflect
ourselves back to ourselves
we came longing for home
with black dreams
sung by poets *black*
like the depths
of my Africa

O Africa
my Africa
i braved the sea again
to return to you
to stand on sacred soil
land of my birth
to feel equatorial sun
catch echoes of childhood
    songs echoing the drum
of my heartbeat

    4
coming home is never easy
it is never the way
you remembered
the house creaks
shards of memories
cut bare feet
walking before dawn

    5
everything seems smaller
now

that tree which once touched the sky

roots grew beneath
cassava and rice fields
markets, dark rivers shaping
their way to the sea

roots shoulder the feet of children
racing between huts
where long black women
shuttle rice with songs for giving

there, fire kindled for food

roots shoulder memory and spirit
and roads lead everywhere
and simply Home.

Job

The Lord let me know early in the day
trouble was coming when He sent a woman
toward me in a tight dress, snapping gum
and working her hips hard. He turned
her head to the right just as I moved close enough
to say hello. She wasn't all that fine,
but I sure could have used a different start to my day.
Seven AM and no love.
The Lord followed up fast with a black man
in a red, double-breasted suit and shoes
with monkstraps. Their high shine sent the sunlight
straight into my eyes, blinding me. The dog
patrolling the front yard where I passed them
tried to run me away from his fence, snarling.
I stared at God's signs. Here's what you can't have:
A regular woman, nice clothes, peace.
My hand in my pocket, fingering change.

Spoken

Mary

My one blood-aunt was kicked out of the house.
My grandfather saw how pretty she was
and guessed she was fast. It kept him up nights.
Worried about that girl. She went after trouble
like it was money and she needed some.
Like there wasn't any at home.
                              He might
Have laughed if it wasn't his family
wrecking his sleep, giving every mouth
in town something to chew on. His own girl.
Her name, the same as his mother's name, Mary.

Bad

bad /baed/ *adj., n.,* (Origin: [Euro] American Culture), *The bad nigger:*
1 defective, inadequate, inferior. 2 evil, wicked. 3 disobedient, naughty ("on
the <u>back</u> seat"—under the censure of the church for bad behavior, such as
"crossing his feet"). 4 disagreeable, disturbing, unpleasant. 5 serious, severe
(of an unwelcoming thing). 6 invalid, worthless.

7a *US sl. adj.* good, excellent, incommensurable, outstanding (Origin: the
linguistic manifestation of the new-world African revolt against Euro-
American cultural, economic, mental, physical, political, social, and spiritual annihilation) Dat bad boy [*bad nigga*] ain nothin nice: Dr. Kenneth
Clark; Nat King Cole; Quincy Jones; Wynton Marsalis; Thurgood Mar-
shall; Oscar Micheaux; Barack Obama; Dr. Neil deGrasse Tyson; Richard
Wright

Comparative adj. 7b (**badder**) Ain nobody got badder skillz than:
Johnny Cochrane; John Coltrane; Jimmy Hendricks; Michael Jackson;
Kasi Lemmons; Sidney Poitier; Ntozake Shange; Anna Deavere Smith;
Kara Walker

superlative adj. 7c (**baddest**) off de chain: Mary McLeod Bethune; Angela
Davis; Frederick Douglass; W. E. B. Dubois; Toni Morrison; W. Purvis
(Inventor: fountain pen); Prince; Oprah Winfrey; Stevie Wonder

badass /baedaes/ *adj. & n.* (also **bad-ass**) formidable:
a Dat's a bad-ass sista right dere: Marian Anderson; Nikky Finney; bell
hooks; Zora Neale Hurston; Mahalia Jackson; Patti LaBelle; Audre Lorde;
Meshell Ndegeocello; Suzan-Lori Parks

b controversial folk figures: Dolemite; Frankie; Stagolee

c rebels: Charles Deslandes; Gabriel Prosser; Harriet Tubman

d revolutionaries: Malcolm, Martin, Medgar

e aesthetics: brown (all variations of the hue; sugar); bountiful (breasts, buttocks, hips, lips, and thighs); braids (all natural hair, including afros, corn rolls, dreadlocks, twists); beads (and cowrie shells); ballet (Dance Theatre of Harlem); black (consciousness); black folks bangin and beauteous in all dey glory.

Inland Sea

Nearly everyone
you meet
in Minnesota
goes up to the lake
up to the shore
(white people that is)
Black people go to Chicago
Cleveland Detroit Gary
     down home
Native American people are home
        within
           without
Many Southeast Asian brothers
dream of home
       often
          dying
             in their sleep
I go with them
       up to the lake
         to the shore
       to Chicago
         Detroit
             down home
     within
       without
          dreaming
           of
           home

Preston's Dream: Version No. 1

Preston came over one Saturday afternoon
with his usual six-pack of Miller
and armful of records. He was in a quiet
pensive mood—almost doleful.
My father caught on and started playing
some Billie Holiday.
"How'd you know I was thinkin'
about Billie?" Preston asked.
"I don't know," my dad said. "A hunch, I guess."
They listened to
Billie's version of *The Way You Look Tonight*.
Billie's version of *Pennies from Heaven*.
Billie's version of *I'll Never Be the Same*.
Finally, Preston said,
"These are all Billie's songs, you know.
She coulda written 'em herself.
In fact, I think she just took 'em
Hokey and corny as they are
'cause nobody wanted 'em anymore.
Like in slavery days, the slaves
gettin' pigs' ears, snouts, feet, and guts
—all the pieces
the massa felt beneath him to eat—
and makin' 'em into delicacies.
She mined songs,
Got the diamonds in 'em that
Nobody cared for or knew how to get.
She got it.
Re-created these songs into her own.
She adopted them.
They were all her children,
and they called her Mama.
Because she was."

My father drank a little beer and smiled.
Billie was singing *Laughing at Life*.
Preston continued.
"I had the strangest dream last night.
I was in this small Midwestern town, all white,
on the Fourth of July. It was sunny,
and a warm breeze blew the flags aloft.
I was watchin' the parade go down Main Street,
bands playin' *Stars and Stripes Forever*
and floats of all kinds advertisin'
the Jaycees and historical society
and people all dressed up in buckskin and Indian outfits.
I was gettin' nervous
'cause I was the only spot in the crowd,
when here comes the last float in line—
I hear Teddy Wilson playing the opening of
I Can't Give You Anything But Love.
And there
on a float made of white and yellow gardenias
—Billie, in her prime—
big and beautiful and leanin' and singin'
into one of those old-fashioned microphones.
and Prez was there, too—pork-pie hat
and shades and cream-white suit
and Little Jazz Roy Eldridge and Joe Jones
and Walter Page and Ram Rameriz! All of 'em!
I couldn't believe my eyes!
I said to a woman holdin'
a big blond baby boy high
over her head and
bouncin' in time to the music
What year is it? I thought
They're all dead—but there they are!
She didn't say anything,
just nodded and smiled
and kept time to the music.
Then I saw Billie turn as she passed us
and smile at the baby
and throw a white gardenia to the mother.
By this time I was cryin' and wanted to catch up—

the float had almost disappeared down the street,
the crowds were too thick,
I couldn't get through.
Then an old toothless farmer in dirty coveralls
put his hand on my shoulder and said
They're gone now,
But they'll be back next Fourth.
You be sure to come back, son,
you're more than welcome here.
I shook his hand, so dirty and gnarled
And hard from heavy farm work.
I said I would, I *will*—
And then I woke up. My heart was poundin'.
I wondered how I could get back, but it was only a dream."
Billie was singing *Why Was I Born?*
"Jesus, Preston, that was some dream."
"James, it was like it was real.
Prez, Billie, Joe, Teddy
—all of 'em alive—
playin' in that hick town somewhere
in the middle of nowhere
on the Fourth of July."

To Be Black in America

I remember rushing home on Friday nights to see "The Brady Bunch" and "The Partridge Family" on ABC-TV, followed by "The Odd Couple" and "Love, American Style." This is the Black experience in America.

I remember having two portraits on the walls in my childhood home, one of Martin Luther King, Jr. and the other of JFK. This is the Black experience in America.

I remember, as a boy, dancing close with shapely teenage girls at house parties in dark basements over at my friends' mom's house. This is the Black experience in America.

I remember the first time that I was called a nigger. This is the Black experience in America.

I remember summer barbecues with great music and all of your relatives and friends singing, laughing and joking. This is the Black experience in America.

I remember too many of my male friends gunned down in the streets and knifed at parties before they were old enough to grow facial hair. This is the Black experience in America.

I remember my father telling me, "You're not like them. Our people came over in slave ships." This is the Black experience in America.

I remember being told that we have two cultures and speak two languages. This is the Black experience in America.

I remember feeling conflicted whenever I had to stand for the National Anthem or the Pledge of Allegiance. This is the Black experience in America.

I remember enlisting and serving proudly in the United States Army, ready to die for God and country. This is the Black experience in America.

I remember my first white friend. This is the Black experience in America.

I remember torn-up textbooks, broken lockers, and crowded classrooms. This is the Black experience in America.

I remember "family summer vacations" being day trips or taking car rides "out there" to see how white people lived and going to day camp at urban recreation centers, while white classmates spoke of going to Disneyland

and meeting new friends at overnight camp while living in many of those big houses that I peered at from car windows, with my parents, with my bare legs sticking to hot vinyl car seats. This is the Black experience in America.

I remember the Black Panthers walking proud through the neighborhood dressed in black leather. This is the Black experience in America.

I remember going to church all day Sunday, starting with Sunday school and ending with a fried chicken dinner at home. This is the Black experience in America.

I remember "American Bandstand" on Saturdays. This is the Black experience in America.

I remember hearing the beginning of hip-hop at a block party when I was a senior in high school jammin' to the clean beats of the Sugarhill Gang's "Rapper's Delight." This is the Black experience in America.

I remember being told by friends, family and society that I had limits. This is the Black experience in America.

I remember rejecting all of that and learning that improvisation is my friend. This is also the Black experience in America.

To be Black in America means always being suspect or being open to the possibility of being suspect. To be Black means frequently having to edit your comments out of fear of offending white America. The same statement articulated by a white person may be deemed assertive—while coming out of a Black mouth, it becomes aggressive. And one must keep in mind that Black success in this society is commensurate with one's ability to make white folks feel comfortable.

The most unbelievable thing to come out of the Rev. Jeremiah Wright incident was that so many white people could be so surprised at the level of anger that could come out of a Black individual. Really? Are whites actually surprised that there is anger in the Black community? Why wouldn't there be? The Black existence in America is a tragic, wonderful, heroic, bitter struggle originally commenced by a horrific forced trans-Atlantic voyage. Can anyone with a reasonable mind not think that a people with our history in these United States might not feel a bit of anger?

I think that the original emotion that Blacks felt vis-à-vis America was hurt. Hurt that we could possibly be in a place where we are so often viewed as a nuisance in the least and with contempt in the worst. And those Blacks who have the time, education, and privilege try to find some way to reconcile conflicting love/hate emotions that are traced back to our origins on these shores.

Anger is only one emotion to derive from the mother emotion of hurt.

Some other derivative emotions are depression, sorrow, self-pity. Many African-Americans have used these emotions as a springboard to succeed against all odds. Others tend to get trapped in despair and follow a journey to destruction borne from the pathology of a system that kicks ass and takes names, caring nothing for the souls that it leaves behind.

I grew up in the Baptist Church. Most Black preachers that I've ever known have a seed of anger within them. It was a combination of this anger and a need to mentally reconcile their societal living conditions that many times led them to Christianity. Religion became a source of comfort, solace, and focus. The most powerful Jesus narrative, for me, is that which illustrates him as a political revolutionary.

The church was also a place where many of these preachers could enjoy control and sovereignty. Since the times of slavery, the church was the only place where Black folks could speak their collective mind with impunity. Our sacred hearts have always been entwined with our political minds. Preachers led their congregants on slave revolts, as was the case with Nat Turner, or on a path to greater human liberty and freedom, as was the case with the Rev. Martin Luther King, Jr.

If white folks truly want to understand how it is to be Black in America they must be willing to listen. They can't start from a defensive adversarial place. They must be open, as if they are learning to speak a foreign language. One wouldn't dream of telling the French teacher that what he or she is learning is incorrect if the accuser had never spoken French before.

We have to start learning to speak each other's language. If Blacks wish to be successful in America, they have no choice. On the other hand, whites have the privilege and the luxury to remain disinterested in Black life. The only loser in that equation is ultimately America.

Don't Blink

Man the feds is out to get me
Because I'm Black
I be lookin out my window they be lookin right back
And if you look like me and you live in The Ap*
Then listen real close cuz we under attack
First of all we aint colored—cuz what that implies
Is to alter the original—but that aint right
that aint right and exact
that aint statin the facts
see we the first ones to ever grace the map
a little history lesson for my people manifestin themselves in the struggle
while they stressin for a blessin
see they want us to give up
put down our weapons and
surrender to the sections 8s and get a crack possession
on our records—then submit to departments of correction
so they can earn a fee for everyday that we oppressed in
the belly of the beast
so don't tell me that it's sweet
when AIDS was introduced only to make us extinct

so keep your eyes open dont blink—dont blink
they get you even quicker when you sleep—dont sleep
see if you think it's sweet or if you think we free
then mentally you six feet deep

I said keep your eyes open dont blink—dont blink
they get you even quicker when you sleep—dont sleep
see if you think it's sweet or if you think we free
then mentally you six feet deep

*Minneapolis

So we got a Black face in the presidential race
and I'm supposed to feel like we came a long way
and then I'm supposed to feel like shit's about to change
like because you switch the poster up—that'll change the frame
I know my people's pain I know we want to keep the faith
I know we see a Black face and it touch a deep place
But we gotta remember that looks can be deceitful
And no I aint sayin that dude is evil
He could have good intentions but he's still a politician
In the most corrupt government—EVER IN EXISTENCE!
and even if he think he can he can't change the system
a system with a mission to keep you and me submissive
and actually—that could be—just one of their tactics
play with our emotions—to turn our thinkin backwards
how quickly we forget how they gangster these elections
but it's a quiet war they gotta use a silent weapon

so keep your eyes open dont blink—dont blink
they get you even quicker when you sleep—dont sleep
see if you think it's sweet or if you think we free
then mentally you six feet deep

I said keep your eyes open dont blink—dont blink
they get you even quicker when you sleep—dont sleep
see if you think it's sweet or if you think we free
then mentally you six feet deep

Unbuckling

> *Dying/ Is an art, like everything else.*
> *I do it exceptionally well./ I do it so it feels like hell.*
> — Sylvia Plath, "Lady Lazarus"

The shackles slosh like galoshes in mud,
dragging history's muck after his feet. He
fixes on them, in this ritual bounce, his head
collapsing like the neck of a bunraku puppet.
He counts his digits, tripping over the one
next to the little toe—would you call that
a ring toe? As he approaches the live throne
he searches the two-way mirror for the faces
of family, and he comes back upon himself.
Oh. He looks at the glass again, a prom-boy
prepping for a picture. He tries on poses,
baring his teeth, scowling, spit spelling
the crease of his lip. Nudged, he draws into
himself, pulling in his turtle head. He sits, waiting.

It is not music that sets him dancing,
though still. His lips skitter, the way bacon
bops on a griddle, burning with Jesus Christ
and Jeremiah Wright. They bounce
and curl, rolling back onto themselves. His
mouth riffles on the lid of a kettle's spout,
the air valve of a coal train, a foghorn.
His face calls out the memories of g-forces
he has never known, sinking through bone
as he tries out the looks babies rehearse
in sleep—the peeled-back toad smile, the furrowed
glare, the toothless gleaming of humor, dread.

The sounds simmer down to the murmuring
skirl of mosquitoes. His tongue tires, twists,
foams, dangling to hang like the tip of
an unbuckled belt, like a barber's strap,
dirty with cream.

Reminders

Michael Montgomery was losing patience with the elevators in this fancy hotel. After attending the client's conference and being bored to death, this brother was tired of long speeches and fancy food. He just wanted to get back to his room and get some sleep.

"Come on!" he said under his breath, loosening the tasteful tie that seemed like a noose around his neck. No elevator would come. Out of the corner of his eye he spotted a service elevator and the sign. *Employees Only*. In defiance, he hopped onto the smaller, plainer elevator. Much to his chagrin, it went down, not up.

When the doors opened, he found himself in what looked like a kitchen surrounded by other kitchens. Where were the elevators that could take him to his room? As he searched, employees of the hotel whisked past him, not noticing that a well-dressed Black man in a navy blue suit was decidedly out of place in the employee basement. He came to a corner where an older Black woman was standing over a stove, wearing a uniform much like the women who had served him at dinner, only in gray whereas theirs had been black. Her white hair was pulled back and tucked beneath a hair net, and she looked very much at peace. She reminded Michael of his grandmother in New Orleans, and he made a mental note to call Big Mama when he got some time.

"Excuse me, ma'am, can you tell me how to find . . ."

"The guest elevators," the woman said, turning around and completing his sentence. "You couldn't wait and decided to take the service elevator, only it didn't go up. It came down. Now you are in the kitchen and wondering how you got here. Am I right, young man?"

Michael smiled. Now that he was on the other side of thirty, people didn't call him "young man" that much. But to this woman, who looked like she ought to be retired, he guessed he was a young man.

"That's right, ma'am," he replied, flashing an embarrassed grin.

"Everyone calls me Miss Gloria. And you are?"

"Michael Montgomery. I was just in the hotel to attend a client's conference, and right now I want to get to my room. Excuse me, Miss Gloria. Is that gumbo I see you cooking?"

"It sure is. I've been cooking at this hotel so long that once a month, they ask me to cook up something for the employee room, not the guests. We put it in a hot pot, and the kitchen workers who want to, help themselves. It's one of the few nice things they do around here the way they used to, before Star Service bought the place out."

"It smells sooo good. Like Big Mama, er, my grandmother, makes down in New Orleans."

"Would you like some?"

"Oh, I couldn't. It's for the employees, and I'm not even supposed to be down here."

Miss Gloria ignored his protest, ladled up some gumbo in a bowl with rice, making certain she included a piece of crab. Quickly, she set a place at the little table to the side and gestured for him to sit down. Surprised at his own obedience, he sat down.

"Ummmmnim . . . ummmmm. Miss Gloria, this tastes like the gumbo Big Mama makes. I didn't know anybody else could make gumbo like this."

"Oh, I'm sure it's not as good as your Big Mama's," Miss Gloria said, beaming. "But the people from the kitchen sure like it. This, along with my Shrimp Creole, Red Beans and Rice, and Stewed Red Fish. Manager has to tell them to wait 'til their lunch or breaks before stopping to eat, when I cook down here."

That reality and Michael's reaction obviously wrapped Miss Gloria in a blanket of pride. As Michael ate his gumbo, she cleaned the area and had one of the young ladies from across the hall place the big pot on a cart and roll it to the worker's area. When Michael looked up, his bowl was empty and Miss Gloria was gathering her things, putting on her coat.

"Now, I'll show you how to get to your room, young man."

"Thank you, Miss Gloria," he responded. He cleared the table, emptying the crab shells into the trash can and placing his bowl in the dishwasher as he had seen Miss Gloria do with other dishes.

"Hmmm . . . somebody sure raised you right," Miss Gloria said.

"Guess that would be Mama and Big Mama."

Taking Michael through a maze of little hallways, Miss Gloria showed him how to get back to the guest elevators. As they passed, all her co-workers said, "Good night, Miss Gloria" and "See you in the morning." She responded in kind. Many asked what she had made for the employee room, and her answer was always the same: "You'll see, Sweetie."

They were so polite and respectful to her that Michael was wondering how a simple cook could gain so much respect. The African-American workers' deference he could understand. Michael guessed that he was not the only one who thought of a beloved grandmother when in her presence. But the white people—some who were dressed for success and looked to be management—were respectful to her as well. Michael's mind drifted to some of the arrogant white folks he worked with, and he wondered how they would respond to someone like Miss Gloria.

"Well, here we are," announced Miss Gloria, pointing to a row of elevators. "I should go back up the service elevator, but I'm tired and will bend the rules tonight. I usually don't do this."

Michael heard himself saying. "Miss Gloria, you have worked here a long time and I can tell they respect you, so the rules really don't apply to someone like you."

Smiling, she replied. "Michael, because people around here respect me and I respect them, the rules *especially* apply to me. But we have been really busy in the kitchen this week, and I hope nobody notices an old cook with a bus to catch riding up the guest elevator with the hotel's most handsome guest."

Michael actually blushed! (Yes, Black people do blush.) How long had it been since he felt his face flush from a compliment? He could not remember.

When the elevator got to the main floor, Michael hopped off with Miss Gloria, telling her for the third time how much he enjoyed the gumbo and thanking her. "Listen, Miss Gloria, I have a rental car in the hotel garage. Let me give you a ride home."

Miss Gloria put up a protest. She explained that she had the bus route down pat. The drivers all knew her and looked out for her, as did the people who worked in the shops and restaurants between the hotel and her little house just twenty minutes away. "Lots of people look out for me, Sweetie."

"That sounds like the old-fashioned community," Michael said. "I didn't know it still existed."

"Why, it does if you look for it and live it. Still a lot of kind people left in this world, Sweetie," Miss Gloria said, sounding, Michael thought, like his favorite elementary school teacher. "But if you want to take this tired lady home, I'll accept *your* kindness."

With that, Michael took Miss Gloria's arm and the two strode across the lobby. Michael felt as if he had the honor of escorting a queen to her castle. Another bank of elevators took them to the hotel garage. Soon they were in his rental car and Miss Gloria was directing him to her duplex.

"How long have you worked at the hotel?" he asked, to make conversation. Twenty-five years, she told him, in a job she initially thought of as "temporary."

"You see, I taught school in Shreveport, Louisiana, for ten years. Then my husband just had to move up North for a better life. Well, it did work out for us. He got a job in the factory helping to build airplanes and made his way up to foreman. It was good money. But I never could get on in the school system up here. They always had more teachers than they needed and promised to call me back. When they didn't call, I found a job working at the hotel, helping to make salads. Temporary became permanent, and here I am."

"You mean you used to teach school and now you're *working in the kitchen?*" he asked, before realizing his tone was rather insulting. Miss Gloria just laughed.

"It's honest work, Sweetie. And I advanced, too. For years I helped run the kitchen. Now I'm what they call a senior cook, which means I make a bit more but don't have to worry about being in charge. Being in charge is one big headache. A lot of the young people still look to me to tell them how things go at the hotel. Honey, I am still teaching!"

Michael could not believe it. No wonder Miss Gloria sounded like an educated woman. She *was* an educated woman. "But what about your education?"

"Michael, I loved school when I was a girl, and later as a young woman," Miss Gloria told him. "At Southern, I stayed on the honor roll. And I used my education to help turn that kitchen into a well-run operation. But just because most people don't consider the job professional doesn't mean I am not a professional. My husband, Wesley, bless his soul, and I raised a son and two daughters and bought this duplex through him working at the factory and me working at the hotel. All three of my children are well educated and have fancy jobs, like you. They also left town and sometimes forget to stay connected. Something tells me you forget to keep in contact with your people, too."

They were pulling up in front of Miss Gloria's neat duplex, and he saw she didn't look the least bit upset. Rather, she looked like a satisfied teacher finishing up a lesson.

For the second time that night, he found himself blushing. "Well, I could call Mama and Big Mama more often. I send them something nice almost every time I am on the road, though."

"And I bet they appreciate those nice things. But what your Mama and Big Mama really want is to hear from their boy. Now, I know you are a man and everything. And if a white man ever calls you a boy, you will let him have it. But you will always be their special boy."

With that, Miss Gloria leaned over and gave him the warmest hug he had received in a long, long time. "Don't you worry about seeing me to the door. I know what a gentleman you are. And stay off that fancy cell phone as you drive back to the hotel. But I need you to do me a favor before you go to sleep tonight."

"Anything at all, Miss Gloria."

"It's not too late. When you get back to your room, call your Mama and Big Mama and just tell them you were thinking about them. Tell them how much you miss them and that good food they cook. They need to hear that."

"Miss Gloria, you are one special lady."

She waved the compliment away, smiled and climbed the stairs to her home. Michael did not pull off until she was inside.

The Stagnant Reassurance in the Communication of the Dead

when my momma comes
she is gentle
walking on air
her flip-flops make no sound
her gown hangs in no breeze
she talks to my mind
showing only soles of shoes
peeks of the bottom of her feet

only at first I saw
her hands doing things
her hands praying
reaching for Chinese food
and wearing Aunt Rachel's ring

momma was the only girl not married

when my momma comes
she is gentle
I am not afraid
she talks quietly
taking the startle in me
she sits on
the sides of my bed
bringing scents of solace

she moves my keys
takes my tapes
flashes my lights
shakes my bed
drops loose coins
saying about men
that "God will choose"

Carrying Home

I am carrying home in my breast pocket:
land where I learned to crawl,
dust that held my footprints,
long fields I trod through.

Home, where Mother baked bread,
where Papa spoke with skies,
where family voices gathered.
In my palm, this heap of earth
I have hauled over hills and valleys.

Releasing dirt between my fingers,
I ask the prairies to sustain me.
May my soil and this soil nurture each other,
may seeds root and develop beyond measure,
may the heartland and I blossom.

Anniversary

There is no clean slate
No blank sheets of paper
To write our lives on
We palimpsestically erase
And rewrite existence like
Painters whitewashing
And rescaping canvas
With images telling new stories
Often by another painter
In some other time
With alterative visions
No story is complete
Life goes on in ways
That tells the same story differently
From other sides of truths
Celebrated narratives previously promulgated
Shading views ancestors left
Our stories don't disappear under
Cover of news but hover like
Ghosts beneath dominant voices
Parchment establishes new anniversaries
With every twist of tongue
Every keyed in message
Penned privet document
Of lives lived on a record
Each year unrolls another scroll
Retelling stories to recover
From the pseudology of war
Every lesson confirms that fighting
Is the absolute right thing to do
In my rear view mirror I see
People with bad ideas
About what the world is made of

They will need to learn for themselves
I will need to fight where I can win
I never thought when
I was an undergraduate
Studying philosophy that aesthetics
Would become an over used word
But every time I turn an ear
In the direction of pop culture
Some artist is talking about life
Values and style
Flipping the script to post modernism
Uncomfortably confronting antiquated myths
Deconstructing master stories with
Post-traumatic truth
Everyday is muffled
In acoustics
Of diamond sprinkled snow
Reflecting how hard
It is to be relevant
Complete
Whole
We thought we knew
What we could not have known
And it made fools of us
Made us overreach and prevaricate
Had we known better we would have done more
But retrospect is false
And the clock is relentless
Secretly I like the story so I'm perpetually
Telling it draft after draft in sequels

Lifeline

Wednesday, January 5

As we approach the Twin Cities, the pilot says, "Ladies and Gentlemen, we'll get to the gate at 10:00 PM, a few minutes ahead of schedule. And you'll be glad to hear that it's a balmy 25 degrees tonight." Some passengers applaud and cheer. Coming from Miami, I consider 25 degrees cold. When I left home several hours ago, it was 72 and sunny. Now, I'm looking out the window at foggy darkness, and I wonder if my mink coat will keep me warm enough.

I can't wait to see my daughter, Rachel, and I wonder if she'll be waiting for me at the baggage claim area. When I walk through the large glass doors, I see her standing there, waving and smiling. I wave and we rush to embrace each other. I'm so glad to feel her in my arms that I almost weep. I hold her tightly. She breaks away first, grinning. Now I feel self-conscious in this coat. Is it too much? I wonder if she thinks I look funny. It's strange to see no one else wearing fur in such a cold place. In Miami, a 55-degree day is a good excuse to sport our minks. Here, everyone's wearing what appears to be thick cotton coats or jackets, brown, blue, or green, with knit scarves. Most people wear no hats. Don't they know that the head is the first place where body heat escapes?

"Did you have a good flight, Mama?" Rachel looks stylish in her black leather jacket and silk scarf, but not warm enough. She grabs my carry-on bag and slings its strap across her shoulder.

"Oh yes, but I feel like I've been flying forever. I'm glad to be on the ground."

"Well, you made it safely. And look at you, all decked out in your mink. You look nice and warm."

"You think so? Is it too much? I didn't want to get cold." I search her eyes to see if she's being sincere or just polite.

She laughs. "Yes, you look fine, Mama. Really," she says, looking at me and then shifting her eyes to look at people rushing around us. "And you'll be okay. But don't say I didn't warn you." She looks at me again, her brow crumpled now. "I told you that it gets too cold up here, and you know you can't drive on slick, snow-covered streets. You didn't have to come."

Before I can respond, she says, "Let's go get your bags. Are you hungry?"

She leads the way, walking with long strides. Given my short legs, I have to practically skip to catch up with her. As I trot beside her, I notice that her dreadlocks are a few inches longer now than they were a year ago when I last saw her. Eight years ago, when she first started growing them, I didn't like them at all. She looked like she had twigs growing out of her head. How was she going to get away with wearing such a hairstyle at work? I was afraid that she might lose her job. I heard about a Black reporter who got fired for just wearing braids to work in California. But now that Rachel's hair is shoulder-length, it actually looks nice and neat.

"I could eat something," I say. "You look real good, honey. How do you feel? You look strong, not like someone about to have surgery."

Rachel smiles and says, "I feel strong."

When we get to the baggage claim area, we find that my bags have already been moved off the carousel. Rachel takes the heavier one and leaves me the lighter one, and we simply walk away with them. I'm surprised that we don't need any claim tickets.

"You guys aren't afraid of people walking off with your luggage?"

Rachel bursts out with laughter. "No, Mama, this is not Florida. This is, as they say around here, Minnesota *nice*."

As soon as we walk outside to the parking ramp, the cold air hits my face.

"So, it's warm for this time of year, huh?" It's startling to see my breath when I speak. After tossing my bag in the trunk of Rachel's car, I hop into my seat and slam the door shut. I feel as if I'm trapped inside a deep freezer, like I'll never thaw.

Rachel shakes her head and laughs.

Friday, January 7

We sit in the reception area of the hospital, waiting to be checked in.

"What's that?" She points to my overnight bag.

"I'm going to stay with you this weekend."

"You mean you're moving into the hospital room with me?" Her eyes flash with disbelief. "No way. They're not going to allow that."

I nod my head. "I'll just tell them that I'm an RN. They'll cooperate with me."

"Oh, Mama, is that really necessary? Why would you do that? I'll be in here for only two days. Diana wants to take you to dinner tonight. Go have some fun." She looks like her father as she crinkles her forehead. I see that little girl I once knew when she pokes out her bottom lip.

"No, I'm not leaving you this weekend. How can I have fun while you're in here?"

Although I want to believe that she'll have a successful operation, I've worked in the medical field for thirty-five years and I've never heard of a myomectomy, a surgical procedure that removes only the fibroids from the uterus. I want to stop her from having this surgery.

When I was in my early thirties, I had a hysterectomy. It was no big deal. Lord knows I didn't need any more babies, so I gladly got rid of my uterus along with my troublesome fibroids. My headstrong daughter, God bless her, should have gotten rid of hers years ago, but she decided to do alternative medicine. Over the last six years, as the tumor grew bigger, making her sicker and sicker, Rachel tried everything under the sun, like chiropractic, acupuncture, and something called "body therapy." Then she changed her diet so drastically she couldn't eat much at all. I'm certain that crazy diet made her anemic. A person could fool around with that weird stuff and kill herself. But what can you do with a stubborn woman who is no longer your little girl?

"Mama," she told me one day during an intense telephone conversation, "I'm not letting them take my womb. I still need it even if I never get pregnant. Besides, who knows? I just might want to have a baby if the right man comes along."

"Okay, honey," I said just to keep the peace, but really I was boiling over, thinking, *You foolish girl! You're nearly thirty-seven with no likely prospects, as far as I can tell. It took me years to get over your divorce and you saying that you don't want to have babies. Now, ten years later, you think you might want to get pregnant? Well, it's a bit too late to think about having children now. You could end up having a baby with Down syndrome!*

When Rachel finally decided to have surgery, I thought God had answered my prayers, only to learn that she had found a surgeon who promised to remove only the fibroids, unless it was impossible to do so. What kind of mess is this? I didn't dare say anything, but I was so angry.

So, I come to Minneapolis to keep an eye on her, to wash and feed her, to maybe change her mind about the surgery. I bring creams and lotions, blue and white slippers that one of my patients knitted for her, good wishes from our family and congregation, and hope.

The operation is scheduled to take two hours. Four hours later, I'm still sitting in the waiting room with my eyes stuck to the monitor, where her name is still listed under *Surgery*. I've tried to read *People* to keep my mind occupied, but it doesn't work. So I pray to maintain my composure, to ward off what feels like a bad omen. Recalling King David's prayer to the Lord in Psalms 22:19, I say to myself: *Be close to me, Oh Lord. Oh my strength, help me.*

Diana and John, Rachel's friends, show up after work and wait with me. Diana engages me in idle chitchat, and I'm grateful for the company.

"Don't worry, Pat," she says, patting my hand. "She'll be all right."

"Mrs. Jones, can I get you anything?" John stands up, finally speaking. He's kept himself preoccupied with the newspaper, shifting from side to side in his seat since he arrived an hour ago. "I'll go get you something to drink," he says before I can answer. Soon he comes back with two sixteen-ounce cups of lemonade. He gives me a cup and a straw. I sip the liquid quickly, realizing I was thirsty after all.

After Rachel has been in surgery for seven hours, Dr. Porter finally brings me the news. Nearly hysterical with worry, I stand up when I see her coming.

"Rachel set a record. I just removed 42 myomas. My last patient had 21, and I thought she had a lot. Look. Here are some pictures for Rachel—she wanted to see them. I'd never imagined finding so many compacted in there."

Although I'm accustomed to hearing this flat, casual tone that doctors tend to use, I can't bear to hear it now, not when she's referring to my daughter. Taking the photographs, I shuffle through them, incredulous at what I see. The bloody balls of muscular tissue are arranged in several lines, ranging from the largest (the size of a grapefruit) to the smallest (the size of a grape). Speaking in an angry, hushed tone, I turn to her:

"Forty-two myomas? That's ridiculous. Why didn't you just take out the uterus?"

Looking into my eyes and speaking in a steady, quiet voice, Dr. Porter says: "Rachel asked me to save her uterus, and I wanted to honor her wishes. When she came to, she immediately asked the nurse, 'Do I still have my uterus?' Keeping it is real important to her. Don't worry, Mrs. Jones. She'll be fine now."

"Did you get them all? And what about cancer?"

"I took out as many as I could, and I found no sign of malignancy."

"All right, Doctor," I say, breathing a sigh of relief. "Thank you for all your hard work."

When she walks away, Diana and John jump up.

"So, she's all right, isn't she?" Diana asks.

"Yes, the doctor says she's fine."

"Did she get what she wanted?" John asks.

"Yes," I say, caught off guard by his question, wondering if there's more than friendship between them. Although they've known each other since college, they haven't been in touch for years, as far as I know.

"I must call home now," I say, leaving the room for some privacy to call my husband, Thomas. I tell him that Rachel is okay and I'll be home Sunday night as planned.

It's 9:00 PM, and they transfer her from recovery to the hospice floor, which they use for overflow. I tell the nurses on duty that I'm an RN and that I'd like to stay with Rachel until she's released. They're kind enough to put us in a big room, where they set up a cot for me next to Rachel's bed.

Later, when the nurse on night duty comes into the room, I stand next to her, observing her every move as she checks Rachel's vital signs. I've hooked up so many patients to IVs and oxygen tanks, but I can barely stand to see Rachel attached to these machines. To complicate things, she also has a catheter in her urethra.

"Could we please get some sanitary napkins?" I ask her.

"What?" The nurse looks at me as if she can't believe her ears.

"Sanitary napkins. My daughter needs some."

"Oh. We don't have any of those up here on this floor," she says, taking Rachel's pulse.

"Where can I get some, then?"

"I guess I'll have to get them from the maternity ward," she says, now taking Rachel's temperature. "Just give me a few minutes."

Eventually she leaves but doesn't come back with any pads, so I have to ask another nurse to get some. My ominous feelings return. Will they be equipped to give her the proper care on this floor?

For the next hour, although I'm exhausted, I sit in the chair beside Rachel's bed and watch her sleep. She seems comfortable, breathing evenly. I wonder about her incision and stand up to raise the covers, lifting her gown. There's some oozing, but the incision appears okay, and her belly has gone down quite a bit. Although I turn her onto her left side and smooth the covers, she remains asleep. I finally feel calm enough to get some rest.

Saturday, January 8

When my cell phone rings, I wake up with a start, suddenly remembering where I am. It's Thomas calling to get an update. We speak quickly and hang up. I get up and float from Rachel's bed, where I watch her breathe, to the chair, where I try to watch television. I then go to the icy window, where I stand looking in total disbelief. According to the news, yesterday's temperature fell to a wind chill of minus 25. I don't understand what that means, and it's worse today than yesterday. How can people actually exist in this place? Now the wind is blowing hard and the snow is falling quietly but heavily. I watch the snowflakes dissolve as they hit the surface. The strangest thing is that when the sun shines, it looks so warm. I cannot fathom this kind of cold.

Two student nurses come to bathe Rachel, but I tell them that I'd like to do it myself.

When I get her up, she's lethargic but in good spirits. While bathing her, I notice that her stomach has grown. I press on it; it feels hard and rigid. As soon as she gets back in bed, she falls asleep immediately, ignoring her breakfast.

When a nurse comes to check Rachel's incision, she turns on the tiny light above the bed, not the overhead light. I wonder how she can see Rachel's stomach clearly in such dim light. I get up from my seat and stand on the opposite side of the bed.

"Her stomach's not right. She's usually not this big. Last night after her surgery, it had gone down quite a bit. Now it's beginning to swell," I say.

"It's probably just gas," the nurse says, changing the bandage.

"But she hasn't eaten anything before or since the surgery."

"I'll make a note of it," she says. But she doesn't write anything on the board for the next shift.

"Could you give her something for the pain? I can tell by the grimace on her face that she's suffering," I say, stroking Rachel's forehead.

"Sure," the nurse says and prepares to give her a shot.

My cell phone begins to ring incessantly, causing Rachel to jump each time. Family, neighbors, and people from church call throughout the day to inquire about Rachel's progress.

Every hour nurses enter our room to check this, to observe that. Each shift brings a team of student nurses, who stream in to watch the head nurse. Then they leave the room and huddle in the hallway.

Suddenly, Rachel awakens and raises her head. "Mama? Why do they look at me like I'm some kind of specimen? How can I rest when they keep touching me?" She closes her eyes and falls asleep before I say anything. Rachel is sleeping too much. I try to keep her awake, but she drifts in and out of consciousness, tossing and turning.

That afternoon the lab nurse comes every three hours to draw blood to check Rachel's blood count. Meanwhile, her hemoglobin drops. During the day they give her seven pints of blood, but the volume doesn't rise because she loses the blood faster than they are able to replace it. Every hour the nurse changes the blood-soaked dressing on Rachel's abdomen. Then a few minutes later, I change the drenched bandage. Meanwhile, her stomach grows, her blood pressure drops, and her heart rate increases.

That night, Rachel begins thrashing about. "Mama, I don't want to die," she cries.

Feeling alarmed, I rush to the nurse's station.

"I'm concerned about my daughter. I can tell that the blood transfusions aren't helping her. I think the doctor ought to see her."

"The doctor's called in today to check on her, so she knows what's going on."

"Rachel is losing a lot of blood for some reason. Something needs to be done. I'd like you to take a look at her."

We walk back to Rachel's room. The nurse turns on the dim light over the bed and checks her chart. Then she looks down at Rachel.

"Look at her stomach. She looks like she weighs 160 pounds now. When she left surgery, she weighed 140," I say, trying not to raise my tense voice. "I pointed this out to the nurse this morning, but she didn't write it on the board. Why aren't you writing notes on the board for the next shift?"

"We're writing them on the chart, Mrs. Jones," she says, looking like she wants to dash away from me. "Rachel seems to be okay now. Let's just wait till morning to see what happens, okay? You look like you could use some rest. Try to get a good night's sleep, Mrs. Jones."

"Wait. You're supposed to switch her position every two hours, and nobody's doing it. She's not supposed to lie in one spot all day. Here, I'll help you move her."

When we lift Rachel, she's so heavy, she feels like dead weight.

I know trauma when I see it, but these nurses don't know because they're not trained to handle critical cases. The patients on this floor are dying, so the nurses are doing whatever they can to make them feel comfortable. My baby's not supposed to be on this floor, preparing to die.

After the nurse bolts from the room, I collapse in the chair, feeling afraid and alone. I can no longer hold back my tears. I want to leave the room so I won't disturb Rachel when I call home, but Thomas will only cry if I tell him how sick Rachel has become. And I don't want to leave her alone. So I stay put, living through what seems to be the longest night I'd ever known. I pray, again recalling King David's words to God: *Don't be far from me, for trouble is near, for there is no one to help.*

Working as a nurse, I've often glimpsed the young face of death, especially when I worked in labor and delivery during the early days of my career. I've seen babies die before their mothers even had a chance to hold them.

And, one spring mid-morning in 1975, I was awakened from a sound sleep when my neighbor's four-year-old son frantically rang my doorbell.

"My mama needs help—my sisters are sick."

When I heard his mother, Mrs. Alejandro, wailing, I sprinted across the street to the garage, still wearing my pajamas. She didn't speak English, but pointed to her daughters, three and five, lying unconscious on a piece of carpet.

While playing hide-and-go-seek, the little girls had gotten trapped in an old refrigerator for one hour. The Alejandro family had just gotten a new refrigerator and had put the old one in the garage for pick up.

By the time I had reached the girls, a small crowd had gathered, and someone had already called the rescue squad.

I kneeled down to check each pulse.

"Can anyone else do mouth-to-mouth resuscitation?"

Realizing I had no help, I leaned over and pressed my mouth against the mouth of the older girl, who lay closer to me. I hoped I could revive her quickly so I could move to the other one. Suddenly another neighbor arrived and began working on the other child. When the older girl began to vomit, the police, who had beaten the rescue squad to the house, rushed her to Baptist Health. Soon the rescue squad followed them with the younger girl, who didn't ever regain consciousness. I watched Mrs. Alejandro clutch her heart, making a stupefying sound that caused my heart to nearly burst wide open. Even now, I can still hear it in my mind and feel sick.

Later that day, I forced myself to get ready for work. Feeling weepy and exhausted, it finally dawned on me that two of my own children could have gotten trapped for one hour in that old refrigerator. How many times that week had the neighborhood kids climbed inside that appliance while playing? I thanked God for sparing my kids, yet I felt guilty that they were alive. To maintain my sanity that night, I kept myself busy with the new mothers and their babies, filling up every second, so I could forget Mrs. Alejandro's twisted face, her child's limp body, and our failure to save her baby girl.

I thought then, just as I think now, that outliving your children is unnatural. Perhaps it's even a curse.

The room is dark except for the flickering light of the television. Sitting beside Rachel's bed, I watch her bloated, pained body thrashing about. I cannot stand to see her suffer like this. Struggling to have faith, I pray to God to have mercy on me for not being a better mother years ago. While growing up, Rachel got less attention than the other two kids—I admit this now. But she was the oldest, the strongest, and I thought I didn't have to worry about her. By the time I was twenty-four, I'd had three kids, and I often relied on her to help me do chores and to babysit while I worked and went to college. Then one day, I looked up and she was eighteen, leaving home for Macalester College. She never complained, but there's a distance between us because I was too busy to get to know her.

What if she doesn't make it? What if it's too late to get to know her now? Although I know that I should not question the Lord's will, I cannot bear to lose my child. *Lord, please take me instead. Look upon my affliction and my pain; and forgive all my sins.*

When the nurse comes back in with another nurse, I jump up, telling them to stay with Rachel while I leave the room to use my phone.

"Thomas," I sob, "Rachel's real sick, honey. Let the kids know. We need everybody to pray."

I hang up and call our minister. "Brother Lewis, something's not right. We need the prayers of the church tomorrow."

Sunday, January 9
When the nurse comes in, I spring from my seat, groggy. When she raises Rachel's gown to check her bandage, it's drenched with blood.

Before she can remove the bandage, I jerk the gown down.

Staring her straight in her eyes, I say: "It's not doing any good to just keep changing it. Call the doctor. I want her to see this."

With a placid expression, the nurse seems to repeat a rehearsed line: "Mrs. Jones, we are not to call the doctor unless there's an emergency."

"This is an emergency. Look at her. Besides losing blood as fast as she gets it, she's retaining the IV fluid—she's blowing up like a balloon. She's got tachycardia and she's short of breath. You nurses traipse in and out of here, paying no attention to my daughter at all. If she were my patient, I would've called the doctor last night." I feel so outraged I could snap her neck.

"When the doctor called, we told her that Rachel's oozing blood."

"No, she's not *oozing* blood. Tell the doctor that I say she's *hemorrhaging.* I'll call and tell her myself."

"I'll be right back, Mrs. Jones," the flustered nurse says, rushing out of the room.

I don't want to leave Rachel alone, but a few seconds later I hurry after the nurse, saying, "And tell her that Rachel's blood pressure is falling and her heart rate is increasing."

When I get to the nurse's station, the nurse has already begun punching the numbers into the phone. When the doctor answers, the nurse speaks fast and loudly.

"Dr. Porter, her mother says she's hemorrhaging."

Suddenly, the nurse hangs up the phone and says, "The doctor said to tell you she's on her way, but the blizzard will slow her down."

When I get back to the room, Rachel wakes up and mumbles to me in a faint voice. I look at her as she reaches toward me.

"Mama, please help me. Please don't let me die."

I move to her side, taking her hand and caressing her face. "Mama's right here and so is God. The doctor is coming soon."

Still holding her hand, I turn away so she doesn't see me cry.

This morning is blustery, that's what I overhear one of the nurses say. So, that's how you describe this kind of raw cold, *below freezing,* something I've never experienced before until I ran out to Rachel's car in the parking lot to get her luggage Friday night. I didn't realize I needed my gloves for such a short time. But my right hand got so cold so fast. I had to pry it loose from the luggage handle. What a shock to my system. Three days later, my hand still tingles. I stand and look out the window, transfixed by all this snow, unable to fathom how my child lives in such harsh weather.

If we'd been closer before she left home, would she have stayed here after college? Thomas says we tricked him, that if he'd known she'd never return home, he wouldn't have allowed her to come to Minnesota. *She should have stayed here and gone to college.* How was I supposed to know that she wasn't coming back to us?

Finally Dr. Porter arrives wrapped up in a striped red woolen scarf and blue parka, carrying her bundled-up baby in a car seat. Leaving the child in the car seat on the floor outside the room, she walks in.

"Mrs. Jones, how's it going?"

By now my eyes are so swollen, and I cannot stop weeping.

"She is so sick, Doctor. And they were going to just let my baby die. I wouldn't let them touch her anymore; I told them you had to get here. I think you need to get my daughter to ICU. She's fading fast. Look. She's steadily losing blood." I raise Rachel's gown to show her the soaked dressing. Rachel's belly is so swollen now that it looks as if she's six months pregnant.

"I ordered the lab to draw blood every three hours, and each time the results turned out fine." Dr. Porter removes the bandage to check the incision.

"You know, Doctor, when I worked in OB, my doctor told me that when you take a blood test, you must wait fourteen to fifteen hours to get an accurate reading."

When she taps Rachel's belly, it makes an echo sound. Feeling the hardness, she says calmly:

"You're right. We need to get her to ICU all right, but first we must get her back into surgery."

She immediately picks up the telephone beside Rachel's bed and calls each of her surgery team members.

Despite the blizzard, the rest of the crew gets to the hospital within twenty minutes, and they rush Rachel downstairs. Dr. Porter invites me to scrub up and come into the operating room, but I refuse. Watching them operate on my child would be too much to bear. I sit outside the room and call Thomas.

"Tell everybody to pray," I say.

Thursday, January 13
Today is the seventh day of Rachel's hospital stay, and I'm still in Minneapolis. Her physical condition has stabilized since Dr. Porter opened up her abdomen again to suction out three and a half liters of blood. Dr. Porter explained that because there were so many fibroids, some of them didn't get cauterized enough; the seepage from each one created internal bleeding.

Now Rachel is having hallucinations and nightmares. Sometimes she doesn't recognize me. Other times, she screams and cries even though she's in a deep sleep. Last night she scared me so much, I leaped out of bed and ran to get the nurse. Neither one of us knew what to do because Rachel didn't wake up despite all the noise she made.

This morning, Dr. Porter comes in while Rachel is eating breakfast. She chats briefly with Rachel and then beckons for me to follow her. We leave the room.

"Mrs. Jones, Rachel is showing signs of *ICU-psychosis*. I think it's best for her to recuperate at home. I'd like to release her tomorrow."

"Maybe it's the medicine. Could the dosage be too high?"

"I asked the pharmacist about that. He doesn't think it's causing the problems. This place is just getting to her. She's been in here too long. Can you stay another two weeks till her follow-up appointment?"

"I'll do whatever's necessary. You're sure she'll be okay at home? She seems to be taking too long to recover."

"Things got really dicey, but Rachel pulled through because she's quite strong. She's already been through the worst of it, so as long as you'll be here to keep an eye on her, she'll be fine at home."

After having breakfast, Rachel takes a slow walk up and down the hall with Dr. Porter. They discuss her condition and release.

"Can you really stay longer, Mama?" she asks, returning to the room and climbing back into bed. "Will you stay for my birthday?" She looks at me with hopeful eyes. When I nod my head, she offers me a smile full of big pretty teeth, her father's smile, and my eyes well up.

Thursday, January 20

Today is Rachel's thirty-seventh birthday. This morning is the first time she's gotten wet since her surgeries, so she's dallying in the tub like she did when she was a baby, just discovering the pleasure of splashing water.

I'm looking out the window at the snow, a new favorite pastime since I've been in Minneapolis. It's warmer this week than last week, but the snow is still falling. The view of the landscape from Rachel's patio window is far better than the view of the hospital parking lot. The snow covering the trees, especially the evergreens, barely looks real to me. The first thing I do when I get up in the morning is look out at those beautiful frosty pine trees. I would love to decorate them with big red bulbs. When the holiday season comes, despite my family's protest, I usually get a large flocked Christmas tree. Years ago, I used to buy the stuff in the can and spray the tree myself. It could be 80 degrees outside, but I'd still have my "snowy" tree. It must be nice to have a light snowfall on Christmas day. This city is especially charming after the snow falls and the sun brightens everything. Then the land sparkles and looks so pristine and tranquil.

But I couldn't live here. Rachel is right. It's too cold for me and I don't dare drive. John, my Godsend, rescues me from disaster, driving me everywhere I need to go, providing me with food and the daily newspaper, taking us to Rachel's doctor's appointments. Today, he's bringing chili and a birthday cake that he's made for the occasion. I now suspect that he and Rachel are dating. He's the only person she'll see during her recovery.

As I move toward the bathroom to check on Rachel, I feel panicky when I hear her sobbing.

"Honey? You okay?" I push the door open. She looks up at me, smiling through her tears.

"I'm alive, Mama."

I sink to my knees and wrap my arms around her.

"This morning when I woke up, I cried tears of joy, too. Happy birthday, honey."

We hold each other tightly.

I pat Rachel dry and lead her to the bed. She lies down and I gently rub her body with a lavender-scented cream, starting with her feet. Her body is regaining its long, lean shape as she begins to shed the twenty pounds of fluid she retained over the past six years and the additional twenty pounds she gained while in the hospital because they pumped a lot of fluid into her body. Finally her heartbeat is normal, but she still looks gray. I'll be happy when she regains a healthy appetite so her hemoglobin will rise and her beautiful ginger color will return.

Examining Rachel's incision, I marvel at the long, neat line that curves below her navel and extends to her pelvis. I think of it as her lifeline. It's amazing that Dr. Porter spent so much time saving Rachel's uterus. What other doctor would have done that? And what other doctor would have listened to me as she did? Together we made a good life-support team.

Dabbing Rachel's sutures with povidone iodine, I'm suddenly reminded of my mother coming to visit me just after I had given birth. Nine days shy of my twentieth birthday, I lay flat on my back, crippled with a spinal headache. It kept me confined to my bed for a month. Because I was too sick to breast feed or change Rachel, Thomas took care of her when he got home from work. Fortunately, my mother came daily to help. She gave me sponge baths and greased my skin with ointment so I wouldn't get bedsores. For the first time in my life, I felt close to her. With each visit, we grew closer, but the following year Thomas and I left Tennessee for Florida. Then two years later my mother died from complications caused by diabetes.

"Rachel, I was just thinking about my mother, Jessie." I prop up pillows behind her so she can sit up. Then I sit at the foot of her bed.

"Really? You never talk about her. Why not?"

"Oh, I don't know. One of my few memories of her is that she cussed like a sailor. She used to embarrass me so much in front of the neighborhood kids . . ." I chuckle and Rachel smiles at me.

"Tell me about her."

"She was something else, that Jessie Rice, wouldn't hesitate to give you a piece of her mind. Always on the go, always working."

"Sounds like you, Mama," Rachel giggles. "You can't be still, either."

"Yes . . . now, I wish I could recall more about her. It used to be too painful to look back, but now I want to remember. I wish, too, that she and

I had been closer." I look at Rachel, whose face tells me that she is eager to hear my stories. I'm surprised that I'm revealing myself to her in this way. I never thought the past mattered or that it was important to speak about my life. But, now I feel happy that I have the chance to talk with her, to spend time with just her. So much time has been lost.

"After what you and I've been through lately," I continue, "I believe that the good Lord has given us another opportunity to get to know each other. It's funny, but even though I've been blessed with nearly fifty-seven years, I thought I'd never live past age thirty-nine, because that's when my mother died."

"Really, Mama? Well, I'm so glad you're still here. I really love you." Rachel reaches for my hand and squeezes it. "You saved my life."

Before she pulls away, I grasp her fingers and don't let go.

Contributors

Davida Adedjouma is a writer of fiction and poetry who has had three musicals produced by SteppingStone Theater in St. Paul. She is also a visual artist represented by Fountain Gallery in New York City.

Writer, educator, activist, poet, and mentor **Louis Alemayehu** has published works in national and international venues. He is a founding member of the poetry/jazz ensemble Ancestor Energy. In 2009 the MN Spoken Word Association gave him an Urban Griot award.

Liberian-born **E. G. Bailey**, an interdisciplinary artist working in film, theater, and spoken word, is a founder of the MN Spoken Word Association, Tru Ruts, and other organizations. He has received numerous grants and awards, including the Hughes Knight Diop Poetry Award.

Conrad Balfour (1928–2008), civil rights pioneer and teacher, was author of *A Sack Full of Sun* (1974) and coeditor of *The Butterfly Tree: An Anthology of Black Writing from the Upper Midwest* (1986). He was Minnesota's human rights commissioner, 1970–71.

Lloyd Brown (1913–2003) was a Communist labor organizer in the 1930s, a writer and editor for the journal *Masses and Mainstream*, a collaborator with Paul Robeson on *Here I Stand* (1958) and other works, and author of the novel *Iron City* (1951).

Philip Bryant has had poems published in *The Iowa Review* and *The American Poetry Review*. He is the author of *Sermon on a Perfect Spring Day* (1998) and *Stompin' at the Grand Terrace* (2009).

Shá Cage is a writer, performer and artist activist who tours regularly. Named a Women's Press Changemaker, she is co-founder of Mama Mosaic Theater for women. Her work has been published and commissioned, and she is the recipient of several awards.

Actress and choreographer **Laurie Carlos**, an original player in the New York avant-garde performance scene, has received multiple honors for her work, including awards from the National Endowment for the Arts, the McKnight and Bush Foundations, and Obie and Bessie Awards.

Gabrielle Civil is a black feminist poet and conceptual and performance artist originally from Detroit, Michigan. She is currently circulating her performance memoir *Swallow the Fish* and developing more, new art. The aim of her work is to open up space.

Taiyon Coleman's work has appeared in numerous journals and anthologies, including *Bum Rush the Page*, *The Ringing Ear*, and *Riding Shotgun*. She is a lecturer in the Department of African American and African Studies at the University of Minnesota.

Kyra Crawford-Calvert is a silver-tongued time traveler who catalogs the lessons of her navigation through script[ure]. Her soul-mission is to water the Seed of Divinity ever present in herself and her fellows, especially those with skin from crimson to midnight.

Mary Moore Easter is a Pushcart Prize–nominated poet and Cave Canem Fellow published in *POETRY*, *Seattle Review*, *Water-Stone*, *Calyx*, *Pluck! An Affrilachian Journal*, and elsewhere; a veteran dancer/choreographer; and emerita professor at Carleton College. Her chapbook is *Walking from Origins* (1993).

Writer, educator, administrator, and tree farmer **Evelyn Fairbanks** (1928–2001) wrote *The Days of Rondo* (1990), her memoir of St. Paul's largest Black neighborhood in the 1930s and 1940s, so that the people who raised her would not be forgotten.

Pamela R. Fletcher, associate professor of English at St. Catherine University and a senior editor of the *Saint Paul Almanac*, has published works of fiction, creative nonfiction, and poetry. She is coeditor of *Transforming a Rape Culture* and *The Way We See It*.

Shannon Gibney is a writer, teacher, and activist in Minneapolis. She is author of the young adult novel *See No Color* (2015). Her creative and critical works have appeared in a variety of publications.

Taylor Gordon (1893–1971) grew up in Montana, worked in Minnesota, then moved to New York City and took part in the Harlem Renaissance as a singer and performer on stage and in movies. *Born To Be* was published in 1929.

David Grant is a Twin Cities–based writer with a diverse palette. He has written drama for the stage, film, and television, as well as fiction and memoir. He teaches screenwriting at Independent Filmmaker Project/Minnesota.

Originally from Ohio, **Craig Green** has worked as a playwright, actor, journalist, and attorney. He has also written a collection of short stories based on Buddhist parables. A father of two, he is currently an assistant county attorney in southeastern Minnesota.

Emcee, poet, and writer **Libby Green** was born and raised in North Minneapolis. Writing stories since she was a child, she truly discovered her gift with words as a teenager. Ms. Green currently lives in New York City.

David Haynes teaches in the writing programs at Southern Methodist University and Warren Wilson MFA. He has written seven novels for adults and five books for younger readers. His most recent is *A Star in the Face of the Sky* (2013).

Kofi Bobby Hickman was born and raised in St. Paul and has remained a lifelong resident of the city. He directed the Inner City Youth League for twenty years and has been a community activist for over forty years.

Kim Hines is a playwright, director, and Equity actor whose works have been produced at the Kennedy Center in Washington, DC, and other local and national venues. She has received many awards, grants, and commissions, including the Bush Fellowship for Playwrighting.

Carolyn Holbrook founded SASE: The Write Place in 1993. She received the Minnesota Book Awards' Kay Sexton Award in 2010. Her book, *Ordinary People, Extraordinary Journeys*, was published in 2013. She won Hamline University's Exemplary Teacher Award in 2014. **Steven Holbrook** has been out of prison for three years and is done with that life. He is sending his daughter to college.

Kemet Imhotep was raised by his great-aunt and -uncle. He attended St. Paul's Central High School and finished at the Unidale Alternative Learning Center, now Gordon Parks High School. He writes to tell the other side of the story.

Andrea Jenkins is a poet, writer, artist, and transgender activist. Her work has been published widely in several anthologies, and she is the author of three chapbooks. She holds an MFA from Hamline University and lives in Minneapolis.

Nellie Stone Johnson (1905–2002), union organizer, civil rights activist, and the first black elected official in Minneapolis, helped form the Minnesota Democratic-Farmer-Labor Party. Her autobiography, *Nellie Stone Johnson: The Life of an Activist* (2001), was written with David Brauer.

Founder and Executive Director of TruArtSpeaks **Tish Jones** is a student of Spoken Word and Hip Hop culture. Her work as a poet, organizer, and educator demonstrates her passion for critical literacy and social change.

Etheridge Knight (1931–91), who turned his attention from reciting toasts to writing poetry while serving in prison for robbery, earned acclaim as a major American poet in the 1970s and 1980s. He lived in Minneapolis from 1972 to 1977.

Arleta Little, arts program officer for the McKnight Foundation, served for eight years as the executive director of the Givens Foundation for African American Literature. Her passions include building effective and humane organizations, supporting artists, and working for social justice.

Roy McBride (1943–2011), one of Minnesota's first spoken-word performers, was the author of *Secret Traffic: Selected Poems of Roy McBride* (2013). A devoted teacher, musician, and visual artist, he worked to help children and adults find voice through writing and art.

Gordon Parks (1912–2003) was a photographer for *Life* magazine; a musician and composer; author of three memoirs and several books of prose and poetry; and director of several movies, including *Shaft* (1971). He received the National Medal of Arts in 1988.

Alexs Pate is the award-winning author of five novels: *Amistad* (1997, a *New York Times* bestseller), *Losing Absalom* (1994), *Finding Makeba* (1997), *The Multicultiboho Sideshow* (1999), and *West of Rehoboth* (2001). He also authored *In the Heart of the Beat: The Poetry of Rap* (2010).

A featured poet-performer in the Panasonic Village Jazz Fest, **G. E. Patterson** lives in St. Paul. His work has garnered a Minnesota Book Award and fellowships from the Jerome Foundation, the Minnesota State Arts Board, and New York City's Fund for Poetry.

Author of award-winning books for children, **Anthony Peyton Porter** is the only person known to have subscribed to, written for, and delivered the Minneapolis *Star Tribune*. He has written from Chico, California, for years now at anthonypeytonporter.com.

Louis Porter II, EdD, is a longtime educator, writer, and consultant. An assistant professor and administrator at Concordia University–St. Paul, he also serves as a teaching artist and specializes in creative writing, performance, and African American literature.

J. Otis Powell‽ is the author of *Theology* (1998), *My Tongue Has No Bone* (2001), and *Pieces of Sky* (2014). His work has earned awards from the Jerome and McKnight Foundations, the Loft, and the Minnesota State Arts Board.

Writer, critic, and photographer **Rohan Preston** authored the poetry collection *Dreams in Soy Sauce* (1992) and several chapbooks. He coedited the anthology *Soulfires: Young Black Men on Love and Violence* (1996). In March 1998, he became lead theater critic at the *Star Tribune*.

Ralph Remington is founder of Pillsbury House Theatre in Minneapolis, where he served on the city council. He was Director of Theater and Musical Theater for the National Endowment for the Arts (2010–13) and has written poetry, essays, screenplays, and plays.

Angela Shannon, author of *Singing the Bones Together* (2003), teaches at Bethel University. Her works appear in *Beyond the Frontier: African-American Poetry for the 21st Century* (2002), *Hip Hop Speaks to Children: A Celebration of Poetry with a Beat* (2008), and other anthologies.

Susan J. Smith-Grier, writer, storyteller, and blogger, enjoys the ever-changing seasons in Minnesota lake country and her awesome kids and grandson. She loves wielding the power of words and story, but tries not to let it go to her head.

Clarence White, a past Givens Foundation Retreat Fellow and a former member of the Central Minnesota Writers' Workshop, writes the arts and culture column "This Week in Saint Paul" for the Saint Paul Almanac. He lives in St. Paul.

Frank B. Wilderson III has received the Loft-McKnight Award of Distinction and the Maya Angelou Award for Best Fiction Portraying the Black Experience in America. His memoir *Incognegro: A Memoir of Exile and Apartheid* (2008) won the Hurston/Wright Legacy Award.

Credits

The following previously published pieces are printed here with the permission of the copyright holders.

"In the City, Homelessness" by Davida Adedjouma was commissioned by Onalea Gilbertson for her off-Broadway show, *Requiem for a Lost Girl*.

"Christmas Tale" by Conrad Balfour from *The Butterfly Tree*, edited by Conrad Balfour (New Rivers Press, 1985).

"God's Chosen People" by Lloyd Brown from *Masses and Mainstream*, April 1948.

"Birth of the Cool: Minnesota," "St. Peter, Minnesota: Barry Harris," and "Preston's Dream: Version No. 1" from *Stompin' at the Grand Terrace: A Jazz Memoir in Verse* by Philip Bryant (Blueroad Press, 2009).

"Ottawa, MN, Cemetery—1992" from *Sermon on a Perfect Spring Day* by Philip Bryant (New Rivers Press, 1998).

"Mama" excerpted from *The Days of Rondo* by Evelyn Fairbanks. Copyright ©1991. Reprinted by permission of the Minnesota Historical Society Press.

Excerpt from *Born to Be* by Taylor Gordon (New York: Covici-Friede Publishers, 1929).

"Glitter Lions" excerpted from *A Star in the Face of the Sky* by David Haynes (New Rivers Press, 2013).

"Kwame J. C. McDonald" and "The Brawl in St. Paul" by Kofi Bobby Hickman from *Saint Paul Almanac*, 2013.

"Stones and Sticks" by Carolyn Holbrook from *The Black Body*, edited by Meri Nana-Ama Danquah (Seven Stories Press, 2006).

"The Bank Robbery" by Carolyn Holbrook and Steven Holbrook from *Black Renaissance Noire* (April 2008).

"My Rites of Passage" by Kemet Imhotep from *Saint Paul Almanac*, 2013.

Excerpt from *Nellie Stone Johnson: The Life of an Activist* by David Brauer (Ruminator Books, 2000).

"Apology for Apostasy?" and "As You Leave Me" from *The Essential Etheridge Knight* by Etheridge Knight. Copyright ©1986. Reprinted by permission of the University of Pittsburgh Press.

"Lilac Week" by Roy McBride. Broadside illustrated by Nick Wroblewski, Powderhorn Writer's Festival 2007.

Excerpt pages 39–46 from *A Choice of Weapons* by Gordon Parks. Copyright ©1965, 1966 by Gordon Parks, renewed 1994 by Gordon Parks. Reprinted by permission of HarperCollins Publishers.

"Autobiographia," "Job," and "Mary" from *Tug* by G. E. Patterson (Graywolf Press, 1999).

"Home Delivery" by Anthony Porter from *Mpls/St. Paul Magazine*, January 1998.

"Sabotage" by Anthony Porter originally performed for Write On! Radio, KFAI, 2000.

"To Be Black in America" by Ralph Remington from *The Minnesota Spokesman Recorder* and *MinnPost*, May 14, 2008.

"Migrations" from *Singing the Bones Together* by Angela Shannon (Tia Chuca, 2003).